ACCLAIM FOR LIS WIEHL

A MATTER OF TRUST

"*A Matter of Trust* is a stunning crime series debut from one of my favorite authors, Lis Wiehl. Smart, suspenseful, and full of twists that only an insider like Wiehl could pull off. I want prosecutor Mia Quinn in my corner when murder's on the docket—she's a compelling new character and I look forward to seeing her again soon."

—LINDA FAIRSTEIN, *NEW YORK TIMES* BEST-SELLING AUTHOR

"Dramatic, moving, intense. *A Matter of Trust* gives us an amazing insight into the life of a prosecutor—and mom. Mia Quinn reminds me of Lis."

—MAXINE PAETRO, *NEW YORK TIMES* BEST-SELLING AUTHOR

THE TRIPLE THREAT SERIES

"Only a brilliant lawyer, prosecutor, and journalist like Lis Wiehl could put together a mystery this thrilling! The incredible characters and non-stop twists will leave you mesmerized. Open [*Face of Betrayal*] and find a comfortable seat because you won't want to put it down!"

—E. D. HILL, FOX NEWS ANCHOR

"Three smart women crack the big cases! Makes perfect sense to me. [*Face of Betrayal*] blew me away!"

—JEANINE PIRRO, FORMER DA; HOST OF THE CW'S DAYTIME COURT
TELEVISION REALITY SHOW *JUDGE JEANINE PIRRO*

"Who killed loudmouth radio guy Jim Fate? The game is afoot! *Hand of Fate* is a fun thriller, taking you inside the media world and the justice system—scary places to be!"

—BILL O'REILLY, FOX TV AND RADIO ANCHOR

"As a television crime writer and producer, I expect novels to deliver pulse-pounding tales with major twists. *Hand of Fate* delivers big-time."

—PAM VEASEY, WRITER AND EXECUTIVE PRODUCER OF *CSI: NY*

"Book three in the wonderful Triple Threat series is a fast-paced thriller full of twists and turns that will keep you guessing until the end. What makes these books stand out for me is my ability to identify so easily with Allison, Nic, and Cassidy. I truly care about what happens to each of them, and the challenges they face this time are heart-wrenching and realistic. I highly recommend!"

—DEBORAH SINCLAIRE, EDITOR-IN-CHIEF, BOOK-OF-THE-MONTH CLUB
AND THE STEPHEN KING LIBRARY

"Beautiful, successful, and charismatic on the outside but underneath a twisted killer. She's brilliant and crazy and comes racing at the reader with knives and a smile. The most chilling villain you'll meet . . . because she could live next door to you."

—DR. DALE ARCHER, CLINICAL PSYCHIATRIST, REGARDING *HEART OF ICE*

WAKING HOURS

". . . an exciting faith-based series that skillfully blends romantic tension, gripping supernatural suspense, and a brutal crime."

—*LIBRARY JOURNAL*

". . . a truly chilling predator and some great snappy, funny dialogue will keep readers engaged."

—*PUBLISHERS WEEKLY*

"One word describes *Waking Hours* by Wiehl and Nelson—*WOW!* A gut-wrenching ride of supernatural suspense that left me breathless and wanting more. The book was a reminder that the battle between God and Satan is not over. Highly recommended!"

—COLLEEN COBLE, BEST-SELLING AUTHOR OF *LONESTAR ANGEL*
AND THE ROCK HARBOR SERIES

"A gripping plot, intriguing characters, supernatural underpinnings, and a splash of romance make *Waking Hours* a fast-paced and thoroughly enjoyable read. I want the next book in the series now!"

—JAMES L. RUBART, AWARD-WINNING AUTHOR OF *ROOMS*

A DEADLY BUSINESS

ALSO BY LIS WIEHL

Snapshot

The Mia Quinn Mysteries (with April Henry)

A Matter of Trust

The Triple Threat Series (with April Henry)

Face of Betrayal
Hand of Fate
Heart of Ice
Eyes of Justice

The East Salem Trilogy (with Pete Nelson)

Waking Hours
Darkness Rising
Fatal Tide

A DEADLY BUSINESS

A MIA QUINN MYSTERY

LIS WIEHL

WITH APRIL HENRY

THOMAS NELSON
Since 1798

NASHVILLE   MEXICO CITY   RIO DE JANEIRO

Published in Nashville, Tennessee, by Thomas Nelson. Thomas Nelson is a registered trademark of HarperCollins Christian Publishing, Inc.

Thomas Nelson, Inc., books may be purchased in bulk for educational, business, fundraising, or sales promotional use. For information, please e-mail SpecialMarkets@ ThomasNelson.com.

ISBN: 978-0-7180-1605-0 (IE)

Library of Congress Cataloging-in-Publication Data

Wiehl, Lis W.
  A deadly business : a Mia Quinn mystery Lis Wiehl with April Henry.
    pages cm
  "A Mia Quinn mystery."
  ISBN 978-1-59554-904-4 (hard cover)
  I. Title.
  PS3623.I382D43 2014
  813'.6—dc23   013049751

Printed in the United States of America

14 15 16 17 18 19 RRD 6 5 4 3 2 1

*For my children, Jacob and Dani, with my
unconditional love. Always. Mom*

CHAPTER 1

MONDAY

There are a million ways to die. As a prosecutor in Seattle's King County Violent Crimes Unit, Mia Quinn had become familiar with far too many. But before the first week of November was over, she would learn there were even more ways than she'd thought.

"Good afternoon, Your Honor," Mia said as Judge Rivas took the bench. Her phone hummed in her pocket, signaling a call or text, but she ignored it. Judge Rivas was a stickler for courtroom decorum.

He inclined his buzz-cut head toward Mia, who stood at attention behind the prosecution table. "Good afternoon, Counselor." He turned toward the empty defense table. "Is Mr. Dockins here?"

The courtroom clerk, Trevor Gosden, answered, "Yes. He's in with Mr. Young."

Despite the formal titles used in court, Mia thought that Trevor's use of *Mister* most certainly did not belong with the name Young. Rolf Dockins was the defense attorney, a gentleman from the top of his silver hair down to his highly polished wing tips. And Bernard Young was the glowering twenty-two-year-old defendant he represented, aka the monster who had raped and strangled two runaway girls.

Today Young was to be sentenced. There were only a few observers in the courtroom, most of them relatives of the girls. Mia had asked for life in prison, and felt confident Young would get it. Her case was airtight. Dockins had done what he could, but she was sure down to her bones that it wouldn't be enough. Young would never be able to hurt anyone again.

A side door opened and Rolf walked in, followed by Young in an orange jumpsuit. A sheriff's deputy brought up the rear.

Mia watched them walk toward the defense table, not thinking about anything except how her phone was buzzing again. Maybe she could manage to sneak a peek as she sat down.

Then Young's upper lip curled back and his eyes narrowed. His face was full of rage. And faster than Mia could react, faster than she could even process what was happening, he broke into a run. Straight for her. Then he lunged.

Young had already fisted her hair in one hand before Mia drew breath to scream. The other hand pressed against her throat. They tumbled backward. She was still screaming when his weight punched all the air out of her.

"Get off her!" Trevor yelled, swearing. "Get off her!" And then he threw himself on top of Young, wrestling with him. Mia's thoughts ping-ponged from the pain in her scalp to the pressure on her throat to the sheer crushing weight of the two men. She squirmed and kicked and pushed, trying to get away, but she was pinned in place.

"Just try it on me, man," Trevor panted. "I'll beat the crap out of you."

Now the deputy was grabbing at Young, yelling, adding his orders to the tumult. Even Rolf, who was seventy if he was a day, knelt next to them and began to yank and grab, trying to subdue his client. Mia found a brief moment to hope that the deputy didn't draw his gun. All of them were so close together.

"Watch out!" yelled Catherine, the court reporter. "He's got a razor blade."

A razor blade? More frantically, Mia arched her back, twisting and kicking. She didn't care if she kicked someone else or if Young tore all the hair out of her head. She had to get loose before he slashed her throat.

For a moment the weight left her neck, but even before she could feel a surge of relief it was back. And then Mia felt a small sharp edge press against her throat.

CHAPTER 2

Everything was moving in slow motion. Mia had all the time in the world to think, even if she had no time to save herself. Time to imagine how the delicate white skin of her throat would part in a red line that would widen into a bloody smile. Time to think about her children. Brooke was only four, Gabe fourteen. Both of them needed their mother. Needed Mia more than ever, since the car accident seven months earlier that had taken Scott from them.

"I got his wrist," Trevor yelled as an elbow pressed into Mia's rib cage. "Cuff him from the other side!"

And suddenly the weight came off Mia as the group of men wrestled a swearing Young back, yanking him to his feet. She sucked in air. With a trembling hand she risked touching her throat, afraid of what she might find.

But no hot blood pulsed from her neck. Her shaking fingers found just smooth skin.

Two more deputies ran into the courtroom with their guns drawn. Everyone was talking at once.

Mia pushed herself to a sitting position and turned to Catherine, who had crept closer. "Did he cut me?"

"No," Catherine said. Her eyes were wide and she had her hands to her own throat. "No, thank God. Should I call an ambulance?"

"I'm sorry!" Young called out, though he didn't look it.

Trevor pushed his shoulder. "It's a little late for that."

Rolf helped Mia to her feet and guided her to a chair. "I'm so sorry," he said. "Just before we came in, he asked me if I thought you had any remorse. I said you were just doing your job. I'm sorry if that had anything to do with it."

"It's the truth," she said, massaging her neck. "And thanks for helping get him off me."

He smoothed down the front of his now rumpled suit. "As soon as Bernard ran past me and I heard you scream, I decided I no longer cared about attorney-client privilege."

Mia was surprised to find that she could still smile.

One of the deputies who had responded knelt in front of her. He had a shaved head and golden brown eyes. "I have first aid training." As he spoke, he pulled on bright purple vinyl gloves. "Where are you injured?"

"I thought he cut me, but I guess he didn't." Lifting her chin, Mia touched the spot where she had felt something sharp. "Like right here."

He bent closer. "From the shape of it, I'd say it's a fingernail mark. But it didn't break the skin. Did you get hurt anyplace else?"

"Some bruises, but that's all." Now that it was over, Mia was starting to shake in earnest. "Everyone piled on him so fast, I don't think he had a chance to hurt me."

"He had a razor blade," Trevor said grimly, "but I knocked it out of his hand."

Rolf said, "Thank God for that. He'd have cut your throat for sure, Mia."

"Okay, I'm going to touch your neck." The deputy gently cradled the back of Mia's head in one hand while he stroked and pressed her throat with the other. "I think you're right. Just bruises. Nothing broken. Your hyoid bone feels intact. You might want to go to the hospital to get checked out. It's up to you. We could call an ambulance."

Mia knew she most definitely did not want to spend the next two hours getting poked and prodded, surrounded by the stress of a busy emergency room. All she wanted to do was go back to her office, pick up her things, and go home to her kids. "I don't think I want to do that." She looked up at the judge, who had come down off the bench too late to join the fray. It was strange to realize the whole thing had lasted only a few seconds.

"You sure you don't want to go to the hospital, Mia?" he asked.

"I'm sure." Everyone was looking at her, including the man who had just tried to kill her. It was one thing to be the center of attention when you were asking the court to take away a man's life, either literally or figuratively. It was another when the tables were turned. When you were the one at risk.

Judge Rivas turned to Rolf. "Obviously, sentencing will have to be delayed. And your client will probably face more charges."

"Obviously." Rolf straightened his tie. "And his family may need to hire a new lawyer. It's one thing to make sure my client gets a fair trial. It's another to have to stop him from killing the prosecutor."

CHAPTER 3

Mia leaned against the elevator wall. Her legs didn't feel strong enough to hold her up. As soon as the doors opened, she would go straight to her office, grab her coat and purse, and get out of here. Right now she couldn't bear to talk about what had just happened. Couldn't bear to have everyone gather around, concerned and solicitous.

Mia wasn't a victim. She had file folders of real victims on her desk. Some with photos of people who hadn't even had time to be surprised before they were dead. And some with photos of victims who had far too much time between the realization that something bad was happening and the end of it.

As Mia walked in, Frank D'Amato was just coming out of his office. He was both Mia's boss and the King County prosecutor. At least he was as of today. The election was only eight days away.

"Mia, I'm glad I caught you. I've got a case I need you to take."

"Can it wait, Frank? There's something I need to—"

"I'm afraid it can't, Mia." He had already turned to go back to his office.

By the expression on the face of their secretary, Mia knew word had traveled faster than the elevator. Judy pulled down her mouth-piece. "Frank, Mia was just—"

"It's all right, Judy." Mia knew there would be lots of questions, lots of discussion, a thorough postmortem designed to prevent some future prosecutor from being slashed to death on a court-room floor. Just not, if she could help it, today. She would put what had happened out of her mind, listen to Frank, and then she would leave. She would wait until she was safely at home behind her closed bedroom door before she would allow herself to break down. Until then, her memory of what had just occurred would go into a box.

Mia was getting pretty good at putting things in boxes.

She followed Frank in. He was already behind his desk, star-ing at his computer screen, his black eyebrows pulled together in a frown. Mia could remember when Frank was the kind of guy who wore Dockers, but now he favored Italian wool suits. His dark hair was artfully touched with silver at the temples. With his athletic body and cleft chin, he looked like an actor hired to play the part of a district attorney—or even president. And Frank was nothing if not ambitious.

"Come look at this," he said, motioning her around his desk. Then he clicked on a file, and a poor-quality video from a security cam began to play. It was black and white, shot from about ten feet above a wide pedestrian bridge.

"Where is this?" Mia asked as a parade of people passed the camera: Moms herding toddlers. Old ladies clutching purses. Young women swinging shopping bags. Adolescent boys sauntering in baggy cargo shorts despite the weather.

"The walkway connects a parking garage to a mall," Frank said.

Her phone buzzed again, and Mia realized she had forgotten to check it earlier. It was probably someone wanting to know more about what had happened in the courtroom.

"What exactly am I looking for?" Ignoring her phone, she mentally put on her prosecutor hat. There would be time to talk about what had happened—and what had almost happened—later.

"You'll know it when you see it," he said grimly.

Two teenage boys entered the frame, wheeling an empty shopping cart. A third trailed behind them. One of the boys wore a white hoodie. The second wore a football jersey with the number 12 on the back, as well as a name she thought started with a *B*. The third boy, dressed in a dark hoodie, walked in front of the cart and began waving his arms. Mia watched the dark spot of his mouth opening and closing. If she had to guess, she would have said he was yelling.

The whole thing was a guess. The picture was so blurry and pixilated, she couldn't really say that all three were boys. Or even kids. The only real clue to their identities was the football jersey. She glanced at Frank, but he was focused on the screen. She just hoped the video wasn't all the evidence they had.

Now the two boys lifted the front of the cart and balanced it precariously on the metal lip of the railing. The front half jutted out into space. Mia caught her breath as it wobbled back and forth. How far above the ground was the walkway? Two stories? More? And what was below? Because she was sure now, sickeningly sure, that the cart was going to plummet. But what was underneath? A child? A bicyclist? A car whose driver would crash?

But the two boys kept both their hands on it, even as the nose dipped and the handle rose. At one point the boy in the dark hoodie grabbed the side of the cart next to the boy in the football jersey, their bodies blurring as they moved. Mia watched in helpless horror as the cart tipped forward and then suddenly disappeared.

All three boys stood for a moment, empty-handed. Each of their smudgy faces held the round, dark O of an open mouth. And then they ran. The boy in the dark hoodie ran to the left. The boy in the white hoodie and the boy wearing the football jersey ran to the right.

"So what happened when the cart hit the ground?" Mia asked.

Instead of answering, Frank raised his hand to tell her to wait. The screen went black, then images from a second video appeared.

This camera was mounted along the side of a narrow road. For the moment there were no cars, just a half dozen people walking in all directions. On the far side of the road were a sidewalk and two sets of glass doors—the entrance to a store. Two people—one taller than the other—were moving toward the double doors and away from the camera. If anything, this video was even blurrier than the first, the figures nearly outside the camera's range.

Although she knew what was going to happen, Mia still gasped when the cart suddenly crashed from above into the frame.

CHAPTER 4

The shopping cart barely missed the shorter person while smash-ing the taller one to the ground. Then the boy in the black hoodie darted into the frame and ran to the injured person, even as the shorter one stood unmoving, seemingly rooted to the sidewalk. More people came, pushing out of the store, stopping their cars in the middle of the road, all of them running to help the person pinned under the cart.

The video ended. Even black and white and blurry, it was still a clear picture of senseless tragedy.

"Who was hit by the cart?" Mia asked.

"Tamsin Merritt. She's thirty-eight. Her fourteen-year-old son, Luke, wasn't injured. At least not physically."

"And Tamsin?" Mia was already using the woman's first name, just as she would in front of a jury to make them think of her not as a victim, but as their friend. Mia was ready to go to war on this woman's behalf. Her breath was speeding up again, not from fear, but from anger.

"I'm told she died right there, at least technically. She didn't have a pulse, and she wasn't breathing." A muscle flickered in Frank's jaw. "A doctor who happened to be in the store gave her CPR. As of a few hours ago, it was still touch and go. But even if she lives, she's more than likely suffered brain damage."

Mia shuddered. "How far did the cart fall?"

"That walkway is four stories up, so about fifty feet."

"And the kids who did it? Do we have them?"

"So far, the only name we have is Manny Flores. That's the boy who tried to stop the other two." Frank pressed his fingers against his temples. "He became hysterical watching the doctor trying to revive her. They ended up having to call an ambulance for him too, and he had to be sedated. He's in Willow Grove, that mental hospital for kids, and right now they're saying he's not in any condition to answer questions. We're hoping to take the other two into custody soon. We're hearing they're around the same age as Manny—fifteen."

"At least that one kid was wearing a shirt with his name on the back," Mia observed. "That should help us find the other two."

"What?" Frank shot her a puzzled look.

"That football jersey with the number twelve. It looked like his name started with a *B*."

"Brady?" A near-smile flitted across Frank's face. "Haven't you heard of Tom Brady?"

Mia shook her head. Had she?

"Of the New England Patriots?" Frank rolled his eyes. "Remind me never to give you a case that revolves around football. There're people wearing that exact same jersey all over the country. I'm afraid it's not much of a clue."

"So where do I come in?" For a second Mia lost her focus on the case and flashed back to what had just happened in the courtroom, her terror when she felt something sharp press on her throat. Pushing the thought away, she leaned against Frank's cherrywood credenza to steady herself, taking care not to knock over any of the framed photos of his two kids. It was rumored that these photos were about as close as Frank ever came to actually seeing them. You had to make certain sacrifices if you wanted to be district attorney. And even more if you wanted to be reelected.

"I need you to decide whether they should be charged as adults or juveniles. And if it's as adults, I want you to prosecute them."

In the state of Washington, youths sixteen or older and charged with certain violent felonies were automatically transferred to adult court. But even younger kids could still be charged as adults.

"Fifteen's awfully young," Mia said, trying to buy herself time. If she took on this case, how much time would she have at home with her own kids?

"We're not talking about little angels," Frank said impatiently. "You saw what they did. It's a miracle the son wasn't injured too. And there's still the chance Tamsin might die."

Making it a second-degree homicide. Part of Mia wanted to throw the book at these two kids who had acted with reckless indifference. At the same time she knew how easily kids were influenced, how little they thought things through.

At the beginning of the school year, her son had fallen in with a new group of friends. Gabe had taken part in a flash mob that robbed a convenience store. He hadn't taken anything—claimed he hadn't even known what was going to happen—but still, Mia was uncomfortably aware of how a single poor decision could have horrifying consequences.

Gabe, the two boys, Manny, even Tamsin's son, Luke—they had all been babies once. How did a baby grow up to be a kid who would set into action a plan that could kill a stranger? For that matter, how did a baby grow up to be Bernard Young? Was there anything you could do to stop it from happening? Juvenile courts were aimed at rehabilitation, but was the direction of these two kids' lives already set? Should they be written off, the energy refocused on protecting those around them?

"I want you to work with Charlie Carlson," Frank continued. "You two make a good team."

Charlie. She wasn't sure how she felt about working with him again. "But, Frank, I don't—"

"Mia," he snapped. "This is my top priority. I need the best people on it. That means you and Charlie. And I need your decision as soon as possible, before the election. I do not need to hear any more from my opponent about this office being soft on crime. Whatever you decide, we need to be able to defend it."

Unlike Frank, his opponent, Dominic Raines, did not look like a district attorney. He was not much taller than Mia and had the pallor of a man who spent all his time indoors. But he had also run a shrewd campaign, using cherry-picked examples to accuse Frank of coddling criminals. According to Raines, far too many were being granted sweetheart plea bargains.

The general public, brought up on prime time courtroom dramas, did not realize that ninety-five percent of felony convictions were the result of plea bargains. Only a handful went to trial. The justice system simply couldn't handle the caseload otherwise.

Raines had been focusing on the cases that sounded the worst, without mentioning any nitty-gritty realities. In some cases there had been a lack of evidence, and a plea bargain had been preferable to a defendant likely getting off scot-free. But on the face of it, probation for a third-degree rape case or nine months in prison for arson did not sound like enough.

"I want you to consider everything carefully, Mia," Frank said. His brilliant blue eyes bored into her. "I'm sure you'll make the right decision."

Her phone buzzed again, and she finally peeked at the screen. The caller ID read Seattle Security. Seattle Security had put the new alarm system in her home when she went back to work. Just one of a million decisions she had made on the fly. But why would they be calling her now?

A fresh burst of adrenaline pumped through her veins. "Excuse me, Frank. I have to take this." She pressed the button to accept the call. "This is Mia Quinn."

A bored man's voice said, "This is Seattle Security calling for Mia Quinn."

Hadn't he heard her? "This is Mia," she repeated, not bothering to hide her impatience.

"We're just calling to notify you that there's been an alert at your home, and no one is answering the phone there."

"Of course not. Nobody's home." Although maybe they were by now. She thought of her phone buzzing when she was in the court-room. It could have been Gabe.

"We've also notified the police department."

She stiffened. "Don't you have someone who goes out to the house and checks?" Why hadn't she read the contract? And she was an attorney.

"No, ma'am. We monitor, we check with the homeowner, and we notify the police department."

Mia had a realistic view of how long it might take the police to respond. More than ninety-five percent of automated alarms were false, so responding to them was a cop's lowest priority.

And maybe that made sense. But not when her kids were due home—Mia checked her watch—*now*. Maybe were already home.

She looked up at Frank. "I have to go. Now."

CHAPTER 5

Coach Harper clapped his hands. "Okay, to finish off this afternoon we're doing some fifty-yard sprints."

Everyone groaned, including Gabe. All he wanted to do was chug a Gatorade and hit the shower. Coach had drilled them hard all afternoon. And now, with the end of practice so tantalizingly in sight, he wanted them to do timed wind sprints.

Gabe gritted his teeth and gutted out the first one. On the faces of the other guys, he saw frustration, pain, and sheer determination.

After the third sprint Marc, one of the linemen, was struggling to come back. Someone yelled from the sidelines for him to hurry up. Gabe was catching his breath, his hands on his knees, so he didn't see who it was. But it didn't seem fair. Marc wasn't a slacker. Before he could think about it too much, Gabe ran back onto the field and started running next to Marc, clapping his hands and cheering him on.

They started their next sprint, and again Gabe was one of the first to finish. And Marc was struggling again, his face red and his chest heaving. But this time five of the team came back to help him finish. The last ten yards, Gabe and Eldon half carried, half dragged Marc to make sure he crossed the line.

When they were all done, Coach had them gather around. He favored them with one of his rare smiles. "I like what I saw out there today. Not only did you strengthen your endurance and your will, you also started thinking about how to be a team. Being a team is all about working together, not tearing each other down. When you get a touchdown, it's not just about the running back who has the ball or the quarterback who throws it or the receiver. It's all of you together working as a unit."

As they headed back to the locker room, Coach clapped Gabe on the shoulder. "Good job, Quinn," he said quietly. "What you did today—that's part of being a leader."

———

By the time Gabe left practice, the weather had changed. The wind was lashing the trees. The rain came in gusts that threatened to tear off his baseball cap. As he walked to his sister's preschool, his legs felt like lead. It had taken everything he had to go back on that field when he himself was finished. Still, it had felt good pushing his body further than he thought it could go. And even better to hear Coach praise him.

Coach Harper did not give compliments lightly. Gabe had worked hard all fall, and it was beginning to pay off. He was getting put in more often, and he was now able to go all out without getting completely winded.

He signed Brooke out and they began the trek home. His stomach growled. He was hungry enough that he could almost forget the ache in his legs, forget the weather. Would his mom be home in time to make dinner, or was he going to be on his own again, reduced to making a blue box of mac and cheese? He sent her a text but got no answer.

Brooke was dawdling, even though a second earlier she had been complaining that she had to go to the bathroom. "Come on." He tugged at her hand, but she pulled away and sloshed through a puddle that came midway up her yellow rain boots.

As they started down their street, he heard a high-pitched whine. It sounded like some kind of alarm.

The closer they got to the house, the louder it got. It was definitely their security alarm. Gabe's heart started beating faster. They stood at the edge of the yard.

"Come on, Gabe!" Now it was Brooke tugging at his hand. "I have to go potty!"

"We can't go in, Brooke. That's the alarm."

"Is there a burglar?"

He didn't answer. The house was dark. All the doors and windows appeared to be closed and undamaged. Nothing seemed to have been disturbed.

What had his mom said to do if the alarm went off? Gabe tried to remember. All he could remember was that if you set it off accidentally, you were supposed to punch in the code—the dates of his and Brooke's birthdays—and hit the "clear" button. They had only gotten the alarm a few months ago, when his mom went back to work and there was no one home during the day.

Taking out his phone again, he called his mom. It felt weird to be holding the phone up to his ear. Mostly he and his friends just texted. The only people he regularly talked to on the phone were his grandparents.

His mom's phone rang three times and went to voice mail.

"Mom, um, hi, it's me. The alarm's going off and I don't know what to do. Um, call me back."

He looked at the neighbors' houses. Those were dark too.

"Gabe—I really have to go!" Brooke was squirming. "Now!" The wind gusted so hard that it caught the hood of her yellow raincoat and blew it back. So hard that the windows in their old house rattled.

It seemed really lame to call 911. He imagined the cops showing up, sirens screaming, and then rolling their eyes when it turned out to be nothing.

Then he thought of Charlie Carlson, the detective who sometimes worked with his mom. Maybe Charlie could tell him what to do.

Gabe had to look up Charlie's name in his contacts. Again he got voice mail.

"Hey, um, Mr. Carlson"—he'd told Gabe to call him Charlie, but for some reason that didn't seem right tonight—"I'm at my house and I can't get hold of my mom. The house alarm's going off and I'm not sure what to do. I think it's been going off for a while. So if you get this message in the next twenty minutes or so, could you call me back?"

Brooke yanked on his hand even harder. "Come on, Gabe! I really have to pee!"

What if he had just set the alarm wrong? Or what if it was just the wind rattling the door? He started towing Brooke along, and she stopped complaining for a second. But when she realized they weren't going in, but rather walking around the perimeter of the yard, she started fussing again.

"Just hold on a sec," he told her. "I need to make sure it's safe." He looked at every window, even the ones on the second floor. None of them were broken. The front and side doors were closed tight.

After they had made a complete circle, they were outside the side door at the end of the driveway. Still holding Brooke's hand, Gabe went up on the porch. He tried the handle, ready to run, but the door was locked. He shook the handle and felt how the door moved in its frame. Stupid wind! That must have been what set off the alarm. Still, he crouched down until his face was on the same level as Brooke's.

"Brooke, I have to make sure it's safe before you can go inside. I want you to stay right here and not move. Can you do that?" He hated to leave her alone, but he didn't know what else to do.

She nodded. "But hurry, okay? I can't hold it for very long."

"I will. But if you see anyone you don't know, do not talk to them and do not let them get close to you. Run away and hide if you have to. Do you understand?"

She swiveled her head from side to side, her eyes wide. At least she was momentarily distracted from her obsession with the potty. "Is there a bad person?"

"Probably not. It's just to be safe."

Gabe wished it wasn't all on him. Then he remembered how he had helped Marc. Remembered how Coach had complimented him.

He put his key in the lock. The door swung open into blackness. Just inside the door, the lights on the control panel were blinking rapidly, some red and some green. He had never really paid attention to them before and didn't know what they meant. He took one step inside and punched in the code.

The silence seemed almost as loud as the alarm.

He took a deep, ragged breath. Should he turn on the light? But if he turned on the light and someone had broken in, they would not only know he was here, but they would be able to move around easily. With the lights off, he had an advantage. After all, this was his house.

Gabe stepped into the darkness.

CHAPTER 6

Charlie sat in his Crown Vic listening to his voice mail before he went back to the office. He had to listen to the third message twice before he was finally able to pick out the hesitant words from some kind of annoying background whine.

"I'm at my house and I can't get hold of my mom. The house alarm's going off and I'm not sure what to do. I think it's been going off for a while. So if you get this message in the next twenty minutes or so, could you call me back?"

It was Gabe Quinn. Mia's kid. Fourteen years old. Charlie had been married three times, but he didn't have any kids. Which was probably a good thing. He didn't even have a cat.

Sometimes, though, he saw a little of himself in Gabe. He'd seen the kid put on an I-don't-care face when he clearly did. Seen him be brave when it might have been better to be cautious. But at fourteen boys were all hormones, impulses, and bravado.

And since his dad had died, Gabe had been forced to grow up. To square his skinny shoulders and be the man of the house.

The kid answered on the first ring. "Hello?" His voice was barely audible, but only because he was speaking softly. The sound of the alarm was gone. Charlie relaxed and pulled the keys from the ignition.

"It's Charlie Carlson. It sounds like you got the alarm taken care of. So is everything okay?"

"No!"

Charlie hadn't known that a voice could be both soft and frantic. He slid the keys back in the ignition. "What's wrong?"

"I turned off the alarm and went inside to check things out. But I think someone else is here in the house too. I can hear them moving around downstairs."

Charlie sucked in a breath, his heart speeding up. "Get back outside! Now!"

"I can't. I think they're right by the stairs." And then the kid put the cherry on the sundae. "And I left Brooke outside."

Charlie started his car again, swearing under his breath. "I'm gonna scramble a unit out your way. Until then, is there someplace you can hide? Under a bed? In a closet?" He couldn't remember what the top floor of Mia's house looked like.

Silence.

"Gabe?"

The only answer was a muffled *thump*. As if the phone had fallen from the boy's hand and onto the carpet.

"Gabe?"

Charlie could hear something in the background. A man yelling. He couldn't make out the words. But he could hear the emotions fueling them. Anger and fear and a little bit of panic.

Hitting the buttons to activate his sirens and lights, he just prayed that the man in Mia's house didn't have a weapon.

CHAPTER 7

To Mia, it seemed to take hours for the courthouse elevator to reach the ground. It stopped on every floor. People held the doors for friends or to finish a conversation. She wanted to scream, but that would only slow things down further.

Many of the people who got on wanted to talk to her, but she just held up her hand and shook her head as she scrolled back through the messages on her phone. Co-workers had reacted to the news of what had happened. Gabe had texted her about dinner. Eli Hall, a public defender who taught with her at the University of Washington Law School, wanted to know if she was okay.

And in the middle was a phone message from Gabe. He had left it just ten minutes earlier. Mia put her finger in her other ear so she could listen to it a second time, trying to tease out her son's voice from the blare of the alarm in the background and from the voices now surrounding her. Finally the elevator doors opened and she pushed her way out, not caring when she stepped squarely on someone's foot. What had Gabe done once he hung up the phone? As she ran to her car, she called him back, but it went straight to voice mail.

"Gabe, it's Mom. Don't go in the house. Go to the neighbor's or something. And call me back as soon as you hear this."

Once she was in her car, Mia raced out of the parking lot, the squeal of her tires echoing off the concrete walls. Her car bounced out onto the street, forcing other traffic to screech to a halt. Ignoring a volley of angry honks, she began to weave in and out of cars.

Her heart pounded in her chest and ears. Her fingertips felt numb. She forced herself to take a deep breath. She was probably overreacting. The term *false alarm* hadn't become a staple of the lexicon for nothing.

But if it was nothing, why hadn't Gabe answered his phone? Why hadn't he called her back? Had her call gone to voice mail because he was on the phone with someone else? Or because he had turned the phone off? Or because someone else had?

As she merged onto the freeway, Mia's hands were slick on the wheel. She drove the way she hated anyone else to, riding people's bumpers until she forced them to move out of the way. The world had collapsed into a single thought, as if she were seeing it all through the sights of a gun. She had to get to her children. Now.

As she raced home, Mia murmured a prayer that was just a single word repeated over and over. "Please. Please, please, please." The rain was coming in gusts, forcing her to constantly adjust the windshield wipers from high to medium to intermittent and then back to high again.

Why hadn't they worked out a strategy for what Gabe should do in a situation like this? They had planned where to meet if they were separated in an earthquake, but wasn't this more important? Of course, Scott was the one who had made the earthquake plan, and that was before they had gotten the security system. Before Scott had died. Accountants were good at making plans, making lists, making sure everything was orderly. Now Mia was trying to take up the slack, be mother and father both, and she feared she was doing a lousy job.

Even if false alarms were common, that didn't mean this one wasn't real. Someone still could have broken in, looking for electronic gadgets or prescription drugs. And since burglars were often users themselves, an encounter with one could be unpredictable, even violent.

And what if it was something worse, someone targeting her specifically? Mia thought of what had just happened in the courtroom. Could this be Young's backup plan? Did he know that her kids were her life? Had he planned to take her life away just as she was taking his?

Being a prosecutor was not a low-risk occupation. No matter how hard you tried to keep your home address and personal details off the Internet, anyone with a little cash could find someone willing to divulge them for a fee. Mia thought of the Denver prosecutor gunned down outside his home, the Texas prosecutor shot by a masked man as he walked to his office. In California a man with a grudge had even killed the daughter of his own attorney in some kind of twisted payback. And then there was Mia's co-worker Colleen, shot down in her basement because she was getting too close to the truth of a scandal.

When Gabe couldn't reach her, what choice had he made? Had he done the smart thing and retreated? But fourteen-year-old boys didn't really believe they might die. Not even when their own dads had.

She heard sirens behind her. Red and blue lights flashed in her rearview mirror. After pulling over to let an unmarked Crown Vic with lights in the grill pass, Mia watched as it took the next exit. The exit for her neighborhood.

Her heart contracted. *No, no, no.* Not her kids. She couldn't take it if anything happened to them too. Scott's death had nearly broken her. But her kids, her kids were her heart. Her life.

Even after she got off the freeway, Mia was still driving at close to freeway speeds. She turned onto her block. In front of her house stood two blue-and-white patrol cars, their light bars now dark, as well as the Crown Vic that had passed her. The door opened and Charlie Carlson got out.

She jerked the car to a stop across the street, then ran toward him.

He turned toward the sound of her heels, then held up his hands. "Stay back, Mia. And don't make any noise. There's someone in the house with Gabe. We don't want to spook the guy."

"Oh my God." It was half prayer, half disbelief. This couldn't be real, could it? "What about Brooke?"

"I don't know." He said it plainly, but in the glow of the street-light she saw the anguish in his face.

One patrol officer was at the side door and the other at the front. Both of them had their guns drawn. The side door was open, and the officer there was yelling, "Come on out with your hands up."

CHAPTER 8

Anticipate the unexpected and assume the worst. That was what his first partner had told Charlie when he started working patrol. Now, years later, he had plenty of ways to fill in the blanks. All of them bad.

He assumed that the person who had broken into Mia's house was still inside. That he—or they—was armed. That he was dangerous. And that he was panicked. Panicked was worst of all. Panic led to poor decisions. Panic led to people getting hurt, even killed. That was why he had asked the responding officers to shut down lights and sirens before they arrived, lower the volume on their radios, and silence their equipment.

"Go wait by your car," he told Mia now.

"But what about—"

He cut her off with a wave of his hand. "I don't have time to argue." He turned away so he could scan the house, looking for clues, for anything out of place. Had he seen movement in the glossy green leaves of the camellia bush next to the side porch?

He stepped onto the porch, keeping out of the line of sight of the open door. In the porch light the cop, with cheeks as red as apples, didn't look much older than Gabe. "Who's inside?" Charlie asked in a voice not much louder than a whisper.

"That's not yet been determined. I found the door open, indicating that we had an active B&E-type situation. I entered, heard movement, and attempted verbal contact. When there was no response, I exited and waited for backup. They just arrived."

"We don't just have a burglar or burglars," Charlie said. "We've also got a fourteen-year-old kid in there. Name of Gabe Quinn. Did you see him?"

The rookie shook his head. "I didn't make visual contact with anyone."

Charlie thought. If he called out to Gabe and the kid responded, would that simply provide the burglar with a ready hostage?

"We know you're in there!" he called into the darkness. "Come on out with your hands up!"

A long silence. Long enough that Charlie had time to wonder just how bad things were going to get. Then a voice came from overhead.

"Charlie? Is that you?"

The tightness in his chest loosened. "It is. Stay where you are, Gabe. Are you alone? Are you safe?"

"Yeah. I'm okay." His voice was shaky. "Are there other cops here? Besides you?"

"Yeah. Two."

"I think they think I'm the bad guy."

"What?" Charlie wasn't sure he was following.

"When I was talking to you on the phone, this guy started yelling at me from downstairs to get my hands up or he'd shoot me. But instead I hid."

He looked at the cop next to him. Now the rookie's whole face was red.

"Did you tell him you were a cop?" Charlie asked.

A pause. "I'm not certain I identified myself as an officer."

He exhaled sharply, then called upstairs to Gabe, "Just to be safe, we're gonna clear the house. Stay put until we say otherwise, okay?"

When it came to the search, the rookie redeemed himself. They worked in speed and in silence, using hand signals, taking quick peeks—alternating high and low—slicing the pie when they went around corners, leapfrogging down hallways, never forgetting about the fatal funnel of a doorway and never turning their backs to an uncleared room.

When they reached the top of the stairs, Charlie called out for Gabe, asking where he was.

"In my room."

"Okay. Just give us a sec."

Brooke's room was clear, as was the bathroom. In Mia's room the bed was unmade, but only on one side, as though she still expected Scott to show up and reclaim his half.

Finally Charlie opened the door to Gabe's room. It appeared empty. The closet door stood open.

"All right, Gabe, you can come out."

The chair in the front of the desk slowly began to inch out into the room, then Gabe unwound himself onto the carpet. Charlie holstered his weapon and reached down to pull him to his feet, marveling that the kid had managed to contort his body into a space not much larger than a milk crate.

"Your mom's outside. She wants to know where Brooke is."

The boy's face paled. "You mean Brooke's not outside? I told her to wait on the side porch. I told her."

There was no point in telling a fourteen-year-old that he had made the wrong decision. Judging by the horrified expression on his face, he had already figured that out for himself.

CHAPTER 9

Mia paced next to her car, her arms wrapped around herself. She couldn't stop shaking. Couldn't take her eyes off the open door Charlie and the cop had disappeared into. Couldn't stop straining her ears to hear the familiar voices of her children. Couldn't stop fearing that she would instead hear something worse. A scream. A cry. A gunshot.

After what seemed like hours but was just a few minutes, Charlie, the young cop, and Gabe came out of the house. Mia flew across the lawn to her son, wrapping his wiry frame in her arms. When had he gotten to be so tall? He submitted for just a second before he stiffened and broke away.

"Where's your sister?" Mia looked behind him for a small figure, maybe hanging back in confusion, but saw nothing. Panic sharpened her voice when he didn't answer. "Where's Brooke?"

"I told her to stay right here." His eyes were huge. He turned in a circle. "Right here on the porch."

"Brooke?" Mia called out into the darkness. "Brooke? Honey?"

Silence. It stretched out, long enough to reach in deep, to hollow her out, and then—"Mommy?" A little voice, and close. *Thank you, God.*

"Brooke? Where are you, honey?"

"Is the bad man still there?" Her voice was coming from deep inside the camellia bush.

Mia tensed again. "What bad man?"

"The one with the gun. He was yelling."

She relaxed as she realized who Brooke meant. "Oh, honey, they're police officers. You're okay. It's safe to come out."

Her yellow rain jacket flashed among the dark leaves, and then she pushed her way out. Mia snatched up Brooke and held her close. Her face was scratched from the branches, but otherwise she looked okay.

"Why didn't you stay on the porch?" Gabe demanded, voice cracking.

"Because," Brooke said, and then stopped.

"Because why?" Mia prompted.

She leaned forward. Her whisper tickled Mia's ear. "Because I had to go pee!"

"Oh, Brooke!" Mia had to smile. Ten minutes earlier she had been sure she would never smile again.

While they had been talking, the patrol officer had been notifying his dispatcher as well as the officer on the other side of the house. Now he cleared his throat. "Um, ma'am, even though there's currently no one in your house, it looked like they must have been interrupted while they were still going through it."

"What?" Her free hand went to her throat, to the place where Bernard Young's fingernail had dug into her an hour before. Charlie cocked his head.

Suddenly her arms felt too weak to hold her daughter, and she set her down. It was all too much. Gabe. Brooke. Coming way too close to having her throat cut.

The young cop gestured for Mia to follow, and they all, including the second patrol officer, trailed after him.

As she staggered forward on hollow-feeling legs, Mia wondered what had been taken. Material things might not matter, but some things were still irreplaceable.

"See." The cop waved his hand at the family room like a game show host extolling the features of a new car. "Someone started to toss it." The room was a mess, as if it had been gone through in a hurry. Half the doors to the built-in cupboards stood open. Brooke's pillow lay next to a wall. Scattered throughout the room were clothes, dishes, sections of newspaper, a single sneaker, a half-filled laundry basket, books, a game of Connect Four, and a random menagerie of stuffed animals.

"They must have been interrupted," the cop repeated. "Do you want to look to see what's missing?"

Mia's cheeks got hot. This kid was too young to know what it was like when you had two kids and worked sixty hours a week. "Actually, um, this is normal. It's how the house was when we left. We've just had a busy week." She hoped no one pointed out that it was Monday.

"Oh." The bright color was back in his face. "So I guess the whole thing was a false alarm. No burglar."

"No burglar," Mia echoed.

"Okay, so when it comes to false alarms, you should know that you're allowed one freebie. But for any additional alarms, you'll be charged a hundred-and-fifteen-dollar fee. Each."

"We should figure out what caused it," Charlie said. "Do you have motion sensors in the house? I've seen cats, balloons, even spiders trigger them. Anything that breaks the beam."

"No. We just have alarms on the doors and the downstairs windows."

"It was pretty stormy out there earlier. And this is an older home." He walked back into the hall, grabbed the front doorknob, and shook it. Even though it was still locked, it rattled in the frame. "That's more than likely your problem right there. With the wind blowing, there's enough play in it that it could have separated the contact from its reed switch for a second. You need to get some weather stripping."

His words were starting to sound like they were coming to her at the bottom of a tunnel. Desperate to steady herself, Mia sagged forward, reaching for the back of the couch.

Suddenly a strong arm was around her shoulders. Charlie started barking orders. "Okay, Mia, I think you need to lie down for a second." As he maneuvered her around the couch, he took out his wallet with his free hand and handed Gabe a credit card. "Call up Pagliacci and order a couple of pizzas to be delivered. Whatever you want. And, Brooke, can you go up to your room and play by yourself for a little bit? Your mom needs a bit of peace and quiet." He turned to the two cops. "And why don't you guys write up your reports outside. If you need to leave her a copy, stick it through the mail slot. If you need her to sign it, come back tomorrow. Right now she needs a little bit of a break."

And because it was Charlie, everyone did as they were told and left the room. Mia plopped on the couch, but even sitting seemed like too much effort, so she ended up stretching out after Charlie cleared a space. She was too far gone even to be embarrassed by the mess. Putting her arm over her eyes, she said, "Thank you. All of a sudden I just felt so dizzy. I don't even understand why you're here. I'm just glad that you are."

"Gabe called me when he couldn't get hold of you. I was on the phone with him when I heard someone yelling, and then Gabe dropped the phone. Must have been the first officer who responded. The one who seems to be trying for rookie of the year award."

"This has been one crazy day." She debated telling Charlie about what had happened, but she didn't want to relive it. What Young had tried to do to her would stay in the box she had put it in, at least for now. Tonight she would take one of the sleeping pills the doctor had given her after Scott died and hope she didn't dream about what might have happened. "And right before all this happened, Frank wanted to talk to me about a case and he wouldn't take no for an answer." She took her arm off her eyes and propped herself up on her elbow. "You'll be hearing about it soon because he wants us to work together on it. Kids dropped a shopping cart onto a woman who was four stories below a pedestrian walkway."

Charlie grimaced. "So they killed her?"

"No. She's not dead. At least not yet. Right now I need to decide whether to charge them as adults or juveniles. I need to figure out what kinds of kids they are. But not until tomorrow." Mia let her head drop back down, reminding herself that she was safe now, that her kids were safe. "I would say this was the worst day of my life, but it wasn't. It's not even the worst day of this year."

Charlie cleared his throat. "There's something I've been meaning to talk to you about."

"Yeah?"

"I've been looking closer into your husband's death. I don't think it was an accident."

CHAPTER 10

Mia's mouth opened, but no words came out. It was like the day the earthquake had rippled up from Olympia all the way to Seattle. Like she was frozen in shock.

But she had always been afraid of this, hadn't she? Scott had been in debt up to his eyeballs, and then he had started secretly drinking again. He must have known it wouldn't be long before the debt collectors began calling the house, before Mia learned about the whole sorry mess. Unable to see a way out of his predicament, had he made an impulsive decision to end it all rather than face the consequences?

If Scott had killed himself, it certainly hadn't been done in hopes of their benefiting. He had let his life insurance lapse, so his death had left them with nothing. Nothing but debts. The kids got Social Security benefits, that was all. But Scott had been spared watching their lives fall apart.

The seven months he had been dead sometimes felt like seven days, at other times like seven years. He had hidden so much from her. Was suicide his final deception? If Scott suddenly were to appear before her now, Mia thought she might be tempted to kill him herself. As it was, she had no place to put her anger.

"I took a look at the accident report." Charlie glanced down at his empty hands and then back up at her. "There are things that don't add up."

Heat rushed from Mia's heels to her hairline. How dare he! What made him think he should stick his big nose in? The knowledge could do nothing but hurt her. She swung her legs off the couch and sat up. "You looked at the report? Let me get this straight. You looked at the accident report for my dead husband, a man you never met?" The skin on her face tightened. "What business is that of yours, Charlie Carlson?"

"After I met you, I got curious. What was supposed to have happened didn't seem to make a lot of sense. Don't you want to know the truth?"

Truth? The truth was that being obsessive might be what made Charlie such a good homicide detective—and maybe a bad human being. The idea of Charlie poring over the details of Scott's death, of smashed glass and smashed bone, seemed nearly obscene.

"What's next, Charlie?" Mia was fisting her hands so hard her nails dug into her palms. She wanted to take one of those fists and smash it into Charlie's nose. "Are you going to start going through my garbage? My underwear drawer? You don't get to go pawing through things that have nothing to do with you. This is my life you're talking about. My life. And my children's lives." Even though she was alive with anger, she kept her voice a low, hissed murmur. If they learned that their father had killed himself, what would that do to Gabe's and Brooke's mental health? "Let the dead bury the dead."

She would never forget that night. Wasn't that hard truth enough?

———

"I won't be home for dinner," Scott had told Mia over the phone. "And don't bother waiting up for me."

"Working late again?" Her stomach twisted. He had been working so many hours lately, sometimes until late into the night. She had asked him a half dozen times if anything was wrong, and he always brusquely assured her that everything was fine.

As Mia waited for his answer, she stared at Brooke's head, bent over the dolls spread over the carpet in the family room. Their daughter would soon turn four, and she had recently become captivated by the idea of friends. She could spend many minutes pairing up appropriate plastic friends. Just pairs, though, no groups of three or more. In Brooke's world, each doll or toy had only one soul mate.

Could Scott be seeing another woman? Mia gripped the phone so hard it cut into her fingers. It would explain his silences, his bad moods, the way he could be sitting right beside her on the couch in front of a sitcom and seem a million miles away when she spoke to him. There were times he came home so late that she was already in bed. But she always roused herself and wrapped him in her arms, nuzzled his neck.

She was sniffing for the scent of another woman, or even another soap, some brand stocked by a hotel.

But so far he had always smelled only of Scott.

"I'm having dinner with a client." His voice was colored with some emotion she couldn't name. Impatience? "I need to go over some things with him, but he's been too busy to meet during the day." His tone didn't encourage any questions.

She went to bed a little after ten and finally fell into an uneasy sleep, futilely reaching out for him every time she shifted. When the doorbell rang just before two in the morning, part of Mia wasn't even surprised. Part of her had known something bad was coming—just not what form it would take. She stumbled downstairs and looked through the peephole. Two cops. One wore a white clerical collar with yellow crosses embroidered on the points. She let out a single sob, then bit her lip. Hard. Gabe and Brooke were still asleep upstairs. When they woke, their lives would be irrevocably changed. Let them sleep as long as they could.

With the taste of blood fresh on her tongue, Mia opened the door.

And now Charlie wanted to rub her nose in the truth. What was true, anyway? That she and Scott had been married for sixteen years and had become strangers? That she now carried an almost unimaginable burden—debts, worries about her children, and the knowledge that Scott hadn't felt he could confide in her?

Or that Scott had abandoned her long before he died?

CHAPTER 11

Mia rounded on Charlie. "Did you ever think that there are some truths people don't want to know? I'd rather believe it was all an accident than to know my husband was in so much emotional pain that he killed himself."

Charlie's forehead wrinkled as he raised his hands as if to protect himself. "That's not what I was saying, Mia. Not at all."

"So what are you saying? Scott was drunk and he went off the road and hit a tree. It was either an accident or deliberate." She took a ragged breath. "I've made my peace with the idea that I'm never going to know why he kept so many secrets from me, like the fact that he'd started drinking again." When he had sworn on the lives of their children that he had stopped. "But this is one secret I would really rather not know."

"He was only .06," Charlie said. Given Scott's body weight, it was the equivalent of about three drinks. "Not enough to be legally drunk."

"But enough to be impaired. And he'd probably lost his tolerance."

"That still doesn't explain what you can see in the reports. Scott's injuries don't make sense." Charlie took a deep breath. "What I'm trying to say, Mia, is that I think he might have been murdered."

Mia tried to take this in, but it was impossible. Murdered? "What exactly did you see in the reports?"

"They're out in the car." He stood up. "Let me go get them."

While he was gone, Mia put her head in her hands. She wished this were a dream. Even a nightmare. Today had been like a nonstop roller coaster, but one with only sickening drops. She heard a car pull up outside.

Charlie came back with a file folder in one hand and two pizza boxes balanced on the other. He called the kids downstairs, then asked Gabe to supervise Brooke while the kids ate in the kitchen. When he returned to the family room, he had the file folder tucked under his arm and was carrying paper plates topped with two pizza slices. Mia was embarrassed to see that Gabe had taken full advantage of Charlie's credit card, ordering two different combos instead of cheaper, single-ingredient pizzas.

From his pocket Charlie produced two crumpled paper towels, handing one over with a flourish. "Your napkin, madam." He settled down next to her. "So have you seen any of the reports?" He kept his voice low.

"No." Mia shook her head. "I figured looking at them wasn't going to change anything. All I know is they didn't do an autopsy." She had been grateful for that. She took a bite of pizza, oddly ashamed that her body could still be hungry after everything that had happened today. Still be hungry when they were discussing her husband's death.

"They don't do an autopsy if they figure the cause of death is self-evident. So what they did in Scott's case was take a chest tap, test his blood for alcohol, snap some photos, and write up a short report about the external condition of the body. I got that and the accident report."

"Okay." Mia waited for the rest.

"In a case like this, when you've got no witness, figuring out what really happened depends on the competency of the CSI who processed the scene and the forensic pathologist who did the exam. Only in this case, there was no CSI, just a patrol officer who responded to the 911 call. And the guy who did the exam wasn't a pathologist, but a death investigator. Who knows how much training either one of them had or whether they're certified and by whom."

He pulled out the accident report, which had a freehand sketch of the accident scene. Mia had to work to swallow what suddenly felt like a wad of cotton in her throat. Two lines curved to the left, indicating a road. A rectangle representing the car sat on the right-hand side just after the curve. A row of triangles showed the line of trees, one of which overlapped the front passenger side of the car.

"How much do you know about car accidents?" he asked.

She lifted one shoulder. "When you work in violent crimes, most of those aren't committed with a vehicle."

"How about physics?"

"Probably not my forte either."

"Accidents basically follow Newton's first law of motion," he said, "which says that an object in motion stays in motion with the same speed and in the same direction unless something acts on it."

"Okay." Mia drew out the word. It was strange to hear Charlie sounding like a professor.

"So. Scott's car failed to completely negotiate the curve and left the road here." He tapped on the illustration. "He hit gravel and then slid into one of these trees. The impact was on the front passenger side door—the right side. The airbags deployed, but he wasn't wearing a seat belt. So he was—"

Mia sucked in her breath. "What did you say?"

"Scott wasn't wearing a seat belt," Charlie continued. "So he was thrown from the driver's seat into—"

"That's not possible." Mia shook her head so hard she felt dizzy for a second. "Scott always wore a seat belt. Always."

"Even when he'd been drinking?"

"Especially when he'd been drinking. He got super cautious behind the wheel when he was drunk."

Charlie paged through the paperwork. "But the first responder told the police that Scott passed him earlier and he was speeding."

"No." Mia knew Scott. "No. He never took chances when he was drunk."

Charlie leaned forward. "Wait a second. You sound like you've been in the car with him when he was drunk."

"I was." She met his eyes. "Not with the kids, never the kids, but sometimes just me."

"So you let him drive when you knew he was drunk?"

Mia tucked in her lips. "We both know that alcoholics can handle amounts that would put other people under the table. Of course if Scott was too drunk, I didn't let him drive, no matter how angry he got. But there were times it wasn't worth arguing with him if it was only a few miles and the roads were quiet. Especially since I knew how careful he was."

Charlie looked disgusted. "Maybe he was only careful when you were in the car."

She sighed. "You could be right. But I know Scott would never not wear a seat belt. The only time he didn't wear one was after the doctor gave him sleeping pills. The whole next day he drove around unbelted, and he didn't even realize it until evening. He told me he was never going to take another one of those pills again. That he couldn't get into as much trouble with alcohol. So for a long time, he used that as his sleeping pill."

Charlie shrugged like he didn't believe her but didn't want to argue.

"Well, for whatever reason, he wasn't wearing a seat belt," he reiterated. "And when the car hit the tree, that part of the car stopped while the rest kept moving, just like Newton said it would. Basically that means the rest of the car started to rotate around the tree. Meanwhile, because Scott wasn't wearing a seat belt, his body kept moving forward at the same speed and in the same direction while the car was starting to move around him. His body hit the interior of the car's passenger side, which caused a lot of damage to the right side—head, shoulder, ribs, and hip." He touched the spots as he named them. "But that's not all that happened. My friend who's a forensic pathologist says that there're really three collisions in any accident, even though they all happen in the same split second. First there's the car hitting something. Then there's the body hitting something inside the car."

"So what's the third collision?" Mia asked. Hadn't everything stopped at that point?

"The internal organs. They follow the first law of motion too. They keep moving until they tear away or hit something hard inside you, like your ribs or your skull. In this case, when the death investigator did a chest tap, he got a syringe full of blood." Charlie touched his chest. "That means Scott's aorta got torn."

"And he bled out inside." Every word was making her flinch. "I know that part, Charlie."

He took a second report from the file. "But in addition to the injuries on the right side of his body, there were blunt-force injuries to the left side of his head. Not the right. The left. His left cheekbone and his left jaw were broken." He again touched the spots as he named them. "Both upper and lower."

"Then he must have hit the dash or the steering wheel."

"I thought of that. Which is why I talked to my friend. The fractures were depressed. He told me that means the head was probably stationary and something moving hit it. Like if you clubbed a block of Styrofoam. The Styrofoam wouldn't crack in half. Instead, the club would leave a sunken imprint in the Styrofoam. And that's what my pathologist friend thinks happened to Scott. He thinks he was hit twice on the side of the head with some sort of club."

"Wait." Mia's thoughts were whirling. "First Scott was in an accident, and after that someone hit him in the head?"

"Well, it's hard to see how it could be the other way around. Because he wouldn't have been able to drive after receiving two blows like that."

"Let me just repeat this so I can get it straight." Mia straightened up. "You think Scott was in an accident."

"I think his car left the road and hit a tree, yes."

"And that hitting the tree caused his death by tearing his aorta."

"Yes."

"Then why would someone come along and hit him in the head if he was already dead? That doesn't make any sense."

"My friend said he might have lived for several minutes, maybe longer. I think someone wanted to make sure Scott was good and dead. Maybe they forced him off the road. Maybe they tampered with his car. But whatever happened, they—"

Mia caught her breath.

Charlie's eyes narrowed. "What?"

"The reason Scott was driving a loaner that night was because his car was in the shop. Its brakes had failed a week before."

CHAPTER 12

Charlie's eyes bored into her. "What was wrong with the brakes?"

"Scott left our driveway, but when he pulled up to that first intersection"—she pointed in its direction—"the one with the four-way stop, he said the brake pedal went right to the floor."

"Was there an accident?"

"No. There weren't any other cars in the intersection. It's always so busy there, but he got lucky that day. He told me he pumped the gas, pulled the emergency brake, and turned into the curb." Mia had been impressed by his quick thinking. "He just bumped along until he came to a stop. Then he walked home, told me what had happened, and called the tow company. He borrowed my car for the day, and at the end of it I took him to our mechanic and he got a loaner. That's the car he was driving when he died."

Charlie cocked his head. "Didn't you put two and two together?"

"Put what together?" Mia's thoughts were racing. "No. Because there was nothing to put together. Our mechanic said the under-carriage of the Suburban had some scrapes. He thought Scott must have driven over something that damaged the brake line."

For a moment Scott rose up in Mia's mind, so strongly conjured it was like he was in the family room with them, leaning against the wall, regarding them with his arms crossed and his face expressionless. She was suddenly aware of how close she was sitting to Charlie, their thighs nearly touching. She scooted a few inches away. The low buzz of a headache was making it hard to think.

Charlie spoke slowly, as if putting his thoughts in order. "The question is—did they tamper with the Suburban's brakes in a failed attempt to kill him? Or did they tamper with the brakes so he'd end up in a car that they knew they could kill him in? Maybe that explains why Scott wasn't wearing a seat belt. Maybe they disabled it."

Wheels within wheels. Charlie was starting to sound like some lonely talk show caller with an elaborate conspiracy theory.

"But how could they know Scott was going to end up in a car from our mechanic? A lot of people would just take a car that new to the dealer, but we've had the same mechanic for a long time and we trust him. The loaner Scott was in when he died was a beater. It had something like two hundred thousand miles on it. I'm sure it didn't have any side-curtain airbags or anything like that. But it wasn't part of any conspiracy."

Scott's Suburban, on the other hand, had been top-of-the-line— and it had also turned out not to really be Scott's. After he died Mia had found out it was leased. And even though Scott was dead, she had still been on the hook to pay it off. She had been lucky to find someone to take over the payments. Even without that burden she was barely making ends meet, struggling to pay all the bills Scott had accumulated.

"I think you're adding one and one and getting eleven." Mia wiped her mouth with the paper towel, signaling to Charlie and even to herself that she was done listening to crazy what-ifs. "Scott ran over something in the Suburban that cut the brake line. Then he got drunk and had an accident in an old car that bounced him around like a pinball. He had a run of bad luck, and he made some stupid decisions. End of story."

"But his face, Mia." Charlie lightly tapped the left side of his face. "Nothing explains the injuries to the wrong side of his head. I want to ask Puyallup County to reopen the case."

"Then go ahead," she said sharply. "You don't need my permission. But I just can't see why anyone would want Scott dead."

"I thought maybe you could help me with the why." Charlie tilted his head. "You were his wife. You knew him better than anyone."

"I only wish that were true." Her mouth suddenly tasted bitter. "I've realized Scott was hiding a lot of secrets from me. About our finances, about his business failing, about his drinking. There could even be more that I don't know about." And did she really want to?

"Can you think of anyone who was mad at him?"

"Mad at Scott?" She almost laughed. "He was so quiet. He wasn't the type people got mad at. If anyone was mad at him when he died, it was me. You never met him, right?"

Charlie shook his head.

"Scott was an accountant. An accountant. The most boring job ever. Staring at columns of numbers with a printing calculator under one hand. Because he was a one-man operation, his clients were people who didn't need much in the way of an accountant, or who only really needed one at tax time. Which was why he was working crazy hours when he died."

Charlie looked down at the papers and then back up at her. "This is an awkward question to ask, but could there have been anyone else?"

"Scott?" Mia tried to buy time to think. What did she want to tell Charlie? Suspicions were one thing, facts another. "We'd been together since college."

"Even people in good marriages sometimes fall into something unexpected."

She bit her lip and said, "To be honest, I used to wonder if he was seeing someone. He was working those long hours, and he was always irritable when I tried to talk to him. I knew he was hiding something from me." Heat climbed her cheeks. She looked down at her hands, twisting in her lap. "After he died and I found out how much debt he left us in, I realized that must have been it. That we were living off credit cards and not what his business brought in. Although I guess it's possible that he had more than one secret. More than two, when you count his drinking again."

"Maybe he tried to break something off and the lady got upset. Or she could have had a husband or boyfriend."

Mia tried to picture it. Was Scott so selfish that he would cheat on her physically and emotionally as well as financially? Of course, this was the same man who had broken his promises to her, lied by omission and commission.

"I guess there's the flip side." Charlie glanced at her and then away. "Maybe some guy had fallen in love with you and wanted Scott out of the way?"

Mia snorted. "If that's the case, then where is he?" She mimed looking around. "No one's exactly eager to put the moves on a widow with a preschooler and a teenager."

Charlie didn't deny it. "How about enemies? Or friends he'd fallen out with?"

"Scott didn't have a lot of friends, but that was by choice. He was sort of a loner." Mia thought of how Scott had pulled back into himself, like a snail retreating into its shell. He must have been afraid that his failure would slip out. "When he wasn't working, he went on long runs or played music." She saw Scott's brown head bent over his guitar, his eyes closed. The memory brought pain so fierce and sharp it was like someone had slipped a knife between her ribs and given it a good twist. "Even when he was drinking, he was a quiet drunk. He wasn't the kind of outspoken guy who made enemies."

"Robbery could be another possible motive. Was anything taken from him? Anything missing from his car?"

Mia thought back. "His wallet was returned to me with all his credit cards—his maxed-out credit cards—and a hundred or so in cash. His phone never turned up, but you know how it is these days—some light-fingered ambulance guy or morgue tech or even the guy who tried to help him might have picked it up. I guess it's possible he had something in the car that someone wanted, but if he did, I don't know what it was."

"Puyallup can probably rule out a hate crime or a gang killing." Charlie tapped the butt end of his pen on the papers. "It's possible someone could have done it just for fun."

Mia's mouth crimped. "In that case, they'll never figure it out." A thrill killing—stranger to stranger—was almost impossible to solve.

"Maybe it was road rage. Someone forced him off the road and then finished him off."

Mia winced. "That's pretty up close and personal." Something else occurred to her as she pictured Scott laboring to breathe, writhing on the car seat. "This is a weird idea, but maybe they felt bad for him. You know, like the person who comes upon a dying dog on the side of the road and puts it out of its misery."

Charlie grunted. "Puyallup needs to re-interview that guy who tried to give your husband first aid. Maybe he saw someone leaving the scene." He looked around. "Did Scott work from home?"

"No. He had an office in a small complex." She remembered her dull surprise at how messy it had been. "I had to empty it out in a hurry or they were going to charge another month's rent. I just dumped everything into banker's boxes and stuck them down in the basement. Oh!" Mia put her hand over her mouth.

"What?"

"His office was a mess. I was too overwhelmed at the time to give it much thought. But Scott was the kind of guy who kept his ties sorted by color. Being neat was in his blood. So why was his office so messy?"

Charlie's jaw tightened. "If someone was looking for something after he died, then maybe somebody really did try to break into your house tonight."

CHAPTER 13

Was Charlie right? Had someone been looking for something in Scott's office?

"It's an awfully big coincidence that a day after I got Scott's records someone tried to break into your house," Charlie said. "We need to look through the stuff you brought home from his office."

Mia put her hand to her temple. "Tonight?"

"I don't think we can afford to wait."

After everything that had happened today, she was never going to get any sleep anyway. She got to her feet. "Okay. Let's go."

To get through the basement, they had to walk through the kitchen, where Gabe had managed to wolf down almost a whole pizza by himself. Brooke, however, seemed to have concentrated on plucking off toppings and piling them on her plate, leaving her with a denuded yellow triangle missing only two small bites.

"Charlie and I are going to look at something downstairs," Mia told Gabe as she tossed Charlie's and her paper plates in the garbage. "Could you do me a favor and get your sister ready for bed and read her a story?"

Gabe looked from Charlie to Mia. "Are you checking on why the burglar alarm went off?"

She didn't want to scare him. Even if she needed to, it could wait until morning. Let him have one good night's sleep. "It was probably just the wind, but we're going to make sure."

The basement was lined with rows of heavy-duty plastic shelves filled with Rubbermaid totes. In one corner was Scott's weight bench, which was now seeing far more use from Gabe than Scott had ever given it. A few months earlier Mia had sold Scott's table saw and some other potentially dangerous tools at a garage sale, so at least now the basement was a little more navigable.

She pointed at a row of cardboard banker's boxes on a bottom shelf. "Those six are from Scott's office." When she leaned down and grabbed the first box, she was surprised by how heavy it was. Then she took off the lid. "Oh, and this one has his computer in it."

"You just left it down here?" Charlie looked around the room, which had a concrete floor spotted with damp patches.

"I haven't really had time to turn around, let alone think about what to do with the stuff from Scott's office." Mia felt a little defensive. "And it's not like we need another computer. We already have one in our room"—when would she stop saying *our*?—"and Gabe's got a laptop. So who would use this one? Brooke? I'm trying to keep her away from screens as it is."

Maybe she should sell it. Even a couple hundred dollars would be a welcome addition to her checking account. Between the fees for preschool and parking and school activities, plus feeding a boy who seemed to need to eat seven times a day, plus paying off the credit card mess Scott had left them in, she needed every penny.

"Why don't you start with the paperwork, and I'll see what I can find on the computer." Charlie set it on top of the workbench. In an official investigation, anything device related would be handled by a computer forensics lab, but that didn't mean a homicide detective didn't have some rudimentary skills.

"What do you think I should be looking for?" Mia took the lid off another box.

"Basically, anything that makes you think twice." He looked down at the screen. "I need a password to get in. Got any ideas?"

Mia's first and second guesses were wrong, but her third wasn't. How could she have known so much about Scott, down to his passwords, but not the important stuff? She turned back to the file box and began systematically examining each piece of paper she took out. Tax forms. Ledger sheets with entries for things like "project sales," "direct labor costs," and "property and premises assets." Ads for exercise equipment ripped from magazines. Payroll records. Utility statements for various businesses.

"So you said we're gonna be working together on that case?" Charlie asked as he clicked through various screens.

Mia was grateful for the change of subject. "The issue is whether the kids should be charged as adults. Frank says they haven't arrested the suspects yet, but he thinks they're close. As soon as they're picked up, we'll want to interview their teachers and neighbors. Maybe the boys themselves, if their lawyers will let us. And I want to talk to the victim's husband and get a feeling for what he wants."

She finished up the first box and moved on to the next. At the top was a misshapen purple vase Gabe had made in preschool and that Scott had been using to hold pens and pencils. It didn't have any special significance to her, but it didn't feel right to just throw it out. She set it aside to bring into her own office. Under the vase were tax worksheets for various businesses. A list of places Scott seemed to be thinking about for vacation, which made her eyes spark with tears. And then she found a file filled with all the agreements for the credit cards he had taken out in both their names, which made her tears dry up.

She flipped through the papers at the bottom of the box. One felt too thick, and she realized it was stuck to the page below it. When she peeled it apart, she saw it was an IRS letter of notification to Oleg Popov, doing business as Oleg's Gems and Jewels. She showed it to Charlie, who made a little humming noise.

"So the IRS wanted to audit one of his clients? A jewelry business is the kind that makes it easy to hide income," he said. "A lot of jewelers offer a twenty percent discount for cash—and then never report the money. And if you don't report it, you don't get taxed on it. Even if a business is losing money, it still has to pay the sales tax it takes in. Seven percent doesn't sound like a lot, but it can add up to thousands every month, and it's on the gross."

Mia's heart sank. "Do you think Scott was helping his clients cheat on their taxes?"

He shrugged. "The audit doesn't necessarily mean anything. That's the kind of business the IRS likes to target. It could range from everything being aboveboard, to Scott just taking his clients at their word and not looking too closely at things, to his actively advising clients on how to cheat." The thought didn't seem to faze him. He turned back to the computer. "Do you know who Scott was with the night he was killed?"

"No. A client. That's all he said."

Charlie tapped on the computer screen. "He kept his calendar online. But all it says is that he had a meeting at eight p.m. at the Jade Kitchen in Coho City."

"He did have a few clients that were restaurants, like that Macho Nacho. I'm pretty sure that Jade Kitchen was another one." Both were small regional chains. As time went on, Scott had talked less and less about his clients. Only after he died had Mia realized it must have been because there were fewer and fewer of them.

"We should go out there," Charlie said. "See if anyone remembers him and who he was with that night."

"Will it matter, though?" Mia asked. "Scott was alone when he died."

"Maybe whoever he was with followed him after he left. Maybe the staff could tell us if they were arguing."

Mia went back to looking through the papers, but for some reason she now found herself aware of Charlie's presence, of the way he breathed, of the slightly sweet way he smelled. She reminded herself that they were work partners, nothing more. It didn't mean anything that he was a man and she was a woman. After all, fifty percent of the population was male. And when it came to the people she worked with, the percentage was even higher.

Halfway down into the third box, she found a printout of a note Scott had sent to Kenny Zhong, the owner of Jade Kitchen, dated only a week before Scott's death.

> In the paperwork you gave me, you're reporting $650,000 of gross sales, but there are only $640,000 of credit card receipts. This lopsided ratio of credit transactions to cash transactions could be highly suggestive that your restaurants are underreporting cash. We need to discuss this immediately.

Mia caught her breath. Maybe Scott *had* been keeping honest books. She turned to Charlie, but he was staring at something on the computer screen that she couldn't see from where she was standing.

"So who's Betty?" he asked in a voice that wasn't quite his regular tone.

"Betty?" It took her a second to remember. "Oh yeah, a couple of months before he died, Scott hired this older lady to help out. It was tax season, which is the crazy time of year for CPAs, especially when you work by yourself."

"Did you ever meet her?"

"No." Mia had had a mental picture of her, though, a lady with her white hair in a bun and wearing mushroom-colored sensible shoes.

"You didn't talk to her after Scott died?"

Mia felt her shoulders sag as she remembered the weight that had pressed down on her after the accident. So many people to tell, so many pieces to pick up, so many things to figure out. "I can't remember. She might have come to the funeral—there were a lot of people there I didn't recognize. I ended up just going through Scott's address book and sending out one mass e-mail with all the names in the bcc field." Mia swallowed down a sudden nausea. "Why are you asking me about her?"

He answered her question with one of his own. "How'd you know Betty was older?"

How had she known? Had Scott ever said? "I guess it was just from the name. I mean, really, who's named Betty anymore?"

"I found a photo on his computer that was downloaded from a phone." Charlie's eyes held an expression she couldn't read. "It's labeled 'Betty,' although it shows both of them."

Mia suddenly didn't want to see. Why had she ever agreed to do this?

Charlie turned the computer screen toward her.

It was a photo of Scott and a young woman. She had a heart-shaped face with a pointed chin, high cheekbones, full lips, and a strong nose. Her blond wavy hair fell past her shoulders. She was beautiful. She also couldn't have been more than twenty-five.

Mia was still standing, but she felt as if the floor were falling away beneath her feet.

"So you don't know her?" Charlie asked.

"No. I've never seen her before."

The expression in Charlie's eyes? It was pity.

Because Betty had her arm around Scott.

And Scott had his arm around her.

CHAPTER 14

Mia must have known. Or maybe, she thought as she stared at the image of her husband and what was obviously his paramour, she must not have wanted to know.

Charlie watched her with eyes that had seen too much and weren't surprised by anything.

She covered her face with cold hands. She wanted to run away. She wanted to hide in a dark place. Curl into a ball, tighter and tighter until she simply disappeared.

Sixteen years of marriage, and this? It wasn't enough that Scott had started drinking again. It wasn't enough he had secretly gotten them into debt that she would now spend years digging them out of. No, he had found another woman, kissed her, laughed with her, whispered to her, caressed her.

Loved her.

And betrayed Mia. Betrayed their family. Lied to Mia every time he claimed to love her.

She dropped her hands from her burning eyes, her shame turning to anger. She couldn't be like Brooke, who still believed she disappeared if she covered her eyes.

"How about at the funeral? Did she come?"

She made herself look again. This Betty, this stupid girl, couldn't be more than ten years older than Gabe. Young. So young it was almost obscene to think of Scott being with her. Mia's jaw started to hurt, and she realized she was gritting her teeth. Why would a beautiful girl like that want to date a married man who was nearly old enough to be her father? He must have given her things, spent money on her. Maybe that was another reason they were so broke.

The funeral had been a blur. Mia had walked down the church aisle on shaky legs, wondering how she could walk at all. How she could breathe. How time could keep heaving itself forward when her life had been destroyed. The only reason she'd been able to stay upright had been the presence of her children on either side. She and her son had stood with their arms across each other's backs. Which one of them was supporting the other hadn't been clear.

"I don't think I remember seeing her there. But I can't be sure."

"Do you remember Betty's last name?"

Mia smiled mirthlessly. "Oddly enough, I do. It's Eastman. I grew up on East Main Street, so when Scott told me about hiring her, her name stuck."

"Puyallup County should talk to her," Charlie said. "Find out what she knows. Find out if there's any way she could be involved."

Mia looked at that face again. Was there something sly and self-satisfied in the set of her lips, in her half-lidded eyes? Or if another man were in this photo, would she be seeing something completely different, something more innocent?

A few years earlier Mia had been hurrying down the staircase when she lost her balance. Rather than falling back and bumping painfully downward, she had tried to keep her feet under her by running down the stairs, her arms outstretched.

She had succeeded. At least for a few steps.

But ultimately she hadn't been able to keep up. The cast she'd had to wear on her wrist for six weeks had served as a reminder that sometimes it was better to accept the pain immediately rather than try to stave it off. Better a bruised bottom than a broken wrist.

Since Scott had died, every day had been like falling down a staircase. Trying to move her feet fast enough that reality couldn't catch up with her. No money? Go back to work. Car too expensive? Find someone to take the lease. No father for her children? Try to be both mother and father.

No husband? Don't stand still long enough to think about it. In the days after Scott's death, Mia had focused on going through the motions. Her children needed her, and she met their needs as best she could, even if at her center she felt ice cold and empty. She thought that maybe if she went through the motions long enough, she could remember how to live.

Maybe it would even become living.

One day became another, and each day it was like she had moved further away from Scott. Even if Mia had wanted to go back, she couldn't. She just kept getting further away, as if she were on an airport's moving walkway that Scott had failed to step onto. And now finally he was so far back she couldn't even see him anymore. Some days she couldn't remember his face without looking at a photograph. Couldn't hear his voice in her head. Some days she called the house when no one was there just to hear him say her name one more time: "Scott, Mia, Gabe, and Brooke aren't at home right now . . ."

But now it was clear that the absence she had felt had been a phantom. A ghost of a marriage past. She stared at Scott's computer screen, at the girl grinning with her face right next to his, while a red-hot flame consumed the empty void at her center. Had Scott been planning on leaving her and the kids, running off with this silly young thing?

He had to have been. Probably leaving all the debt behind for Mia to clean up.

Charlie was watching her. She could see the sympathy in his

tired blue eyes. She wanted to rage and moan and scream until her throat was raw. But the kids might hear, and they had already experienced more than enough stress for the day.

But if she didn't do something, she would burst. Her eyes fell on the vase. It was nothing special, nothing that Gabe had labored over, nothing that she had even remembered until she saw it again in Scott's office.

She picked it up, raised it high overhead, and threw it down on the floor, intending to smash it to satisfying smithereens. But it was made of some child-friendly clay that dried in the air, not in a kiln. The only noise it made as it fractured into four or five big pieces came from the pens inside as they clattered onto the cement floor.

"You okay?" Charlie said mildly.

"Just mad," Mia said. "Mad and sad." She half laughed. "I sound like one of Brooke's early readers. The cat sat on the mat."

Charlie gave her a crooked smile. "I'm sorry you feel bad. And that Scott seems to have been a cad."

"I don't think it's 'seems to.'" Mia dropped to her knees and began to clean up the mess she had made. "I think he was. And I just didn't want to know it." The last piece she reached for was the bottom section of the vase. When she picked it up, she heard a faint rattle.

She peered inside. Her eyes widened. At the bottom was a small black velvet box.

"What is it?" Charlie asked, but Mia was too engrossed to answer. She hooked it out with a finger, then opened the box. She tugged at the glittering thing inside. Then it fell from her grasp and rolled away.

It was a diamond ring.

CHAPTER 15

As the diamond ring rolled across the floor, Charlie muttered an amazed-sounding expletive. Mia was frozen, but she could feel her eyes getting wider.

"Do you think that's real?" she finally asked.

"Why would he have hidden it if it wasn't?"

The ring came to rest under one of the plastic shelves. She knelt down but couldn't see it. Charlie took a flashlight from the top of the workbench and joined in the hunt.

Mia finally fished it out with one of the pens that had been in the vase. "Is it an engagement ring?" she asked as they both stared at it.

The ring itself was made of some silvery metal, white gold or platinum. Six prongs held a large round diamond. Rectangular-cut diamonds were set into the band on either side.

Charlie let out a low whistle. "I guess. But I run in circles where nobody could afford to even look at a ring like that."

Mia was glad she had taken off her rings a few weeks ago, including the one with a tiny chip of a diamond Scott had given her when he proposed.

Her jaw clenched so hard her teeth hurt. If she had wanted proof that Scott was really cheating on her, here it was. In glittering carats.

"I wonder why he hadn't given it to her yet?" Charlie asked.

Mia unclenched her jaw. "Wouldn't we have to be divorced first?"

"Not if you think of it as the world's most expensive promise ring."

In Mia's dream she and Scott were hiking along a narrow track winding above a rocky coastline. A hundred feet below them, the ocean crashed over boulders. In real life it had been years since they hiked, but in the dream they were fully outfitted in layers of fleece and Gor-Tex, hiking boots on their feet. Scott was ahead of her, clambering over a large rock that blocked the path. Mia called out for him to be careful.

Suddenly Scott slipped. In slow motion he cartwheeled down the steep slope, bouncing off boulders like a rag doll before his body finally hit the water. He sank out of sight. For one moment his head broke through the waves, his arms windmilling, but then he disappeared completely.

The area was deserted, without even a seagull to witness what was happening. Mia didn't know what to do. She didn't have a rope. There was no way down, and even if she were able to get there, there wasn't even a sliver of beach. With a feeling of unspeakable horror, she understood she could not save Scott.

And then the water began to rise.

It was more than just the tide coming in. She realized it was a tsunami, a growing wall of water that quickly swallowed the boulders and then ate up the space that had separated her from the waves. Soon it would pick her up and smash her against the rocks, or push her down, down, down, so deep she would never come up for air.

A small insistent voice slowly roused her.

"I wet the bed, Mommy. And now it's cold."

With a groan Mia pushed herself up. Brooke was standing next to the bed, pushing her shoulder with one of her little hands. There was no ocean, no tsunami. Scott was long dead, even if the repercussions of what he had done weren't.

Mia had had nightmares about the ocean since she had nearly drowned when she was five. She hadn't learned to swim until Gabe started clamoring to go to the pool. She had found an adult learn-to-swim class, and every Wednesday she forced herself to go. After nearly every lesson she threw up, but she persevered. She still hated it, but she could do it. The irony was that Mia lived in a city defined by water, bordered by Puget Sound on one side and Lake Washington on the other.

Now she shuffled down the hall to the laundry closet. It seemed oddly empty. Shouldn't there be more sheets and blankets? Were they stuffed in one of the laundry room's baskets? Or had Brooke built a fort someplace that she hadn't noticed? But that didn't explain the shelf that was normally stacked with toilet paper. Half of it was missing.

Was Gabe sneaking out to TP people's houses? Did kids even do that anymore? And if they did, and he did, how was he getting out without waking her? Her bedroom was on the other end of the hall, but these days it seemed like she slept as lightly as if she'd drunk two cups of coffee before going to bed. Which sometimes she had.

Mia remade Brooke's bed while Brooke curled up on the carpeted floor. It only took a few minutes, but still her daughter was asleep by the time she finished. She picked her up and laid her down, pulled the quilt over her shoulders. Too tired to carry the soiled sheets down to the basement laundry room, Mia compromised by tossing them down onto the tile floor of the first-floor foyer.

She meant to return to her room, but when she went back to check on Brooke, the temptation proved too much. She curled up beside her on the toddler bed. Brooke was usually a restless sleeper, flinging her arms and legs about as if she were performing jumping jacks in her dreams, but for once she was still. And oh, how Mia missed the warmth and companionship of another body in bed. She curled around her daughter and held her close.

She closed her eyes, but sleep eluded her. The day ran through her head again in a series of frightening images. Young's contorted face as he ran toward her. The squad cars outside her house. The cops with their guns drawn. Charlie talking about the unexplained injuries to Scott's head. Betty's beautiful, complacent face. The glittering diamond ring bouncing across the floor. Scott drowning.

What secrets had he taken to his grave?

And what would happen once she started to uncover them?

CHAPTER 16

TUESDAY

Vin opened the closet door to get his coat. He paid no attention to the figure lying on the floor, jackknifed at the waist, dark hair covering its face. Its right leg stuck out at an odd angle.

He had bought the girl on Craigslist. You could get anything there. Even girls made of plaster, girls who had once been painstakingly dressed in the fashions of the day, posed to entice customers to buy what they wore. Girls who had eventually been discarded to make room for newer, lighter models made of plastic.

Up close, she didn't look that real, what with the chip missing from the tip of her nose and her oddly pink skin. But if you laid her out at night in front of a car that you had skewed across the road, a car with its hood up and its flashers on, she looked real enough.

Real enough to make a man's heart stutter in his chest when he rounded a corner and saw her lying there. Especially if his drink had been spiked.

Real enough to make him jerk his car to the right to avoid running her over.

Real enough to make him plow into a line of trees.

Real enough to kill him. With a little help from Vin.

CHAPTER 17

Where was she? Mia's eyes flew open. Her panicked breathing echoed in her ears. Her heart was beating like a windup toy. She scrambled back until her shoulder blades were against the wall, her teeth bared, ready to fight.

Then she blinked, finally absorbing where she was. She wasn't on the floor of the courtroom with a razor blade at her throat. She wasn't fighting off Scott's killer or saving Gabe from an armed intruder or trying to rescue Scott from the waves. She was in Brooke's toddler bed. From the wall, stenciled images of bunnies and puppies smiled down at her. Brooke was still asleep, the deep sleep that only a small child was capable of, one undisturbed by Mia's panic.

It was early in the morning, early enough that the sky outside Brooke's window was still dark.

With a groan Mia got to her feet. Her back ached as if she had slept like a contortionist. The bathroom mirror revealed scattered bruises on her neck and torso, from both Bernard Young and the men who had tried to save her from him. A few were shaped like fingerprints, and one faint mark on her throat was the half-moon shape of a fingernail. Mia shivered as she thought of how close she had come to dying.

Last night Charlie had given her copies of the accident report and the external examination report, but she hadn't looked at them yet. She didn't have the emotional strength. Today Charlie planned to ask Puyallup County to reopen the investigation into Scott's accident. And when the detectives came to talk to her, she would show them everything they had found. Even the photo of Betty. Even the diamond ring.

She stayed in the shower for a long time, trying to wash off the residue of her dreams, the memories of yesterday. Twenty-four hours ago she would have said she had known Scott, had known even his flaws. Now she wondered how much one person could ever know another.

Downstairs she put Brooke's sheets in the wash. It was still early, so she didn't need to get the kids up yet. Weekday mornings were usually a stressful blur. If she wasn't careful, all her kids' memories would be of her barking at them to get up, hurry up, clean up.

In this new reality Mia was always running late, catching up, taking shortcuts, forgetting something, making do. Juggling a half dozen cases, worrying about Gabe and Brooke, trying to put more or less healthy meals on the table, overseeing homework, doing laundry. Keeping to a budget while she slowly repaid the debts. Every night she fell into bed thinking of all the things she hadn't accomplished during the day.

Now she checked the flour canister. The envelope she had put the ring box in was still buried in the bottom, a temporary hiding place until she could figure out what to do next.

For right now, she decided that *next* meant making pancakes.

Fifteen minutes later Gabe shambled into the kitchen, alternating yawns with sniffs of the air. "Pancakes? Is it somebody's birthday?" Since she had gone back to work, breakfast meant cold cereal for the kids. Mia was lucky if she remembered to grab a granola bar to eat in the car.

"No. I just felt like making them." She sprinkled chocolate chips over the batter she had just poured on the griddle.

Deftly avoiding a swat from her spatula, Gabe grabbed the top pancake off the finished stack. "I'm sorry I went inside yesterday after the alarm went off," he said with a full mouth. "That was kind of stupid."

It was a rare apology.

"We're just lucky it all turned out okay. Next time, though—well, I hope there isn't a next time—but if there is, and you feel like something's not right, stop. And then talk to an adult about it. Me, Charlie, or at least one of the neighbors . . . even if you think you can handle it by yourself."

"I wish Dad were still alive." Gabe reached for another pancake, and this time she didn't try to stop him.

"You and me both, buddy." Although if Scott were to appear before her now, her first instinct would be to slap him. The second? That . . . she still wasn't sure of.

Gabe cut his eyes sideways at her and then away. "What were you and Charlie really doing downstairs last night?"

Had he overheard them? Mia had to tread carefully. She didn't want Gabe to know about Betty.

"There's some stuff about your dad's old business that I need to clear up."

He nodded, but she wondered if he believed her.

"Can you get your sister up? I want to make sure she has enough time to eat." Brooke was a dawdler.

"Sure." He looked at the clock on the stove. "Maybe you can even eat with us today?"

Something squeezed her heart. How many fourteen-year-old boys would ask their mom that? And how many studies showed that a family sitting down to eat together was better for kids? These days Mia ate most of her meals on her feet as she tried to keep one step ahead of the chaos.

"I'd love to."

Mia was one of the first people into work. When she opened the door to her office, she smelled the flower arrangement before she saw it. Surrounded by a cloud of pink cellophane, it sat in the middle of her small conference table. Pink roses and mini carnations provided the backdrop for showy stargazer lilies. Each pastel petal was outlined in white and dappled with red.

What was wrong with Mia that when she leaned over to sniff and saw the red dots, the first thought she had was of blood splatter?

She opened the card. It was signed by Judge Rivas, as well as everyone who had been working in the courtroom yesterday, including Rolf Dockins, Young's defense attorney. They all wished her well, praised her for being a trouper, and complimented her on her strength. The lid on the box where she had put the experience threatened to pop off, but she pushed it back down. Someday she would have time to process what had happened, but not now.

Knuckles rapped on her open door. She turned to see Frank.

"I heard about what happened yesterday, Mia. I wish you would have told me. Should you even be here today?" His brown eyes were filled with concern.

Still, she was sure that right above those eyes his brain was busy calculating what her taking off a day or two would do to the shopping cart case. Frank knew her home and cell phone numbers. If he had really wanted her to stay home, he would have called.

"I'm okay. Just a little banged up. It all happened so fast, I didn't really have time to be scared." She pushed her memories of screaming in terror, barely pausing to draw breath, out of her head and back into storage.

How was she going to have the energy to work today and then teach? *Fake it until you make it,* she told herself. She was an actress playing Mia. The Mia everyone needed her to be.

CHAPTER 18

In a glass-walled ICU room, Tamsin Merritt lay surrounded by a tangle of tubes, wires, and machines. Mia stepped lightly across the threshold, unconsciously holding her breath, as if she might waken her. In part she had come here to escape the parade of concerned co-workers, but now that she was here she found herself even more off balance.

Tamsin's face was swollen and discolored, her eyes shallow, purple slits. White gauze was wrapped around the top of her head. The edges of the gauze were marked with a brownish ooze of bloody fluid. The air smelled of disinfectant mingled with other, deeper scents that Mia couldn't name.

A narrow foam pad was wrapped around the back of Tamsin's neck, cushioning her from the tie that held in place the flexible white breathing tube inserted into the hollow of her throat. Two more large flexible tubes were joined to it, one white and one blue, and they were connected to an accordion-like pump on a stand by the bed. The room was filled with the sound of its rhythmic wheezing. The machine's pace was much slower than normal breathing, so it seemed to Mia as if Tamsin were holding each breath. The long pause before the air was released in a *whoosh* heightened Mia's anxiety.

From a pole, three IV bags dripped into Tamsin's arm. At the far end of the bed hung another bag half filled with pale urine. Above her head, a monitor showed various numbers and graphs that constantly changed. The woman at the center of it all, the one being kept alive by the beeping and whooshing machines, lay as still as if she were already in her grave.

When Mia thought of the two boys who had done this, her heart hardened. Anyone who was capable of inflicting this kind of terrible injury certainly deserved to be punished to the fullest extent of the law.

She stepped closer. Tamsin was covered by a doubled sheet. A folded blue blanket, splotched with dried blood, rested under her head and on top of the pillow. Half her dark hair had been shaved, and the remnants were matted together with more blood. Large black stitches ran across her forehead and then back along the stubbled part of her skull.

A doctor entered the room. He was in his midthirties, with a muscular physique that loose blue scrubs couldn't hide. A stethoscope was draped over his neck, and under his blue cloth cap his head was shaved. He frowned at her. "Are you a family member?"

"I'm from the King County prosecutor's office," Mia said. "We'll be handling her case."

"You do know she can't talk to you?" he asked as he leaned over to check Tamsin's IVs.

"I just wanted to see her for myself. So I can fully understand what they did to her."

He turned toward Mia and his upper lip curled back. "They dropped a shopping cart on her from four stories up. And why? For fun? Even animals don't do that to each other."

Mia didn't say anything, but she wondered if the doctor was right. When she was growing up, their cat, Applesauce, had liked to play with his prey. He would let a mouse run off a few inches, squeaking desperately, then pounce on it again and idly bat it about or carry it in his mouth for a few yards. Then he would drop the mouse and start the game all over again, turning with a hiss on any human who tried to intervene. And when the poor thing was finally dead, half the time he wouldn't even eat it.

Mia gathered up her courage and stepped closer to Tamsin. It was hard to look at her and think of the woman she had been only a few days ago. Just heading to the store with her son to do some shopping. How many times had Mia been in her shoes? Now she was a seemingly lifeless body on a bed.

"So that's where the shopping cart hit her?" Mia said in a near whisper, pointing at the stitches.

"There?" the doctor answered, making no effort to keep his voice down. "Yes, but we also had to remove a piece of her skull." Mia must have made a face, because he said, "If your brain starts to swell, it has no place to go. So we do what's called a hemicraniectomy. We removed a portion of her skull to allow her brain to swell beyond the confines of the bone without causing further elevations in brain pressure." One of the numbers on the monitor went higher, to ninety-five.

It wasn't so long ago that Mia had nursed Brooke, watched her heartbeat pulsing on the soft spot of her skull. But eventually her fontanel had knit together, as it was designed to do. How could you go out into the world with only a stretch of skin protecting your brain?

Mia shivered. "So she's always going to be missing part of her skull?"

He shook his head. "No, no. We froze it. Once the swelling has resolved, we can suture it back onto its original place."

She had no desire to learn how you sewed bone to bone. "And she's still in a coma?"

"Yes, but remember we put her in it. So it's a medically induced coma, not one caused by the trauma to her brain. We did it to slow things down. While she's in the coma, her brain doesn't need as much energy. So hopefully it's less likely that parts of it will die." He sighed. "Still, even if she recovers, anyone surviving a cranial injury of this magnitude should expect to contend with some degree of permanent disability. There could be memory problems, difficulty with solving problems or planning actions, changes in personality, physical impairment—it's a wide range, and hard to predict. She's going to need extensive physical therapy at a minimum, and probably some type of long-term care."

Mia wondered if they should be talking about Tamsin like this right in front of her. Wasn't it true that hearing was the last sense to go?

The doctor was looking up at something, and Mia followed his gaze. The numbers on the monitor kept going up even as she watched: 99, 102, 108, 115. An alarm began to sound. He reached up to turn it down and then leaned over Tamsin. "I don't like this tachycardia. It can cause blood clots, and she could have a heart attack or a stroke. I need you to leave. Now."

Mia hurried out of the room as a half dozen people in scrubs ran toward it.

CHAPTER 19

Why didn't you tell me?" Charlie demanded as soon as Mia climbed into his car. Part of him wanted to throttle her. They were going to meet with Tamsin's husband, Wade, and their son, Luke, but right now his focus was only on Mia. "Someone tries to cut your throat with a razor blade in court yesterday and you don't even think to mention it?"

When another detective asked Charlie this morning if he had heard what happened to Mia, everything had stopped for him. He hadn't been able to move or even think until he learned that (a) she was unhurt and (b) the attack had occurred the day before.

"A few other things happened after that. As you might remember." Mia managed a faint smile, but her face was so pale her skin appeared nearly translucent. "It didn't come up."

"Were you hurt at all?" Charlie's hands tightened on the steering wheel.

"Just a few bruises, but I think most of them came from everybody piling on, trying to get that guy off me. Trevor Gosden knocked the razor blade out of his hand before he could do any damage. I just don't know where it came from."

"It's possible to tuck a razor blade between your cheek and gum." Charlie poked his tongue into his cheek.

"Like chewing tobacco?"

"Only more deadly. Then you just put your hand up to your mouth, like you're coughing, and spit it out." If Trevor hadn't been there, Young might have slit Mia's throat from ear to ear. Charlie made a mental note to buy the guy a beer.

"The only good thing about yesterday was it was *all* so stressful," Mia said. "I couldn't really take any one part of it in. There was no time to think about what had just happened because something new and equally bad was happening. In a way, maybe that was actually better." She scrubbed her face with her hands. "I did have a lot of nightmares last night. Only they were all about Scott. He was drowning in the ocean. And I tried and tried, but I couldn't save him."

If Charlie had been in her dream, he would have thrown that jerk a cement block.

"When I was a kid, some nights I couldn't go to sleep for thinking about what it would be like to drown." Mia looked over at him. "Did you know that parts of the ocean are over seven miles deep? I used to lie in bed thinking about sinking down, down, down." One hand touched her neck. "And no air."

"The atmospheric pressure would kill you long before you reached the bottom. And around here, even if you floated, you'd die from hypothermia in an hour or two."

She rolled her eyes. "You know, Charlie, that doesn't actually make me feel better."

"Sorry," he said. Sometimes being around Mia severed the connection between his brain and his mouth. "Anyway, I called Puyallup County this morning, asked them to reopen Scott's case. I told them about the Suburban's brake line being cut."

Mia bit her lip. "Did you tell them about what we found in the basement?"

"I mostly said they should look at the medical evidence again. Between that and the brake line, I think that's more than enough for them to start with." Charlie had begun by contacting the traffic division, but they hadn't been very responsive. He had finally asked to be transferred to the sheriff, who had listened without much comment. He had promised to look into it himself and get back to Charlie.

"Before we get to her house, you should know that I went to see Tamsin today," Mia said.

"What? Why?" Charlie asked. "Is she conscious?" Mia couldn't conduct interviews on her own, because she couldn't put herself on the stand to testify about what she had learned.

"I just wanted to see her for myself. And I also wanted to get out of the office. I couldn't get any work done. Everyone wanted to talk about what happened yesterday, and right now I don't want to think about it." She pressed her lips together. "But looking at Tamsin was hard. Her head's all stitched up, her face is puffed up, and they had to take out part of her skull until the swelling goes down. They ended up kicking me out of the room because her heart started beating too fast." She sighed. "When I think about Gabe, I know that kids make mistakes. But when I think about Tamsin in that hospital bed, I feel like these boys deserve the maximum."

When Charlie saw the Merritts' house, he let out a low whistle. Although if this was called a house, then what Charlie lived in would be considered a hovel. A cardboard box.

It was four thousand square feet, easy. Charlie's house could have fit inside twice, with room to spare. But in this neighborhood, which he was pretty sure had once been a Seattle Street of Dreams project, the sprawling two-story house with its four-car garage was not even the biggest house in the development.

When he pressed the doorbell, it played a snatch of something classical. He and Mia looked at each other, eyebrows raised, and then the door opened. He was half expecting a maid in a starched black dress and white apron, but instead it was a tall man Charlie assumed must be Tamsin's husband. On the rare times Charlie was home, he was usually dressed in gray sweatpants and a T-shirt, but this guy was wearing a navy-blue suit cut close to his athletic body.

Mia had said Wade worked in investments, and although she hadn't been sure what that meant, to Charlie it was clear: lots and lots of money.

"Charlie Carlson," Charlie said, putting out his hand. "Seattle police." He left out "homicide." No need to spike the guy's worry about his wife.

"Wade Merritt." His grip was a little too firm.

"And I'm Mia Quinn with the King County prosecutor."

Charlie noticed that Mia didn't wince when Wade shook her hand, so he had either taken it down a notch or she was good at hiding pain.

They followed him into the living room, which had a gleaming pale wood floor and floor-to-ceiling windows. In the middle of the space, two brown leather couches flanked a matching love seat and ottoman. It took Charlie a second to figure out what was missing. Instead of a big-screen TV, the furniture was grouped in front of a stone fireplace.

Unlike Charlie's house, the space was totally uncluttered by half-read magazines and newspapers, dirty dishes, teetering piles of mail, takeout boxes, or discarded clothes. But it also didn't seem to be a place where people actually lived.

"You have a beautiful home," Mia told Wade as he sat down on one couch and they took the other.

"Thank you." He sighed and nodded. "All Tamsin's doing."

"Is she a homemaker?" Mia asked. The word sounded so old-fashioned, but in this case it certainly fit. Something this beautiful could not have happened by itself.

"She's that, but a lot more." Wade's breathing hitched for a second. "She's also something of a philanthropist. She's very passionate about her causes. Health care for the homeless, low-income housing, helping single moms go back to school, cheering up kids with cancer . . ." He squeezed the bridge of his nose and was silent for a long moment while he blinked rapidly. "She says we've been given so much that we have to give back. She has a soft heart."

"Your wife sounds like a very generous person," Charlie said.

"She is." He leaned forward and rested his elbows on his knees. "Not only with money, but with time. You want someone on your board, it's Tamsin. And I'm not just talking about schmoozing with folks like us. No, she'll plan the event, arrange the venue, write the newsletter, photocopy it, fold it, and stick the copies in the envelopes." He took a long, shaky breath. "She's helped so many people, and then those two punks go and drop a shopping cart on her."

Mia leaned forward. "The reason that we're here, Wade, is I'm the prosecutor assigned to your wife's case. We anticipate that the boys who did it will be arrested in the next day or two. After they are, I'll need to decide whether to charge them as adults or juveniles."

"They're not boys," Wade said. "They're not kids."

"They're not?" Charlie echoed mildly.

"They're animals." The word exploded out of his mouth.

Mia sat back in her chair, as if to put some distance between them. "I'll need to do some investigation to understand their frame of mind," she said as if he hadn't spoken. "What they were thinking. How well they understood the consequences of their actions."

"What is there to understand?" Wade's face was red. "Animals like that aren't capable of thinking. They just wanted to hurt someone. Wanted to destroy. They didn't care what damage they did. They dropped nearly fifty pounds of metal onto my wife's skull from four stories up. Even an idiot, even an animal, would know what that would do."

"The law hinges greatly on intent," Mia said carefully. "A person who means to run someone over is treated very differently from a drunk who hits someone accidentally."

"But either way, my wife is still lying in a hospital bed with part of her skull in a freezer. At my company we make decisions based on the bottom line. The intention doesn't mean squat. The only thing that matters is the results. And the result of their actions is that my wife is in a coma in intensive care."

"We understand that this is devastating, Wade," Mia said.

Charlie nodded. If it were his wife, he would feel the same.

"It's a lot more than that." Wade took a ragged breath. "It's my duty to speak for Tamsin now. So I will say what she would not be able to, because of her soft heart. I want them tried as adults and prosecuted to the fullest extent of the law. Those punks destroyed my beautiful wife. Even if she lives, she'll never be the same."

"Thank you for telling me how you feel." Mia's words were even. "That's exactly why we came to see you. I also went to see your wife a few hours ago."

Wade jumped to his feet and grabbed his keys from his pocket. "What? She's conscious? Why didn't they call me!"

CHAPTER 20

Silently, Charlie swore to himself. Wade Merritt thought his wife was awake.

"No, no," Mia said hastily. "Your wife is still in the medically induced coma. I just wanted to get a better understanding of what happened. That's why I visited her in the hospital, that's why we're talking to you, and that's why we'll also be talking to those boys' teachers and counselors. Maybe the kids themselves, if their lawyers will let us."

Merritt sat back down heavily. "When I first saw her, I didn't even recognize her, and we've been married for seventeen years. Her face is so swollen, and they shaved off half her hair." He raised his hand to touch his own dark hair, threaded with silver.

"It must have been a terrible shock," Mia said softly.

"She was actually dead. Did they tell you that?"

They both nodded.

"If it weren't for that doctor, the one who was shopping in the store, she might have stayed dead. As it is, she is never going to be the same. They can't even tell me if she'll ever be able to walk or talk. She could be lying in a bed like that for the rest of her life."

It was Charlie's worst nightmare. To be neither dead nor alive, but something in between. The legs drawing up to the chin as the muscles stiffened and contracted, the hands curling into claws, the skin breaking down from bedsores.

"Our son, Luke, was standing right next to her." Merritt's mouth folded in on itself. "It's only sheer chance that he wasn't hit. As it was, he's traumatized."

"We'd like to talk to him too," Charlie said. "Just for a few minutes."

"No." Merritt's jaw clenched as he shook his head.

"Trust me, your son is already thinking about what happened whether anyone talks to him or not," Charlie said.

"He's also a witness," Mia said. "He'll be called to testify. I need to know what he will say, and it's better if I talk to him now."

Merritt was silent for a long moment. Finally he nodded and got to his feet. They followed him down miles of hallway. Most of the doors were closed, although Charlie did catch an envious glimpse of a home gym that looked better than the one he paid a monthly membership for and kept swearing he'd visit.

Merritt stopped in front of a door with a poster of a wolf taped to it. Some kind of rap music was playing, but it stopped abruptly after he knocked.

The kid who answered the door was in that awkward stage, lanky and slumped, cheeks stippled with red acne. "What?" He stood so that his body blocked their view of his room.

"This is Detective Carlson from the police department and Ms. Quinn from the prosecutor's office. They're here to talk to us about what happened to Mom."

"Actually, we'd rather talk to him alone," Charlie said. "It won't take more than five or ten minutes."

Wade looked at his son and back at them. "I guess that's okay. I'll be just down the hall if you need me."

Or, Charlie guessed, right outside the door trying to listen.

Luke stepped back to let them in.

"Luke!" Wade said as he caught a glimpse. "Your room is a pig-sty. You have to clean it up."

"I will." He said it with just enough conviction that everyone could pretend they believed he was telling the truth.

It was true that his room was far more lived-in looking than the rest of the house. The bed was unmade. Cast-off clothes lay in a pile next to a hamper. His desk held an open laptop, a skate-boarding magazine, a copy of *The Catcher in the Rye*, a half-eaten slice of pizza, three open cans of Monster energy drink, and a crumpled bag that had once held Doritos. The room smelled like feet.

The kid sat down at his desk, but there were no other chairs in the room. Rather than perching on the edge of his unmade bed, Charlie and Mia remained standing.

"We wanted to talk to you a little bit about what happened," Mia said. "We believe the boys who did it are about your age, maybe a year or two older. It's my job as the prosecutor in charge of this case to decide whether to try them as adults or juveniles."

His nod was almost imperceptible. His eyes—and even his fingers—were on his computer, which was open to Facebook. He was scrolling through status updates.

"Can you tell us more about that day?" Mia said in a soft voice.

"Me and my mom went to the store." His fingers stilled, but he kept his face angled toward his computer. "They were having a special on T-shirts. Three for the price of two, plus she had a store coupon."

Charlie couldn't help but think of the beautiful house that surrounded them, the Lexus and the Audi in the driveway. He was willing to bet that Tamsin had grown up poor.

"And then what happened?" he prompted.

"We were walking across this, like, little road. I heard some kids shouting above us, but I didn't pay any attention." He pressed his lips together until they turned white. "I didn't even look up. And then one of them like yelled something, and I heard a scraping noise and all of a sudden this big metal thing came crashing down out of nowhere. I didn't even know it was a shopping cart at first. And Mom got hit by the bar in front—you know, on the bottom? She got pushed to the ground and there was, like, like a dent on her forehead." He was choking back tears now, his face as red as his zits. "And she wasn't moving. I was afraid to touch her. Afraid it would make things worse."

Mia stepped forward and cupped her hand over Luke's shoulder. He looked down at it, but he didn't move away.

"And then this dude in a dark hoodie ran up. He was crying so hard there was snot running down his face. He just kept saying how sorry he was. He was going to touch my mom, but I shoved him and made him get away from her. Some lady kept yelling that she had called 911. And then there was a guy who said he was a doctor, and he started helping my mom. And when I looked around for the kid in the dark hoodie, I didn't see him anymore." His voice broke. "Is she going to live? Do you know? Dad won't tell me. He took me to see her yesterday, but she looks like she's dead."

Mia and Charlie looked at each other. Her eyes looked panicked. Was she picturing Gabe in a similar situation? He leaned in. "She's made it this far, buddy. I think that's a pretty good sign."

The boy's shoulders loosened a little.

"Could you identify either of the boys who dropped the cart?" Mia asked.

Luke bit his lip. "I don't think so. Not even the one who ran up. I maybe saw one of them look over the edge after it happened, but it just happened so fast it's like a blur. I was mostly just wanting to help my mom."

Charlie had been afraid of this. Between the kid's testimony and the fuzzy videotape, they just had to hope that Manny's testimony would put both boys firmly on the scene.

"The thing is, what I heard before the shout? I think it was the sound of them laughing." Luke blinked and tears ran out of his eyes. "Laughing."

CHAPTER 21

For the past few weeks, Eli Hall had been looking forward to watching Mia go after a witness. Not just because she was by far the most attractive woman he had met since moving to Seattle. But he had also heard that Mia Quinn was an excellent litigator, smart, fast on her feet, and good at coining turns of phrase that stuck in a juror's head like advertising jingles.

Eli and Mia were both adjunct professors at the University of Washington's law school. This evening they would be modeling cross-examination for the law students, using "facts" provided by Titus Brown, the program's director, for a fictitious case about the murder of a clerk at a grocery store. First Eli would do a direct examination of his witness, a memory expert (really a student playing the part). Then it would be Mia's turn. Using the same set of imaginary facts Eli had been given, Mia would try to take the witness apart.

But when he saw her in the staff break room before class began, Mia seemed less than present. He touched her arm. "Are you sure you're okay to be teaching today? After what happened?"

"I'm fine." The blue shadows under her eyes put the lie to her words. "They got that guy off me right away and he didn't hurt me."

After a moment's hesitation, she added, "There're some other things going on, though."

"What's wrong? Is it Brooke or Gabe?" His Rachel was sixteen. Eli knew what it took to raise a teenager on your own.

"No. It's not the kids. It's my, my"—she stumbled over the words—"my husband. There's a possibility his death wasn't an accident."

"What do you mean?" As soon as he said the words, Eli wished he could call them back. Of course she meant suicide.

"It's possible he was murdered."

He blinked. "I thought he died in a car accident."

"Supposedly the injuries don't add up. It looks like he was beaten after the accident."

"Do you think it's really possible he was murdered?"

"I don't know." She sighed. Her eyes looked wet, and Eli had to resist the sudden urge to put his arm around her shoulder. "I honestly don't know." She looked at her watch. "I guess we should go in." She turned toward him. "Don't say anything to anyone, okay?"

Eli nodded, but that didn't stop him from wondering. In the classroom, he half listened as Titus began to lecture about cross-examination.

"The purpose of cross is to corroborate your case." Titus had a preacher's cadence. "If you've watched too many movies, you might think your goal is to have the witness dramatically break down on the stand and admit his own guilt." He wagged a finger. "No. Because that will never happen. Instead, you use the cross to tell your story to the jury. You highlight inconsistent statements, suspect motivation, and lack of truthfulness. On the direct, the witness is the star. But on cross-examination, it's the lawyer.

"Remember that you control the witness." He pointed at the students. "You must maintain the upper hand. Keep the cross brisk. Don't give him time to think. Lead the witness by getting him to agree with you. Then build one fact on top of another, like bricks.

And remember to ask short leading questions. Now, I know it's not easy for a lawyer to ask a short question, but you must.

"Learn to use your head. No, not by thinking, but by simply moving it up and down." He demonstrated. "Humans are hard-wired to mirror each other, so if you nod, the witness will too. And never get into an argument with the witness. There's an old saying: 'Don't argue with a fool, because the jury may not be able to tell the difference.'" Laughter rippled through the students. "Whether you like it or not, the truth is that many times the jury is look-ing for form, not substance. If you can make a witness backtrack, babble, or even just look confused while you look calm, you'll have the upper hand."

He stepped back. "And now, without further ado, may I pre-sent you the case of Bill Jones. Mr. Jones has been charged with attempted murder in the shooting of a grocery store clerk. Both the clerk, John Doe, and a customer, Mary Smith, have positively identified Mr. Jones as the shooter. Mirroring real life, Mr. Hall will play the part of defense counsel, and Ms. Quinn will play the part of prosecutor. The witness they are interviewing will be played by your fellow classmate, Jocelyn Daugherty. And I will be the judge."

To a smattering of applause, Titus took the judge's chair while Eli and Mia sat at their respective tables. The room was designed like a miniature courtroom. Jocelyn took her seat in the witness box. Eli got to his feet. "So, Dr. Daugherty, we met for the first time yesterday?"

This was actually true, aside from the "Dr." part. Jocelyn was in Mia's class, and she and Eli had met to review her testimony.

"Yes."

"And we've talked on the phone, of course?"

"A few times."

If he were Mia, he would bring up how much the witness would be paid for testifying. The best defense was a good offense, so he raised the issue himself. "And, of course, Dr. Daugherty, you expect to receive compensation for the research that I've asked you to do and for your time appearing here?"

She nodded. "I hope so, yes."

"But your compensation is not based upon whether we win or lose, is it?"

"No, absolutely not," she said firmly.

Eli took her through a series of questions about how a witness's testimony could be affected by the way questions were asked, by how lineups were conducted, or even by something as small as a cop's facial expression or tone of voice. Jocelyn answered confidently.

It was a line of questioning Eli had taken dozens of times in real life. He was trying to negate the eyewitnesses' testimonies, not by impugning their character, but by showing that memory was far from a video camera that accurately recorded events for later review. That memory was, instead, malleable and suggestible.

He went on for another ten minutes before turning the witness over to Mia.

Mia strolled over to the other woman, but her first question was anything but casual. "A lot of people in your field—psychologists and psychiatrists—would say it's just kind of a commonsense thing that you come in and testify about, right?"

Jocelyn tried not to fall into the trap. "I think it's misleading to say a 'lot of people.'"

Mia cocked her head. "Reputable people in your field say that, though, don't they?"

Jocelyn hesitated. "A few reputable people might express that opinion. A few."

"But basically what you testify about is not really hard science, is it? It's more soft science, right?" Mia nodded her head as she spoke.

Jocelyn caught herself before she was halfway through her first reciprocal nod. "I don't think people in my field would call it that, no."

"You don't?" After her rhetorical question, Mia didn't pause. "Okay. In your vita, I see a list of the many articles and books that you've written. You've also testified in 171 trials. All of these have to do with all sorts of things around memory and perception, right?"

Jocelyn was back on more comfortable ground. "Yes."

Mia took another swipe. "Is there anything at all about memory or perception that you don't make money off of?"

Indignation straightened Jocelyn's shoulders. She was fully invested in her role. "There's plenty that I don't make money off of, like freeing innocent people from prison pro bono."

Mia cocked her head. "I'm sorry. What was that answer again?"

"Some of my pro bono work is freeing the innocent."

"Are you here today pro bono?"

A pause. "No."

Mia said, "When did you arrive in Seattle for this case?"

"About four o'clock yesterday."

"And who paid for your plane ticket?"

"The defense."

Mia leaned in. "Who paid for your hotel room?"

"I did," Jocelyn answered.

Mia feigned surprise. "They're not going to reimburse you?"

"Well, I hope they will, but I paid for it when I checked out this morning."

"And where did you stay last night?"

"At the Hilton."

Mia echoed her words. "At the Hilton." She raised her eyebrows and looked at the students who were playing the part of the jury, inviting them to think about how nice a stay at the Hilton might be. After a moment she added, "And all of your meals, while you're here in town, you're going to be reimbursed for?"

"Yes."

"And all the time you spent on the phone with the defense counsel—you get reimbursed for that?"

Jocelyn was struggling not to fall into the trap of answering yes, yes, yes. "I hope to be compensated for my time, yes."

"And any research you did for this case, no matter how unimportant it was, you hope to be reimbursed for?"

"I hope so, yes."

"What is your typical charge by the hour?"

"Well, it depends. If I'm doing it pro bono, it's nothing. I sometimes charge five hundred dollars an hour for my time." Even the make-believe jury murmured a bit at the number.

"Does that include while you're on an airplane?"

"Well, generally I charge for up to a maximum of twelve-hour days when I'm out of town." Jocelyn shot Eli a desperate glance before trying to blunt the force of Mia's charges. "Even if I spend sixteen hours on a given day, I would only charge for twelve."

Mia would not be deterred. "So that could possibly include time spent going to the bathroom in this courthouse?"

"I hadn't looked at it that way."

"It could?"

"It could," Jocelyn finally conceded. On direct examination, she had calmly answered questions. But now she was flustered, and it wasn't just that she was a law student playing an expert. Even a real expert would probably be reacting the same way.

Mia summed it up. "So when you add all that up, plane ticket here, hotel room, meals, plane ticket home, telephone calls, any research, going to the bathroom, putting on your makeup this morning, sitting up there in that chair, the grand total that you're going to submit to defense counsel when you're all done with this is going to be how much?"

If this had been a real case, Eli would have been sweating bullets by now. As it was, he made mental notes. And was oddly thankful that a public defender's budget rarely ran to that kind of money.

Jocelyn answered, "On the order of ten thousand dollars. Approximately."

The jury would now be considering the amount of work done and asking themselves if she was worth $10,000. And if she wasn't, then why was the defense willing to pay for it? They would wonder if Eli was, in effect, buying her testimony.

Mia was dismantling the witness, and there was little he could do to stop it.

"You've already told us that you have testified over 171 times," she said. "I guess the meter's ticking. Is this 172?"

After a pause, Jocelyn found her voice. "Approximately."

Eli jumped to his feet. "Judge, I object to the sidebar remark about the meter ticking. It's disrespectful."

Titus said, "That's sustained."

But the damage had been done, and everyone in the room knew it. As a witness for Eli, Jocelyn had shown that memory could be influenced by many things. But once Mia had gotten her hands on her, Mia had also shown that money could influence testimony.

Maybe even buy it.

CHAPTER 22

When Mia came home from the law school and opened the front door, tendrils of eye-watering gray smoke swirled out, undulating under the porch light.

She burst into a run. Where were the kids? Why wasn't the smoke alarm going off? Coughing, eyes stinging, she followed the source of the smoke into the kitchen, where she found Gabe standing on a chair underneath the smoke alarm. He was holding the battery.

"What happened?" A charred lump that looked like it had once been a white paper bag lay in the sink, floating in water gray with ash.

"I was making popcorn for a snack." He jumped down from the chair. "I guess it cooked too long." He looked so nonchalant that Mia wanted to scream.

Her heart began to slow down. "Where's your sister?"

"In the family room."

"How many times have I told you to wait by the microwave so you can hear if it's stopped popping?"

Gabe looked at Mia blankly, as if this admonition was falling on the same deaf ears her original advice had. Smoke was still curling from the vents of the microwave oven.

"Never mind. Just turn on the fan and then open the front and side doors. Maybe we can get some airflow going." On the way to the family room, she jabbed the thermostat button until it dropped to fifty-five. No point in trying to heat the outdoors.

The smoke was making her cough, but Brooke seemed oblivious. At the sight of Mia, her face lit up.

"Mommy, Mommy, look! I learned how to do a headstand." Her pink pillow, the one with a cartoon princess on it, was against one wall of the family room. Brooke knelt and pressed the top of her head on it, her hands braced on the floor for balance. She kicked up her legs, got about halfway up, and then fell back.

Undeterred, she demanded, "Hold my legs!"

Mia thought of everything she had to do. The smoke that had to be shooed out somehow, the dinner yet to be made, the pile of unopened mail, the clothes that had to be washed if Brooke was going to have clean pants to wear to school.

And then she remembered yesterday, of how she had thought she'd lost both Gabe and Brooke.

"Okay, honey."

She stepped forward, and when Brooke tried again, Mia grabbed her legs and lifted them into place up so that the little girl was doing a headstand.

"Wow! Look at you!"

A huge grin split Brooke's reddening upside-down face. "I know! I'm an expert at this."

"Great job!" Mia loosened her grip.

"No! You have to keep holding me up, Mommy!" And then Brooke fell silent, seemingly content to work on setting the world's record for longest assisted headstand.

After what seemed like five minutes, Mia tried to twist her wrist to look at her watch, but Brooke listed sideways. Mia let go. As soon as her feet hit the ground, Brooke started to pout.

"I want to do it again. I need you to help me stay up, Mommy."

"I can't right now, honey. I have to make us dinner. And help your brother get the smoke out of the house."

"But I need you to help me now!" It was the simple logic of kids. For that matter, it was the simple logic of most of the people in Mia's life. Frank didn't care what else she had on her plate, just that she take care of the shopping cart case. Even Charlie wanted her to start digging into Scott's past until it yielded up all his secrets.

"It will have to wait until after dinner." Which she had better make fast if she wanted to have Brooke bathed and in bed by a decent hour. Which meant checking the freezer and seeing what she had on hand that was heat-and-eat. Preferably nothing that needed to be microwaved.

Gabe was still in the kitchen, but now he was swinging the door open and closed. She wasn't sure how much it was helping, but the smoke was lessening. Or maybe she was just getting used to it. After rummaging through the freezer, she came up with some frozen orange chicken, Asian mixed vegetables, and precooked brown rice. God bless Trader Joe's.

"Why don't you just concentrate on getting rid of the popcorn bag and cleaning out the sink?" she told Gabe. She put a frying pan on the stove, opened all three bags, and dumped them in.

There were days she looked at his dark hair and eyes and saw Scott so strongly she had to bite her lip to keep from crying. But today she also thought of those boys on the videotape. A poor choice, an impulsive mistake—what fourteen- or fifteen-year-old didn't make them? What good would trying those boys as adults do? She could fill Gabe's ear with threats about what would happen if he didn't look both ways, wear his helmet, pay attention to the popcorn in the microwave. But half the time, it seemed to her, the words slithered out his other ear without his even being aware of them. It was hard to believe that bringing the hammer down on those two boys would actually make other kids stop and think.

But if it didn't deter crime, then what was the purpose of

the justice system, the institution Mia had dedicated her life to? Rehabilitation? In that case, only the juvenile justice system was really geared to try to straighten out wrongdoers, regarding kids as more malleable. Adult prisoners were largely forgotten, especially in these days of budget cuts.

Or was the system really about punishment? She thought of the Old Testament, with its eye for an eye. Or one of those countries where thieves were still punished by having a hand lopped off. Could she justify locking up two kids for years and years for a prank gone wrong? Even a prank that had left a woman in a hospital bed? No matter what happened to them, it wouldn't reverse Tamsin's injuries.

Gabe came back from throwing the burned bag in the trash. "Mom. I think your food's burning."

She had been so engrossed in thought that she had stopped stirring. "Oops!" She avoided Gabe's eye as she turned off the burner, then divided up the food. Would Brooke eat much of it? Doubtful. To supplement, she put a bagel on her daughter's plate. What did they have for fruit? Was there some canned pineapple in the cupboard?

The shelves were far less crowded than she remembered. Where were the chili and canned soup and even the SpaghettiOs only Brooke liked? Mia had to go grocery shopping, and soon. Did all fourteen-year-old boys eat as if they had a hollow leg they had to fill up first?

Dinner passed in a blur. She got Gabe to load the dishwasher while she assisted Brooke in two more headstands, then gave her a quick bath and helped her brush her teeth. Mia was so tired that when she lay down by Brooke to read her a story, she worried she might fall asleep before Brooke did.

She had finished one book and was about to start on another when Brooke looked at the photo of Scott that Mia had framed and put by the bed. Her round blue eyes swung back to Mia.

"Are you still mad at Daddy?"

CHAPTER 23

What?" Mia asked as a bubble expanded in her chest. "I'm not mad at Daddy."

Did Brooke even understand that Scott was dead? Really dead? Sometimes it felt as if her daughter thought the whole thing was temporary.

Brooke didn't answer.

"Do you think I'm mad at Daddy, honey?" It was getting harder to force out the words past the growing pressure. "Because I'm not."

Brooke just looked at Mia for a long moment, then closed her eyes.

"Brooke?"

"Be quiet, Mommy. I'm sleeping."

Are you still mad at Daddy? She was mad at Scott. Mad at him for dying. Mad at him for drinking. For drinking and driving and dying. And now she was mad at him for cheating on her. For spending money he didn't have—had never had—to buy his girlfriend a diamond ring. And if Charlie was right, Mia would probably soon be mad at Scott for whatever secret had led to his murder.

Before she went to bed, Mia made sure the house was locked up tight and the alarm set. Normally she only set the alarm when everyone was away from the house. But things were no longer normal, not even the new normal she had fallen into since returning to work. When she passed Gabe's room she stuck her head in to say hello. He mumbled an answer, his eyes on his computer screen, but then he shook the hair out of his eyes and gave her a sweet smile.

In her room she took a deep breath before opening up the copies of the reports that Charlie had made for her. But she saw only print and the freehand illustration of the accident scene that he had shown her earlier. He hadn't copied the photos. Mia was grateful for that.

The first page of the accident report contained the sketch of the scene, as well as boxes and blank lines that the responding officer had filled out. Mia's eyes skittered over them.

> Weather condition: overcast
> Road condition: damp
> Restraints in use: no
> Airbag deployment: both driver and passenger side
> Accident classification: fatal

The second page held the meat of the report:

Summary of Accident:

V-1, driven by Scott Quinn, was n/b in the n/b lane of Vollhanger Road, when his vehicle veered to the right, drove off the unpaved shoulder, then struck a tree, causing major damage to the right front end of V-1. There were no other vehicles involved. Quinn was declared dead at the scene. POI was 1150 feet south of the north curb line of Hillcrest Drive, and 7 feet west of the west curb line of Vollhanger Road.

Responding Officer's Statement:

On 4-09-2013 at approximately 11:17 p.m. I was dispatched to a single-car accident in the northbound lane of Vollhanger Road. I arrived at scene within 10 minutes of the original call to find a 2007 Buick LeSabre with extensive damage off to the north side of the road. It was occupied by a deceased male. I photographed the scene, then the Medical Examiner's Office removed the body and took it to the Coroner.

I interviewed Alvin Turner, who stated that he was traveling north on Vollhanger Road when he observed a blue Buick LeSabre pass him at what appeared to be a high rate of speed. He honked his horn but was ignored. He said the driver appeared to be swerving. About 10 minutes later, he came across the Buick LeSabre, which had left the road and hit a tree. He stopped to assist the driver but found him deceased. He then called 911.

On 4-10-2013 at approximately 2:15 p.m. I interviewed Quinn's wife, Mia Quinn. She stated that he was in excellent health. She also stated that he had stopped drinking three years earlier.

On 4-11-2013 I received the Toxicology Report from the County Laboratory. The report states that Scott Quinn had a blood alcohol content (BAC) of .06g/110ml.

Conclusion:

Investigation into this matter has concluded that this accident was caused by the actions of Scott Quinn who was on an unfamiliar road late at night and possibly also fatigued, traveling at least 10 miles above the posted speed limit, with a blood alcohol level of .06%. Primary collision factor: Unsafe speed. Associated collision factor would be driving while intoxicated.

How could Charlie read this report and think Scott had been murdered? When it was clear that he had been drunk and careless? With shaking hands, Mia turned to the report the death investigator had prepared.

External Examination Report:

The body is clad in black dress pants and black underwear, a sleeveless white undershirt, and a white-and-blue striped dress shirt.

In her mind's eye, Mia clearly saw that shirt. It had been Scott's favorite as well as hers. The stripes were three slightly different shades of blue on a white background. The cuffs and collar were lined in crisp navy-blue paisley, which Mia had always thought of as a little surprise, like an inside joke.

When she learned he was dead, she had wanted him to be dressed in that shirt before he was cremated. She had imagined its smooth cotton wrapping him tight, skimming over his muscled arms and torso. Before she had gone to the funeral home that morning to make the arrangements, she had searched the house high and low for it, even gone to the dry cleaner.

Only when Mia had given up and gone to the funeral home empty-handed had she realized he had died in that shirt. The manager of the funeral home had brought her Scott's things in a stained brown paper bag and asked what she wanted him to do with them. When she opened it, there was the shirt, stiff and dark with blood, sliced next to the buttons and up the sides where the paramedics had cut it off him. Mia had let out a little cry and then pressed it against her lips for a moment, while the manager averted his eyes.

Eventually she folded up the shirt and put it back in the bag. She took Scott's wallet and told the manager to throw away the bloody clothes.

> The body is that of a well-developed, well-nourished white male,
> 72 inches, 181 pounds, appears the 36 years as reported. The body
> is cool.

But Scott was always so warm. She still missed the sheer comforting warmth of him at night.

> The corneas are clear, irises brown, conjunctiva pale and have no
> petechial hemorrhages. The ears have normal shape (see injuries

above and behind the left ear). The nasal septum is in the midline and the nostrils have some blood. The lips are unremarkable.

Unremarkable lips? Then they couldn't be talking about Scott. His lips were anything but unremarkable. They betrayed every emotion, full when he was relaxed, pressed together in a tight white line when he was angry. Sometimes Mia still imagined she could feel them touching the back of her neck. When she was working in the kitchen or holding one of the kids on her lap, he had liked to come up behind her, lift her hair off her nape, and kiss her there.

The teeth are natural. Several loose teeth are found on the tongue in the mouth. The neck is symmetrical. The abdomen is flat. The lower extremities are symmetrical. The upper extremities are symmetrically formed and the right has deformity due to injury. The fingernails are short, evenly cut, and intact.

There are injuries to the right side of the chest, abdomen, pelvis, and ribs. There are blunt-force injuries to the left side of the head. The facial bones, including nasal, left cheekbone, left upper jaw, and left lower jaw, exhibit depressed fractures.

A chest tap yielded 100 ml of blood, indicating a torn aorta.

Probable cause of death:

Multiple blunt-force injuries due to vehicular accident.

Mia cupped the left side of her face while she moved her head to the right. In her mind's eye she saw Scott's unbelted body slamming into the passenger side door. It didn't seem possible that the injuries to the left side of his face had happened in the accident.

So was Charlie right?

But if Scott had been beaten to death, they would never be able to match a suspect weapon to the depressed fractures the death investigator had noted on the left side of his skull.

Not when Scott was now fine gray ash.

CHAPTER 24

Scott Quinn had been pretty handy. At least for a while. He could take a business that was turning a profit and make it look poor on paper. That way you could keep your money and not have to share it with the various city, county, state, and federal governments that always had their hands in your pockets. For a price, Quinn would even keep a second set of books, a more accurate accounting that you could show the bank but not the tax man.

Then, far too late, the idiot had decided he should get a conscience. That certain things weren't acceptable. Like he could pick and choose. Fraud and tax evasion were okay, but selling coke wasn't?

Despite his skills, Quinn had quickly become a liability. One that Vin had had to eliminate.

Now he had been dead for months.

So why wouldn't his wife let him stay dead?

CHAPTER 25

WEDNESDAY

Mia felt like she had just gone to sleep when her phone rang. She forced one eye open, then the other: 5:37. The caller ID on her phone read *Frank D'Amato*.

"Hello?" Mia tried to sound awake.

"Two things." No preface, no apologies for waking her. "First, I just got a heads-up that KNWS has the footage of the cart being dropped as well as of it hitting Tamsin. They're going to lead with it on the six o'clock morning news."

Mia groaned. "Who gave it to them?" The last thing they needed was a media circus. Once it was out, the video was bound to go viral.

"Who knows? All I know is that people are going to be asking a lot of questions, and I want to have answers for them."

"Do we have names yet of the kids who dropped it?" She resisted the urge to pull the covers over her head.

"That's the second thing. We not only have the names of the kids, we've got the kids. They were taken into custody about an hour ago. Their names are Dylan Dunford and Jackson Buckle."

The only paper she had handy was Scott's accident report. Mia turned it over and scrawled their names on the back, getting Frank to spell them. "How old are they?"

"Fifteen. Both of them."

As Frank had guessed, too young to be automatically tried as adults. Now Mia had a little less than forty-eight hours to decide what charge was best: for Tamsin, for her family, for the boys themselves, and for society.

"I'll call Charlie." Mia rapidly made a list of what needed to be done. "We'll start with their schools, and then we'll interview the neighbors and family members." She wanted to begin with the most objective observers and work her way in to the boys' families, who would probably offer her a less than unbiased view of them.

"You got lucky. I understand they live in the same apartment complex and go to the same school. In fact, it's the same school Manny goes to."

"We already talked to Tamsin's husband yesterday. He said that even if they were under the age of sixteen, he wanted them charged as adults. He was fairly vehement about it."

"Be sure to keep me in the loop," Frank said.

When Mia called Charlie, he kept interrupting the conversation with yawns, not bothering to hide that he had been asleep. He agreed to pick her up at her office. Then Mia called and requested the arrest records for Dylan Dunford and Jackson Buckle. And, after a moment's hesitation, for Manny Flores.

By now she was wide-awake. She got dressed and left a note on the kitchen counter asking Gabe to walk Brooke to preschool—and to be certain to set the house alarm.

———

An hour later Mia climbed into Charlie's car carrying the file on the shopping cart case. She had printed out the boys' records, but she hadn't had time to do more than skim them.

"I got you a coffee." Charlie pointed at a sixteen-ounce paper cup nestled in a holder. "Nonfat latte." With his other hand he hoisted what had to be at least a thirty-two ouncer to his lips. He seemed to be steering the car with his knees.

"Thanks." Mia picked it up gratefully, trying not to pay attention to whether Charlie was actually staying in his lane or how close the other cars seemed.

Charlie took another sip of his coffee and then wedged it back between his thighs. "So what information did you come up with for those boys?"

"I just got the records for all three." She opened up the file folder. "So let's start with the one who has the least amount of paperwork." It was sad to think that such young kids had already amassed records. "That would be Dylan."

"Wait a minute." Charlie glanced over. "Don't you mean Manny?"

"No. His file is actually a little thicker than Dylan's. Oh, and speaking of Manny, his psychiatrist just told me that he still wasn't up to being questioned."

Mia picked up Dylan's records. Once they turned eighteen, all three kids' records would be sealed, unavailable to anyone but law enforcement or the courts. In some cases, it was even possible to petition to have them expunged, wiped away as if they had never been. Juveniles, the thinking went, shouldn't have the records of their youthful mistakes follow them into adulthood. The law recognized that an adolescent was not as capable of making the same reasoned decisions as an adult. That children deserved a fresh start.

Unless they were tried as adults. In which case the law regarded them as adults from start to finish. Including housing them in prisons with adult offenders who were often twice their size and three times their age.

"Dylan has had only a couple of contacts with law enforcement.

He was caught shoplifting." Mia assumed it had been something he could sell on the street. She ran her finger down the lines of type. "From, uh"—her heart broke a little as she kept reading—"from a Safeway."

"You mean he stole food?" Charlie signaled for the exit. "Like steaks and seafood?"

"Like frozen burritos," Mia said, still reading. "He told the officer who took him into custody that he was hungry. The charges were ultimately dropped and the family was referred to social services. A few months later he was picked up on a playground with a forty-ounce can of beer. He said it was a present for his fourteenth birthday from his stepdad. The stepdad—who was actually the mom's boyfriend—was charged with furnishing alcohol to a minor. A few months later Dylan accepted a plea bargain on a breaking and entering charge—it looks like he didn't actually steal anything—and ended up spending two months in a therapeutic foster home."

Mia turned the page. "As for Manny, when he was in sixth grade he was caught with a joint and let off with a warning." Looking at the birth date on the top of the page, she did the math. "He hadn't even turned twelve yet."

"They start young around here." Charlie had to raise his voice to be heard over a car in the next lane. The two boys in the car—and they were boys, not even out of their teens—were playing rap music so loud that Mia could feel the bass vibrating her ribs. Charlie turned and gave them a look. Even though she didn't think he looked all that much like a cop, with his hair that had to be within a millimeter of the maximum length the Seattle PD allowed, they glanced at each other nervously. At the very next corner they peeled off.

Mia looked back down at the records. "There's more. In seventh grade Manny asked to use a neighbor's bathroom. She said yes, but then she caught him with his hand in her purse. The charges were dropped in exchange for his receiving counseling."

"Maybe the counseling actually worked," Charlie said. "He tried to be one of the good guys. Too bad he didn't succeed."

"I hope we can talk to him soon. Manny's key. He can clearly link the other two to what happened, but more importantly he can tell us what they said to each other right before they dropped it."

She turned to the next record, which was Jackson's. It was also the thickest. She flipped through page after page, trying to hit the high points. "Jackson's been charged with minor in possession. Both alcohol and weed, multiple times. Caught in a neighbor's apartment stealing jewelry. Broke into another guy's house and stole liquor and video games." Her eyes skimmed over the entries. "Shoplifting, loitering, even littering. He's had to attend anger management classes, an outpatient mental health program, and he's even been required to go to school." She tsk-tsked. "You've got to wonder about the family dynamics if the judge thinks going to school isn't a given for a kid. What kind of parent lets a kid treat school as an optional activity?"

"Just because you watch them walk out the door doesn't mean they're attending school," Charlie pointed out. "In middle school I used to take off as soon as I was out of sight of my house. Luckily I got serious a couple of years later."

They were driving past block after block of cheap apartments with views of each other or five-lane freeways rather than the Space Needle or Puget Sound. Fast-food litter clogged the gutters, and any stretch of wall bore a spray-painted graffiti tag. In her nightmares, the ones in which the house slipped out of her grasp, Mia was forced to move to a neighborhood like this one.

At the end of one block, she saw two boys smoking. School was about to start, but they seemed in no hurry to be anyplace, even though they didn't look any older than Gabe. She wasn't even certain that what they were smoking were cigarettes.

If she got behind on the mortgage, what would happen to her kids? Since Scott died, Gabe had been teetering between bad and good, between acting like a child and trying to be a man. If she tore him away from his roots, would he join those boys on the corner? Brooke loved her preschool, but its emphasis on art and education and individual attention didn't come cheap. It was hard to believe anything like that even existed here.

A woman was pushing a baby in a stroller down the street. The child looked no more than eighteen months old, but it was gnawing on a corn dog. The young mother leaned down and offered the kid a sip from her huge cola. In Mia's neighborhood, with its stately homes and families with nannies and private tutors, such behavior would get her reported to children's services. Here it fit right in with the pawn shops and used-car lots.

Mia tore her gaze away from the vista of her possible future.

CHAPTER 26

At South High, Charlie parked the car in a visitor's spot. As he walked with Mia down the main hall of the school to the office, he heard conversations in English, Russian, Korean, Spanish, Vietnamese, and a few languages he didn't recognize.

Mia looked like what she was, a nicely dressed mom. Even though his rumpled black overcoat hid the holster on his hip, Charlie stood out. Half the kids regarded him warily, and a few people pointed and whispered. Did they know why he was here? The names of the kids who had been taken into custody couldn't be released by the media, but gossip didn't need TV to spread.

The school's office was a hive of activity, with phones ringing, students signing in and out, and teachers checking mail slots. They finally managed to catch the attention of one of the ladies answering phones behind the counter, who then directed them to the office of the vice principal, Peggy Alderson.

A middle-aged woman rose from her seat behind the desk. She wore a navy-blue suit, and her shoulder-length hair was blond slowly going gray.

Charlie introduced them, and the other woman held out her hand.

"Call me Peggy." Her hands were small, and as if to make up for them, her grip was strong enough that he had to hide his wince. It was one thing that Wade's handshake had caused him to flinch, but a petite older woman's? Maybe he needed to start hitting the gym again.

"Please, sit down," she said.

Aside from the chair behind her desk, there was only one free chair. Two more chairs, a small round table, the tops of two book-cases, and Peggy's desk were all covered with stacks and stacks of paper: loose, bound, rubber-banded, teetering. So much for the paperless office. She scooped up a pile from one of the chairs, turned in a circle looking for a place to put it, and finally set the stack on the floor before returning to her desk.

Charlie took the chair she had just cleared. The window behind her desk overlooked a city bus stop, but what caught his eye was the round hole in the middle of the pane. It was about an inch across and cracks radiated out from it. Made by a .45, if he was any judge.

"I appreciate your being willing to give up your office so we can interview these students' teachers." Mia opened a notebook. "Why don't you tell us a little about the school and whatever you know about the boys before we talk to the first teacher?"

"We have our challenges here." Peggy steepled her fingers and then pulled them apart to lift her hands, palms up. "Around ninety percent of our kids qualify for free or reduced lunch. We have lots of immigrants, or kids who are seventh-generation poverty. A lot of single-parent households. It's particularly hard for the boys. Many of them have no male role models. I'm always trying to hire male teachers, but forget it. Especially male teachers of color."

Charlie glanced over at Mia as they both nodded. They heard the subtext. These boys might have done something terrible, but Charlie and Mia needed to look at the whole picture.

"Other Seattle schools have parents who work at Microsoft or

Boeing." Peggy's mouth twisted. "They can fund-raise to fill in the gaps from what they get from the city. Here we're nothing but gaps, and the kids are lucky if they have one parent with a job, even if it's just pushing a broom at night. There's a lot of social poverty too. Homes where the TV is on all the time but there's not a single book. Where the parents are in and out of jail and the kids are cared for by a succession of aunties and really tired grandmothers. Where lots of people you look up to sell drugs or their bodies or at least plasma. Where there's no expectation you'll finish high school, let alone go to college."

Yeah, yeah. Charlie got it. These kids were poor, they had no role models, they deserved a break. He cut to the chase. "How well do you know these boys? Jackson Buckle and Dylan Dunford?"

"Jackson's fairly bright, at least I suspect he is, despite his grades. Bright enough that he doesn't always get caught. Dylan is a little more"—Peggy hesitated—"borderline. He's struggling. He may be a candidate for a more intensive program."

"What does that mean?" Mia asked.

"Dylan may have a learning disability that's been previously undiagnosed. Washington mandates that all children with a disability have an IEP—individualized education program—so they have the opportunity to learn the EALRs—essential academic learning requirements—which enable them to meet the GLEs—grade-level expectations—for reading, writing, and science, as well as the PEs—performance expectations—for math."

Charlie snorted. And he thought he worked in a bureaucracy. The endless acronyms made his head hurt. "What does all that even mean?"

"In a nutshell, special education. Perhaps if he were in a smaller classroom, maybe with an aide, Dylan might flourish."

"Are Jackson and Dylan friends?" Mia asked.

"That could be too strong a word. But I have seen them together. That's about all I can tell you. Those two and Manny."

"Flores?" Charlie shouldn't have been surprised, but he was. "They're all friends?"

"They're part of the same loose group of boys." Peggy held her hand up and tilted it back and forth. "As I said, neither the best nor the worst."

Charlie thought about the three boys' records. "Have you ever had to discipline them here at school?"

"Dylan stole a teacher's purse last year. We found it in his locker, but everything was still there. He said he had no idea how it got there. I had my suspicions." She raised an eyebrow.

"Which means?" Charlie prompted.

"Things have gone missing around Jackson too, but somehow they never turn up in his possession. At least not that we can find."

"So you think Jackson took the purse and hid it in Dylan's locker?"

"I didn't say that," Peggy said. "It's just that it seemed out of character for Dylan—and it was Jackson's teacher."

"How about Manny?" Mia asked.

"I suspended Manny three days last month for throwing a trash can at another kid. He said he was being picked on." She shrugged. "He may well have been right."

———————

The first teacher they talked to, Stacy Michaels, wore skinny jeans, a hoodie, and red Nikes. She didn't look much older than the students.

"This is my second year with Teach for America," she said with a sigh. "I came in here all starry-eyed, thinking I was going to save the world. Frankly, I was an idiot. I can't even save myself, let alone these kids."

Charlie nodded. A verbal response seemed unnecessary. The floodgates were already open.

"They're not the least bit grateful. They talk back. They're disrespectful. Don't they think I know what they're doing, texting under their desks? Nobody just smiles down at an empty lap. And you don't even want to know what they get up to in the bathrooms. They run wild. The only thing this job is doing is helping me pay off my student loans. I don't dare turn my back on them. I lock my purse in my desk, and even then I don't bring any credit cards to work anymore. Last year one of the kids managed to slip my Nordstrom card out of my wallet and charge $630 worth of stuff before I'd even sat down to dinner that night."

"Okay." Mia drew the word out. "What can you tell me about Dylan and Jackson?"

"Don't forget Manny. None of those kids are angels. All three of them skip school. Dylan stole another teacher's purse last year, and I can't count the number of times I've seen Jackson out on that sidewalk"—she pointed—"smoking a cigarette. Sometimes he'll be flashing something around, like a CD, and you just know he stole it. And there're times the way he looks at me just makes me shiver. His eyes are so cold. Even Manny, the one they're calling a hero? I know for a fact that he assaulted another child this year."

"Do you think either Dylan or Jackson is capable of understanding that his actions have consequences?" Mia said.

"To be honest," Stacy said darkly, "I wouldn't put anything past either of them. And I think they know exactly what they're doing."

Gloria MacDonald looked like she was in her late forties, but Charlie had to recalibrate her age when she said she had been teaching for thirty-nine years. She had coffee-colored skin and wore her black hair in a bob. The bangs set off her large, deep-set eyes.

"What can you tell me about Jackson and Dylan?" Mia asked. "I understand you're teaching both of them."

"Honey, I've taught everybody." Gloria flapped one hand. "I even taught Jackson's mom. And it's not because I've been in this school for a long time, although I have. It's because the two are only fifteen years apart." She raised one eyebrow and gave her head a little shake. "If Jackson applied himself, he could graduate high school. Even college. But I'm afraid he's not applying himself to the right things."

"What about Dylan?"

She shook her head. "That boy's got nine brothers and sisters, and there's not enough love, food, or space in that family for half that number."

Charlie exchanged a look with Mia. He couldn't imagine raising one child, let alone ten of them. With that many siblings, Dylan must basically be raising himself.

"He's not a bad kid. I had him to my house for dinner a few weeks ago. I think he came back for fourths." Gloria smiled at the memory. "He played with my little grandchildren. Now would I have done that if I thought he was a danger to others?" She leaned forward, her face fierce. "Look, his IQ tests out at eighty-five. Couple that with the fact that he's a juvenile and you've got no case. I've been around the block more times than I care to count, but I really can't see him doing this. Deliberately dropping a shopping cart on that poor lady? I find it hard to believe."

"We have him on video," Mia said.

"I heard that. But Dylan's suggestible."

"Are you saying you think it was Jackson's idea?"

She pursed her lips. "All I'm saying is whenever something bad happens, I always check to see where Jackson is."

CHAPTER 27

Lost in thought, Mia walked with Charlie through the school's parking lot and back to his car. It had all seemed so clear yesterday, when she was standing at Tamsin's bedside, vowing to punish those responsible for such unthinkable violence.

But the pictures the teachers and the vice principal had painted of the boys were more nuanced. Dylan was troubled. Jackson was trouble. Even Manny was something of a question mark. Dylan and Jackson might both be fifteen, they might both have helped heave the shopping cart over the wall, but it was clear Mia would have to weigh the fates of the two boys separately. Was one a vulnerable boy and the other a thug? Or were they both victims of their own circumstances?

It was hard enough to know with her own child if she had set him along the right path. As Charlie got into the car, Mia used her cell phone to check on the location of Gabe's.

"Whatcha doing?" Charlie glanced over curiously.

"I have an app on Gabe's phone that lets me see where he is. I just wanted to make sure he got to school okay, since I left the house before either of them was up." She relaxed when she saw that he was right where he should be.

Charlie's own cell began to ring.

"Detective Carlson." Charlie pressed the Bluetooth earpiece into his ear as he put his keys in the ignition.

"What?" As he listened, his mouth drew down into a frown. "How can you say that?" His voice rose. "Did you even read the report? . . . Then how do you explain the fact that he had injuries on the left side of his face but all the other injuries were to the right side of his body?"

Mia froze.

"No, bodies don't move in unexpected ways." Charlie was nearly shouting. "Haven't you heard of the laws of physics?"

A sour taste filled her mouth. She bit her lip to keep from retching.

"What about the problem with his brakes that I told you about yesterday? Huh? Did you take that into consideration? Someone tampered with his car before the accident. Someone wanted this guy dead and they didn't stop until he was. Only I guess you guys don't want to hear that." Charlie tried to say more, but it was clear that the person on the other end wasn't letting him get a word in edgewise.

"Don't think this is the end of this," Charlie finally said, but by then Mia could tell he was talking to a dead connection.

Mia swallowed her nausea. "So that was Puyallup County?"

"They're not gonna reopen the investigation into Scott's 'accident.'" Charlie's sarcastic spin on the last word made it nearly a growl. "They said his death was clearly due to driver error exacerbated by alcohol, and that his injuries were consistent with the accident. They said they didn't see anything 'new' or 'more' to investigate. To them, it's a single-car crash where the only person who was injured was the deceased driver, so there's no one left to prosecute. They just shrugged at the evidence. I guess since nobody wrote on the wall, 'I did it,' they're gonna cut it loose. When I talked to them yesterday, they even asked about my relationship with you. It's like they think there's a hidden motive."

Mia could imagine how he had approached the whole thing. Charlie could be a little too . . . focused. He was the kind of guy who sometimes battered down the door before he even tried the knob.

So it was possible that he had rubbed them the wrong way.

He exhaled forcefully and then started the car. "Besides, if they came back and said oops, they were wrong, what good would it do them?" He answered his own question. "None. There's no advantage in reopening it, not as far as they're concerned. You've heard what they call Puyallup County. Mayberry with Audis." Once filled with farms, the county had become a bedroom community for Seattle, for people who wanted a little acreage so they could dabble in wine grapes or stable their kids' horses. "They've got a low crime rate, at least on paper. And they seem determined to keep it that way."

"So it's over then." Mia felt an odd sense of relief. Did she really want to know what had happened that terrible night Scott died? Even if the truth was different from what she had been told, Scott was still dead. And if learning the truth did change anything, it would probably be for the worse.

"It's not over, Mia." Charlie's jaw tensed. He was driving too fast for her taste, but she decided not to say anything. "Nobody says we can't look into this on our own."

Mia remembered the day she and Scott got married. How badly her hand had shaken when she put the ring on his finger. They had repeated the ancient vows, promising to love in sickness and in health, for better or for worse. Only a few weeks ago she had stopped wearing her wedding ring. But even though death had parted them, even though Scott had cheated on her in so many ways, didn't she still owe him something?

Mia took a deep breath. Let it out. "You're right."

"First off we need to talk to the guy who discovered the accident. If we get lucky, it's possible he even saw the killer leaving the scene."

She nodded.

"I'll see if he'll meet us where it happened. We can check out if there're any houses nearby, any other potential witnesses."

"Are you going to tell the guy that this is unofficial, just two citizens asking questions?" Mia raised an eyebrow.

"I might let slip where I work."

"Be careful, Charlie. You don't want to be accused of abusing your badge."

Charlie nodded and shrugged at the same time. "I also want to see if the owner of the Jade Kitchen in Coho City will meet us. We can see what his explanation is for the low cash receipts. And if they have surveillance cameras, they might still have footage from that night."

"From seven months ago?" Mia thought it unlikely.

"You never know. We can also see if anyone working there remembers who Scott was talking to that night."

Mia took a deep breath. "I might stop by Oleg's Gems and Jewels. Give him back the paperwork. Say I found it in Scott's things. See what he has to say about the IRS and how Scott handled his finances." She took a deep breath. "And I want to ask him about the ring."

Charlie grunted and shook his head. "Nuh-uh. I don't want you going by yourself."

"No offense, Charlie, but it's pretty clear you're a cop even when you're in plain clothes. I'm talking about dropping by his store in the middle of the day. Very casual. In and out. I just want to see how he reacts, and you'll skew it."

"I don't like it." His jaw was set.

"I didn't say you had to."

He made a little humming noise. "That app you had on Gabe's phone?"

"Yeah?" Mia didn't know where he was going.

"Can you set it up so I can keep tabs on you?" Charlie parked across the street from the boys' apartment complex. "Just until this is over?"

"I don't know, Charlie." Mia's mouth twisted. "Isn't that kind of weird? Big Brother-y?"

"Oh, and it's not weird when you have it on Gabe's phone?"

"I just want to make sure he's safe and not getting into any trouble."

He pointed at her. "Bingo."

"Okay, okay." She pulled out her phone and started tapping on it. "I'll set it up on mine first."

"I'm gonna track down Betty and talk to her," Charlie said. "Find out what she knows. And for that, I figure it's better if I go alone."

The nausea was back. "You think Scott was whispering sweet nothings in her ear?"

"Maybe." Charlie's eyes flashed over to hers. "Or maybe she killed him."

CHAPTER 28

L ook. Let me say this as clearly as I possibly can. This isn't personal. This is business. You owe my client money." Vin tapped the end of the baseball bat into his palm. Slap. Slap. Slap.

"Yeah? And?" the kid with the earring asked. He was as skinny as a toothpick, with lank blond hair he had hooked behind his ears like a girl. "You really think I'm supposed to be scared of you?"

At least the kid had finally stopped asking how Vin had gotten into his apartment. Had finally realized he had more important things to worry about.

Despite his bold words, the kid did look scared. His face was pale, his eyes were skipping around, and his feet wouldn't keep still. He threw a glance over his shoulder. Was he looking for help? But Vin knew he didn't have a roommate. Or even a girlfriend. Although that last thing was no surprise.

And the only way out of this apartment was through the door Vin was standing in front of. Sure, there were windows, but they were four stories up.

Clearly the kid hadn't learned a few basic facts about how the business world worked. One was that if you had been entrusted with a certain amount of cocaine to put on the retail market, then you had better come back with the right amount of money.

And another basic fact: If you looked weak, the wolves would take you down. Rip your throat right out.

In about five seconds, the kid was going to figure that out.

CHAPTER 29

The apartment complex was a dingy ivory, two-story, three-sided box that held a small parking lot. Charlie and Mia started by knocking on the neighbors' doors. At the first two, no one answered. The third was opened by an olive-skinned woman who looked at them through the chain, muttered, "No English," when Mia asked if she could ask a few questions, and then closed it firmly.

At the next two apartments, Mia heard soft footsteps as someone came to the door, looked out the peephole, and quietly crept away. Did they not want to get involved? Did they not trust anyone who looked official? Did they think she and Charlie were there for something else?

The sixth door belonged to a young woman who lived directly over Dylan's apartment. She wore a red-and-gold sari. Bracelets clinked on her bare ankles. "I don't know them, but there is screaming a lot. Screaming and arguing. Too many people." As if to punctuate her words, someone under their feet hollered, "Shut up!" The three of them looked at each other.

After they showed her a picture of Dylan, the woman said, "This summer he had a . . ." She paused, then covered her eye. "A dark eye."

"A black eye?" Charlie prompted.

"Yes." Her mouth twisted as if she were annoyed at herself. "A black eye," she repeated. "Yes. A black eye."

"Who gave it to him?"

She shrugged. "Someone who lives there, probably."

When they knocked on the next door, they heard fumbling, and then finally it swung open. A young girl, not more than five, stood staring at them with huge dark eyes.

"Where's your mommy?" Mia asked. "Your daddy?"

The only answer was a blank stare.

"Hello?" Charlie leaned in to holler past her. "Hello? Is anyone home?"

Nothing but silence. They could enter if this was an exigent circumstance, if there was concern about the child's welfare. But she appeared clean and well fed, and the apartment was no messier than Mia's own house.

Mia crouched down to bring her face level with the girl's. "We're going to go now, sweetie. Don't answer the door again unless you know who it is. And give this to your mom or dad." She took out a business card and scribbled *Please call me* on it. Then she sent up a wordless prayer for the girl's safety.

A plump, middle-aged woman answered the door two doors from Jackson's apartment. Her blond hair had been dyed so often it looked like straw. After offering them seats on a wine-colored couch, she settled down into a recliner.

"I've seen that Dylan around, but I don't know him well. The family hasn't lived here long, and from what I hear they might be gone soon enough."

"What do you mean?" Mia asked.

"I heard they were behind on rent. They have so many mouths to feed, I'm not surprised. Jackson and his mom have lived here two years. Maybe more. I used to let him come by, but I stopped about a year ago."

"Why?" Charlie asked.

"Because he started changing."

"What do you mean, *changing*?" Mia pushed her feet into the floor, trying to move into a more comfortable position. The couch was so overstuffed she and Charlie were in danger of rolling into each other.

"These days he hangs out at the mini mall a couple of blocks away." She waved a hand over her shoulder to indicate the direction. "Sometimes late at night. Sometimes even during school hours. And half the time he has a cigarette. Once I said hello to him and he said something disrespectful back. I'm sure it was because he was with a couple of other boys, but still . . . As a mother, I feel he's been given too much freedom."

She turned out to be the last person who was home and willing to answer the door. It was time to go to try the boys' apartments.

There was no answer at Manny's. Charlie raised his hand to knock at Dylan's door but then held off. A woman was yelling at someone, her voice rising and falling. As far as Mia could tell, it was a one-sided rant.

When Charlie did knock, it was more than a minute before anyone came to the door. The woman was scrawny, with thin, greasy-looking brown hair. It was hard to imagine how one baby had managed to come out of those skinny hips, let alone ten.

The apartment behind her was dark, all the blinds drawn. Two stained couches were jammed into the living room, facing a darkened TV and a coffee table piled with dirty dishes. Mia squinted. Were there other people in the room?

Charlie was only halfway through introducing himself and Mia when the woman shook a finger in his face.

"I know who you are! My baby's gone and it's all your fault."

"I'm not the one who dropped a shopping cart on someone's head, Mrs. Dunford," Charlie said mildly.

She gritted her teeth at that. "It's Clark now. Ms. Clark. And

Dylan didn't do it either. You've got the wrong boy. Even if he says he did it, that don't mean anything. That boy will say anything people tell him to."

"And will he do what anyone tells him to do?" Charlie asked.

"Yes," she said, then realized the trap she had fallen into. "I mean no. I mean, he's not right in the head. But he would never do what you people say he did. And I don't have to talk to you and I don't have to let you in."

A familiar stench reached Mia's nose. Her eyes had adjusted to the lack of light. In the far corner of the room, a little kid who couldn't have been more than five was changing a baby's diaper.

"But we want to hear your side," Mia said. "We want to learn more about Dylan."

"I'm sick of you people. You always think you can make things better by sticking your nose in. Well, not this time." And with that she closed the door in their faces.

"No electricity?" Charlie said as they turned away.

"It looks that way. And I think I smelled more than poop in there. Maybe rotten food. So it might have been that way for a while." What would it be like to live in a place where the fridge and the oven were nothing but useless boxes? Where having too many people in a bed was a plus because at least they kept each other warm? She pinched the bridge of her nose. "When we're done here, I'll call someone I know at Children's Services. They can at least do a welfare check."

Finally they knocked on the door of the apartment Jackson shared with his mom. She answered so quickly that Mia wondered if she had been secretly watching them go from door to door. She was a slight woman who covered her mouth with her fingers when she talked. Her nails had sparkly purple polish. She invited them inside, where they sat on a brown plaid couch that had seen better days. Better decades.

"My son is a good boy," Regina Buckle told them. She must think they hadn't seen Jackson's records. Or maybe in her world a kid could have the kind of record Jackson did and still be a good boy. "But I haven't been the best mom. I've had to work all kinds of hours at all kinds of jobs. It's hard to find anything that pays good when you've only made it through ninth grade. That was why I was so proud of my baby when he started tenth grade this year. It means he's doing better than me." Her hand slipped, and for a moment Mia saw her teeth. One of her eyeteeth was missing.

"Are you working now?" Charlie asked.

"No. I was working at a food cart, but it, um, closed."

"And Jackson's dad?" Mia asked, even though she already had guessed the answer.

"He's not in the picture." Regina bit her lip and then looked up at them through thick dark lashes. "I should tell you something, though. My boyfriend just got busted for selling pot. He's the one who owned the food cart. Now I don't know how I'm going to pay rent this month."

"So if your boyfriend smoked pot, what about Jackson?" Charlie asked.

"No! He knows I don't put up with any of that." She seemed unaware of any contradiction.

"Hasn't he been picked up with pot and alcohol?"

"Those weren't his. He has bad friends who asked him to hold things. He's too trusting."

And that's how it went with Regina. Her son was a good kid who sometimes made honest mistakes. She didn't believe—couldn't believe—that he had done what they claimed he did.

As Charlie was driving them back, Mia's phone rang. She listened without asking many questions, then hung up, her heart heavy.

"Who was that?" Charlie asked.

"Someone from my office. I guess the inpatient facility that was treating Manny decided he was ready to talk to us, but Manny must not have agreed. He locked himself in the bathroom and tried to cut his wrists."

Charlie swore softly under his breath. "Did he succeed?"

"They said he didn't cut deep enough to do any real damage." Mia sighed. "But no matter what end of this case you look at, all you see is pain."

CHAPTER 30

"his coffee smells good and burnt." In the squad's break room Charlie dubiously sniffed the cup he had just poured. He was talking to Andy Gibbons, another homicide detective. Yellowing reminders taped to the walls exhorted them to clean up their spatters and to remember that their mother didn't work there. Despite the homemade signs, the space was a mess, had always been a mess, and would always be a mess.

"It'll put hair on your chest," Andy said, reaching for the glass carafe.

"How's it going with that double murder?" Charlie asked.

The other detective shrugged. "Seems pretty open and shut. Two dealers fighting over territory and the girlfriend was in the wrong place at the wrong time." He threw back a swallow of his coffee as if it were rotgut whiskey. "How about you?"

"I'm working that shopping cart case."

"I saw that on the news this morning. So stupid. So the lady died?"

"No. At least not yet. Right now the focus is on deciding whether to charge the kids who did it as adults or not." Charlie took another slug of his coffee. "And I've been looking into a traffic accident in

Puyallup County that I'm pretty sure was no accident. But I guess they don't see it the same way, even though the death investigator should have picked up on some discrepancies."

"Good luck with that," Andy said. "That place is positively inbred. If I remember right, their death investigator is married to the sheriff's sister."

Charlie blinked as a piece of the puzzle fell into place. No wonder the sheriff had been so adamant that no mistakes had been made. It wasn't a cover-up. Or at least not a traditional one. Puyallup was covering up their own incompetence. They might have done the same no matter who was in the accident. And minus a literal smoking gun, nagging them to reopen it was not going to do any good.

Back at his desk, Charlie called the number listed on the accident report for the first responder. He had debated about using his work phone but decided on his personal cell.

"Hello?" The man had a thin voice with a bit of a quaver. Charlie pictured an old guy in a fishing cap.

"Is this Alvin Turner?"

"Yes?" He sounded suspicious, as if Charlie had interrupted his dinner hour to try and sell him something he didn't need.

"This is Charlie Carlson. I'm a friend of Mia Quinn. Last April you were the first person on the scene after the accident that killed her husband, Scott Quinn."

"Oh yes. That was a terrible thing. Terrible."

"Mia is just now coming to terms with what happened. She is wondering if it might be possible to meet with you."

After a long pause, the old man cleared his throat. "I'm not sure there's much I can tell her."

"It would really help to ease her mind."

"But he was dead—or at least very close to it—when I got there."

"Even knowing that would be good for her. And I promise it won't take much of your time," Charlie said, not knowing if that was true or not.

Turner continued to sigh and demur but finally agreed to meet them at the site of the accident the next day at six p.m.

Next Charlie turned his attention to the woman who might have best known Scott at the time of his death. Not Mia, but Betty Eastman, the young woman with the old lady's name. It didn't seem that long ago that Charlie would have started his search by looking up Betty's phone number and street address in the white pages. Did anyone use a paper phone book anymore?

Sometimes Charlie felt like a dinosaur. He usually wasn't home in time to watch the nightly news on TV, but when he was he got the feeling that no one under the age of fifty was in the audience. The ads were all for drugs for shingles or erectile dysfunction.

Newsweek was no more. Same for the *Seattle Post-Intelligencer.* And the *Seattle Times* seemed awfully light these days. Even books had been turned into ones and zeroes.

Everything was online, but only when he was actively working a crime was Charlie allowed to search the law enforcement databases. Requests were audited, and if anyone saw activity that didn't look like it belonged, they'd contact Internal Affairs in a heartbeat. He could get days off, maybe even fired. Technically he shouldn't even have requested the reports about Scott's accident. At least he had done that over the phone, so he hadn't left any electronic footprints.

But luckily the Seattle PD also subscribed to LexisNexis. And since it was available to anyone willing to pay the subscription fee, requests to it weren't audited. Charlie typed **Betty Eastman** into the search box. Up popped several choices, but only one in Seattle. Five seconds later he had more than enough information on Betty to track her down. Phone numbers, addresses past and present, education, marriage records, licenses, criminal records—even death records. Twenty-two years old, Elizabeth Eastman had never been married, and she hadn't died. She had a Washington State driver's license and had lived at a string of addresses. She had one criminal conviction, for drunk driving a year earlier.

With his personal cell, Charlie tried the phone number listed, but all he got was a message saying it had been disconnected. He went back to the computer.

Under education it showed that Betty had been an accounting student at the University of Washington. That might explain where Scott had met her. But it didn't explain where she was now. Because the most recent term she had attended was last spring, and she hadn't finished.

Betty's job history was even older, a patchwork of various fast-food jobs ranging from McDonald's to Pizza Hut and Taco Time. The last had been about a year ago, and the work she had done for Scott didn't show up.

So, if Betty wasn't working and she wasn't going to school, what was she doing now?

All he was left with was her address. Because it included a unit number, Charlie assumed it belonged to an apartment. He clicked on it, which brought up other names associated with it.

There was just one. Jared Johannsen. Another U-Dub student, only he was majoring in marketing. He had lived in the apartment about three months longer than Betty. She had moved in about a year ago, about the same time she stopped working at Taco Time.

If Betty wasn't working and she wasn't at school, she might be at home.

Charlie pulled his keys from his pocket. It was time to take a little jaunt.

Was he stupid to be chasing after a theory he might never be able to prove, let alone arrest anyone for? But someone had left two children without a father, a good woman without a husband. Someone had wanted Scott Quinn dead and then made sure he was. A lot of murders were personal, stemmed from relationships gone wrong. And any relationship between a married man and a girl about half his age was sure to go wrong.

And there was Mia. Lately Charlie found himself thinking of

her far more than he should. Of the way she nodded her head. The little humming sound she made when she was thinking. He had seen her angry, intent, questioning. What he most wanted was to see her happy.

The building where Betty and Jared lived had all the charm of a complex that catered to students. Low-slung, it was made of cement blocks and painted in various shades of beige that probably reflected an ongoing effort to cover up tags. A Hispanic guy dressed in a silvery-gray coat and with a leaf blower on his back was determinedly blowing approximately half a dozen leaves across a strip of muddy grass in the center of the courtyard.

Charlie knocked on the door of unit 103. The young man who opened it was tall, six two or six three. Straight black hair parted on the side. Piercing blue eyes. With his square, cleft chin, he looked kind of like Superman.

"I'm looking for Betty Eastman," Charlie said. "Is she here?"

The kid tilted his head. "You're him, aren't you?"

Charlie decided to go with it. He nodded.

The last thing he saw was the kid's fist.

Heading straight for his face.

CHAPTER 31

Mia had never been in Oleg's Gems and Jewels before, even though the shop was only a few blocks from her office. She must have driven or walked past it hundreds of times, but all that was visible from the street were two heavy wooden doors with no windows, just the name of the store spelled out in ornate gold script. The O in Oleg had been replaced with the drawing of a diamond.

Now Mia pushed open one of the doors and caught her breath. Inside it was so light and airy it felt like stepping into a sunlit meadow. The carpet was a pale gold. Rows of recessed spotlights lit up the long display cases. Adding to the open feeling, the bottoms of the cabinets weren't made of wood but mirrors. At the back of the room, a large white globe lamp glowed like the sun itself.

But what really drew the eye were the golden cutouts of butterflies and birds strung on clear filaments that ran from ceiling to floor along the sides of the room. As she moved they fluttered in the air, catching the light.

Mia was the only customer. She hadn't heard any bell or buzzer, but a few seconds later a girl glided in from a door set flush with the wall and painted the same color. Her dark hair was pulled back into an elaborate low bun that showed off her long neck and dangling earrings. Her tall black sandals were held in place by two thin straps, and she wore a black, formfitting, cap-sleeved dress slivered with black lace inserts.

"Are you looking for something in particular, madam?" Her accent sounded Eastern European, the *l* coming from the back of the throat. Her skin was so smooth and poreless that Mia felt desiccated by comparison.

"Is Oleg Popov available?"

"Whom shall I say is inquiring?"

"Mia Quinn. You can tell him that my husband was Scott Quinn."

Not a flicker marred the girl's face. She simply nodded and turned away. While she waited, Mia leaned over one of the glass cases. Inside were necklaces, earrings, and bracelets. They ranged from large stones in simple settings to elaborate pieces covered with dozens of glittering diamonds. A king's ransom in a single glass case. Scanning the room, she spotted three cameras, and guessed there must be more that were hidden.

A stocky man entered through the same door the girl had used. His cheeks were red and round, and his hairline had receded into a perfect M, leaving a prominent widow's peak. He wore a pale turquoise shirt open-necked under a black wool suit. When he walked around the counter, Mia saw the red Prada stripe on the heel counter of his shoes.

"Mrs. Quinn," he said, stretching out a square hand that bore rings on every finger. "My heart broke for you when I heard about Scott's accident. I am so sorry for your loss." The syllables fell out of his mouth one by one in a low, slow monotone.

"Thank you." She glanced over her shoulder. Even though they were ostensibly alone, she couldn't help feeling they had an audience. "Is there a place we could talk in private?"

"Of course." If he was curious, his still-smiling face didn't show it.

He led her back through the same door. Mia was reminded of

being backstage. Behind the scenes, the glamour fell away. Here the lights were fluorescent, the painted walls marred with scuff marks. Two old desks that didn't match faced each other. A plump older woman sat at one of them, talking on the phone in a low voice. No one sat at the other desk, where the computer screen showed rotating scenes of the shop from a half dozen camera angles. It reminded Mia of the shopping cart case and the decisions she needed to make.

A second dark-haired young woman was signing for a delivery, but it wasn't from UPS or FedEx. The driver was dressed all in black and wore a gun on his hip. Oleg paused to murmur something in the woman's ear. The woman looked up at him with heavily lined dark eyes and nodded.

Oleg led Mia to the end of the hall, past a bathroom and a tiny kitchen area. His big office was cluttered and windowless. On top of the desk sat both a microscope and a magnifying lamp. The wing-back leather chair behind the desk looked like it belonged in a home, not an office. The leather was scarred from hard use, although there was a shiny spot in the middle where Oleg must rest his head.

A black-and-chrome chair faced the desk, but a woman's black leather jacket was draped across it. "So sorry," Oleg said as he picked it up and hung it on the back of the door. "My girlfriend can be very careless with her things."

Mia nodded. What was the best way to approach this? "It's actually Scott I wanted to talk to you about," she ventured.

"He was my accountant for two years. A very good one. I put everything into his hands and I trusted his advice." Oleg smiled, one side of his mouth moving higher than the other.

Mia thought of the IRS letter. Was he saying that any errors had been Scott's and Scott's alone?

She took a deep breath. "After Scott died I cleaned out his office, but I didn't have time to go through the paperwork until a few days ago. I found some papers I think are yours."

She had sorted through it all a second time, setting aside anything with Oleg's name or the name of his business. She had gathered ledger sheets, receipts for various bills, utility statements, and bills of lading for shipments of jewelry from all over the world: Belgium, Columbia, South Africa.

And before she had come here, she had photocopied them all.

Mia handed over the file. "I know it's not really my business, but I couldn't help but notice that the IRS sent you an audit notice about two weeks before Scott died. I hope he was able to get things resolved before, um, before the accident."

Oleg waved one hand. "Yes, yes, we had a meeting, but it was all a simple mistake. Once your husband went over the paperwork with the IRS agent, he realized they were in error."

She nodded. Had Scott told the IRS the truth? She remembered what Charlie had said, about how easy it would be to hide profits in Oleg's line of work.

"There's something else I wanted to ask you about," she said slowly, reaching into her purse. She brought out the black jeweler's box and handed it to him. "Can you tell me how much this is worth?"

Oleg snapped it open. His face betrayed nothing. He turned on the light on the magnifying mirror and began to examine the ring, turning it back and forth.

"I know this ring," he said, turning off the light. "It is very well made. For what it is."

"What do you mean, for what it is?" Mia's stomach started to churn.

"The band is eighteen-karat white gold, but the stones—I am afraid they are cubic zirconia." He slipped the ring back into its box and snapped it shut.

"You mean they're fake?"

"I am so sorry." He looked at her pityingly, and Mia realized he thought that Scott had given her the ring, told her it was real.

"Scott bought it from me a few months before the accident. We have another store that sells well-made costume jewelry. Not everyone wants or appreciates the real thing." He made a face. "But as I said, for what it is, it is well-made. Often you will see these types of rings made with cheap silver and flimsy settings, but I will not carry those. Even if it is costume, it is high-quality costume. Of course, if it were real, with that cut and clarity, it would be worth about thirty."

"Thirty what?" Mia asked incredulously.

"Thirty thousand."

She started to laugh. It all seemed so ironic. Ironic and stupid. Scott had bought his girlfriend a fake ring to commemorate their equally false relationship.

Oleg pushed back the magnifying mirror. "Are you all right?"

Mia was still laughing. But when she put her hand to her cheek, it came away wet with tears.

Oleg looked alarmed. "If there is a problem with money, I could buy it back. It cost seven or eight hundred."

Mia knew that this time he meant dollars. "No, no. I'll keep it." And every time she was tempted to feel sorry for Scott, she would take it out and look at it. Remember how he had cheated on her. And how he had planned to cheat his stupid, starry-eyed girlfriend with a ring that only looked like the real thing.

Oleg cleared his throat. "Is there anything else I could help you with today?" He appeared anxious for her to leave.

"No. I guess that's it."

They got to their feet, and he ushered her out into the corridor. The young woman had opened the top box of the delivery she had signed for. Inside were large rhinestone-encrusted pendants in bright yellows and blues, so gaudy they could qualify as bling.

Oleg barked a few words in Russian, and the woman hurriedly closed the box and set it aside. He turned to Mia. "For our other shop. Costume jewelry. No one dresses up anymore. Women do not want the cocktail rings, the tennis bracelets, the statement neck-laces. They don't understand the value of having something real. It's all disposable these days."

Mia raised an eyebrow. "Yes. It certainly seems that way."

CHAPTER 32

With a groan Charlie opened his eyes. He was on the ground, and someone was leaning over him. An astronaut? He blinked, and the figure resolved into the gardener in his silvery-gray coat, the air tank his leaf blower. He was dabbing at Charlie's nose with a crumpled tissue, now spotted with bright red blood.

"You want I should call the police?" the gardener asked.

"I am the police." Charlie put his hand to his nose and gingerly moved it from side to side. He didn't think it was broken. When that happened, it felt crunchier. He was just lucky that he had landed next to the walkway instead of on it.

Jared was leaning against the concrete wall with his head in his hands. Now he stared at Charlie. "Wait. You're not Scott?" If he was acting, he was doing a good job of it.

"No." He slowly got to his feet, ignoring how the world swayed and righted itself. The gardener stretched out his arms as if he were either going to catch Charlie or prevent him from hitting Jared in turn. Charlie pinched just below the bridge of his nose, but when he swiped the fingers from his other hand underneath, the blood already seemed to have stopped.

There was a way to mumble his name so it was a single blur. He did that now, since he wasn't exactly here in an official capacity. "I'm Charliecarlson." Then he turned to the gardener. "It's okay. You can go back to your leaf blowing. Everything's fine."

"I'm really sorry, dude," Jared offered, looking miserable. "Are you a real cop?"

Charlie started to nod, then stopped because he didn't like the way it made him feel.

Jared shook his hand, winced, and blew on his knuckles. "I've never done anything like that before. It's just that I thought you were the guy my girlfriend left me for."

"Is her name Betty? Betty Eastman?"

"I called her Bets, but yeah, that's her." His eyes got wide. "Why? Is she in trouble?"

"Can you tell me where she is?" Charlie persisted.

Jared made a noise that was not quite a laugh. "I wish I knew. Awhile back she left me for some guy named Scott."

"We're looking for her because she may have witnessed an accident."

"The last day I saw her was back in April. April fourteenth."

Charlie blinked. That was the day Scott had died. "Would you mind if we went inside? I kind of feel like I need to sit down." He also wanted to see the interior of the apartment for himself, look for any clues that Jared was lying.

"Oh, shoot, of course. I'm sorry, man."

The small apartment was decorated in flesh tones—pinks and beiges and ivories. Everything was jammed together. They walked in through the kitchen, where gold-speckled linoleum peeled up at the corners. What passed for a dining room was a space about five feet across, just big enough for a tiny round table and two armless chairs. In the corner, a fake fern provided the only spot of color. The whole thing was fairly tidy. Messy, it would have been claustrophobic.

Jared offered him some water, which Charlie declined. They sat at opposite ends of a small cream-colored couch.

"How did you and Betty meet?" Charlie corrected himself. "Bets."

"We had an anthropology class together. I told her I liked her laugh. Of course, I liked a lot more than that. But I figured 'laugh' was the best thing to say." Jared smiled at the memory. He seemed as pretty as a Ken doll, but just as empty-headed. "Have you ever met her?"

"I've seen her picture."

"It's not the same. Sometimes she would talk to me and I wouldn't be able to hear her." Jared raised his knuckles to his mouth and absently kissed them. "I would just watch her mouth move and get lost."

That certainly sounded like the basis of a solid relationship. "Why did you think she was with this guy you mentioned? This Scott?"

"He's an accountant. She got a part-time job working for him. An internship. She said she was getting hands-on experience. Hands-on." He snorted. "Now I know what that meant. And then she started sneaking around, being mad at me, pushing me away if I even tried to hug her." His mouth twisted.

"Did she know that Scott was married?"

"She wouldn't care about that." He shrugged. "She's very single-minded. Her full name is Elizabeth, but when she moved in with me she started calling herself Bets. She would say that with her, all bets were off. She said if you saw what you wanted, you should just go for it." His ears reddened. "That's how we ended up together. I sort of had a girlfriend, but Bets said she knew she wanted me. At the time she was dating her manager at Taco Time and he was married. When I met Bets, I kind of let her think I had more money than I did. After she moved in with me, she never paid for anything. She never even asked if she could. She was very good at getting people to buy her things."

Mia had told Charlie that Scott had left her in debt. How much of that money had gone to Betty, gone on her back or in her mouth or, for all Charlie knew, up her nose?

Jared encircled one wrist with the thumb and middle finger of the other hand. "One day she came home wearing this diamond bracelet."

"A diamond bracelet?" In his mind's eye, Charlie saw the diamond ring go skittering across the floor of Mia's basement.

"She got mad when I asked about it, where it had come from. Tried to tell me it was an old family heirloom." Jared snorted. "Which was such a crock. I know she grew up with nothing and nobody. Just bouncing around from one foster family to another."

Unexpectedly, Charlie felt a flash of sympathy.

"She started being gone a lot, and when she came home her mouth was swollen, like from kissing. And I'd see her talking on her phone and she would be all giggly and flirty, and then when she saw me she would hang up."

"Did she tell you she was leaving you?"

"No. She just didn't come home that night. And the next day she sent me an e-mail. She said she wasn't coming back, that I should just forget about her, that she would only cause me unhappiness." He snorted. "Like leaving me wasn't going to hurt."

"Have you talked to her since then?"

"No."

"Communicated with her in any way?"

Jared shook his head.

"Let me ask you something," Charlie said slowly. "And think about it before you answer. Are you 100 percent certain it was Bets who sent that e-mail?"

"Who else would know my e-mail address?"

"Just think about it."

Jared was only able to keep still for a few seconds. Then the words tumbled out of him. "It sounded like her. She was always kind of dramatic. She should have majored in acting instead of accounting. But she said she liked accounting because it was about money, and she'd never had any."

"Did you keep the e-mail?"

"No. I deleted it."

That meant Charlie couldn't look at the IP address, at least not without a warrant. And since this wasn't an official case, he wasn't going to get one.

"Did you e-mail her back?"

"I did a couple of days later, but it bounced back, saying it was an unknown user. She must have closed the account."

"So she just packed up and moved out and left you nothing but an e-mail?"

"No. She left her things here."

A chill went down Charlie's spine. It was beginning to sound as if someone just wanted Jared to think Betty had left.

"In the e-mail she said I could just sell her stuff at a garage sale or give it to Goodwill—that she didn't need it any longer."

"And did you?"

"Not yet. I put it all in a box in the closet."

"Can I see it?"

"Sure." He got up and came back a few seconds later with an old banana box.

Charlie sorted through it quickly. Nothing but clothes, a few textbooks, makeup, a dozen photos of herself, both with and without Jared. Charlie lifted up a few pieces of clothing. They all seemed absurdly small. Although maybe on Betty they had been just right.

Jared held a blouse to his nose and sniffed deeply. "They still smell like her."

Had Betty run because she was worried she would be next?

Or had she run because she was the one who did it?

Or had she been unable to run?

CHAPTER 33

Mia inched the car forward, gaining a whopping six feet before the car ahead of her again put on the brakes. The University of Washington was only five miles from the King County Courthouse, but today was one of those days when it might be faster to walk. From the seat beside her, she grabbed a handful of Lay's barbecue chips and stuffed them into her mouth. She hadn't had time for lunch today, but before climbing into her car she'd ducked into the convenience store that was kitty-corner to the courthouse. She'd bypassed the cheese sticks, the glossy apples, and the sole sad, bruised banana and gone straight to the junk food aisle.

In twenty minutes she would be teaching the ten students in her law school session the finer points of cross-examination, expanding on what she and Eli had modeled on Monday. She reminded herself not to get too close to anyone in case her barbecue breath overwhelmed them.

In the cross, she would tell them that each question needed to be brief and limited to a single topic. The more complicated a question was or the more loaded with clauses, the more easily the witness could quibble or deny.

If only she could reduce Scott's death into a simple yes or no, up or down, black or white. She stuffed another handful of chips into her mouth.

Her phone rang. "Mia Quinn." Pressing the Bluetooth into her ear, she tried to chew more quietly. She eased her foot off the brake and slowly rolled forward, gaining a few more yards.

"How's traffic on the 405?"

Her scalp prickled. And then she recognized the voice. "Charlie?"

"Just trying out that phone tracker app. Plus I wanted to see how things went with Oleg."

"Things went . . . okay. Scott had already straightened out things with the IRS before he died." She took a deep breath. "I also showed Oleg the ring."

"What did he say?"

Mia managed a laugh. "Get this. It's a fake. The stones are cubic zirconia." If only it had been real, she could have sold it and used the money to fill in the hole Scott had dug her.

"Maybe he bought it to match Betty's breasts."

Trust Charlie to be coarse, but right now she welcomed it. Much better to be coarse than to cry. "What I don't understand is why he bothered to hide it." Putting on her turn signal, she managed to sneak into the middle lane, which promptly stopped moving.

"He must have been afraid that you would drop by the office and find it."

Mia thought of the girl's pretty, sulky face. "Or that Betty would, prematurely. Maybe he was planning some big dramatic presentation." She wondered when he had been thinking of giving it to the girl. Before or after he asked Mia for a divorce?

"The thing is," Charlie said, "Betty hasn't been seen since April."

"What do you mean?"

"I tried to track her down, but she doesn't seem to be anyplace. She's not working. She was going to school in accounting, but she stopped attending classes in the middle of spring term. The closest I came to finding her was finding her boyfriend."

A tiny pulse of hope beat in Mia's chest. "Betty had a boyfriend?" Maybe she hadn't understood the photo or the meaning of the ring. Maybe the photo had shown two friends at dinner. Maybe he had planned to replace Mia's ring.

"It sounds like she has a history of overlapping relationships. The boyfriend, Jared, was a student at U-Dub with her. He said that when he met her, Betty was dating her Taco Time manager. After that she moved on to—and in with—Jared. Then she started out as Scott's intern, but he said it was clear she was seeing someone else. He was sure it was Scott."

"So Betty was cheating too? She and Scott made quite a pair." Mia let out a little bark of a laugh. Even to her own ears it sounded ugly. "So our girl Betty was working her way up the food chain. Taco Time manager to student to accountant. So who's she with now? Some midlevel manager?"

"The thing is, Mia," Charlie said, "Jared said the last time he saw her was the night Scott died."

"Then where is she?" A shiver ran over her skin.

"Jared said he got an e-mail from her the next day, saying he should just forget about her. But anyone can send an e-mail. Plus, she left all her stuff behind."

"Do you think Betty was murdered too?" Her thoughts were whirling.

"I don't know what to think. But if she was killed, then why hasn't her body turned up?"

"Maybe she's the one who killed Scott, and then she ran off?" Mia startled as someone behind her honked. A space the length of three cars had opened in front of her. She jackrabbited forward, then hit the brakes. "Maybe Betty figured out that he was all flash and no substance, just like that fake engagement ring he was planning on giving her even though he was already married."

"But why go to all that trouble to make it look like an accident?" Charlie said.

"What if it wasn't planned?" Mia was feeling her way. "What if they were going someplace that night, they started arguing, and she jerked the wheel or he overreacted and they crashed?"

"There was some intrusion into the passenger compartment," Charlie said. "But if she was wearing a seat belt, he could have hit the passenger door ahead of her, or even the dash. If his body had hit hers, Betty would have been pretty badly hurt too."

"But then why would she hit him in the head?" Mia was only a mile away from the law school now. The answer came to her, the one that had sounded so outlandish only a few days earlier. "Maybe she saw how badly hurt he was and thought she should put him out of his misery?"

Charlie's voice sped up. "And she found a branch or a rock or— does Gabe play baseball? Could one of his bats have been in the car?"

Mia didn't know, but she thought about Betty's boyfriend. "Or what about this Jared? Do you think he could have forced Scott off the road and killed him?"

"He seemed more sad than mad," Charlie said. "And that wouldn't explain where Betty is."

"Maybe he killed her someplace else. Or maybe this Jared and Betty did it together. Or he's covering for her." All they had were questions and no answers. Suddenly Mia was so, so tired. She stuffed another handful of chips into her mouth, not even trying to hide her chewing. "But I guess the bottom line, Charlie, is why should I care? The more I learn about Scott, the more I wonder."

Mia did care, but it wasn't in the right way. The only emotion she felt was anger. Not just at Scott. She was angry at herself. Angry at her own naïveté. How could she have been such a fool? She kept remembering the pitying look in Oleg's eyes when he looked up from the ring. The way Charlie had looked at her when he showed her Betty's picture on the computer screen.

"I was married to him for sixteen years. It's pretty clear I was an idiot. I just don't know how long I was one." How many other couples had she seen go through an affair when she secretly thought to herself that the other partner had surely known and turned a blind eye? Only now it was her. She must have wanted to be blind.

"Scott was smart," Charlie said. "He covered his tracks. He had two sides and he only showed you one."

"That's because I only wanted to see one. I knew he was cheating on me, Charlie, I knew it in my bones, but I never confronted him. I just went bleating after him, trying to get him to love me again. I was pathetic, like some beaten dog crawling back to its owner." Tears flooded her eyes, making it hard to see the road.

"Look, don't put this on yourself." Charlie's voice sharpened. "You're a good person. You gave Scott your trust because you yourself are trustworthy. Do you really want to be the kind of person who doesn't trust their partner, who goes onto the computer and checks the browser history, who figures out their passwords and snoops?" He was silent for a moment. "Because I've been that person. And it brings you no joy."

Mia could only nod and stuff more chips into her mouth to try to keep the sobs from coming out. She pulled into the faculty parking lot.

Right next to Eli Hall.

CHAPTER 34

Eli was just gathering his things to get out of his car when a dark blue Toyota pulled in next to him. It was Mia Quinn, her mouth moving as she spoke to someone on the phone. She was steering with one hand. With the other she seemed to be knuckling tears from her cheeks.

When she saw Eli, her eyes widened, then she pasted on a smile. As he got out of his car, she swatted something off the passenger seat.

It looked like an empty bag of chips. Not that Eli would point fingers. He knew what it was like to juggle being a single parent with two jobs. And then there was her being attacked on Monday.

He waited for her as she leaned into her car to gather her things, making an effort to avert his gaze from how her skirt tightened across her legs and backside. "Are you okay?" he asked when she emerged.

Mia looked at him and then away. "Yeah." She was walking fast. Eli matched her stride for stride, although it felt like he was nearly running to keep up. And she was wearing heels. "I just wish I'd been here ten minutes earlier. I don't like to cut it this close."

"And that's everything that's bothering you?" he prompted gently. Lydia used to complain that he interrogated her.

"Maybe I'm just a little stressed out."

"Are you still wondering if your husband was murdered?"

"I've been digging around since then." There was a catch in her voice. "Let me just say I haven't liked what I've found. The evidence is still pretty circumstantial, but it all points in the same direction."

"Do you know who did it?"

"Not yet. Probably someone who was mad at Scott." Her laugh sounded like it had been crossed with a sob. "Which I guess would include me. I'm starting to feel like the biggest fool who ever lived. How can I see through criminals when I couldn't see through my own husband?"

"Because a marriage has to be built on trust. It should be a place where you can relax." Eli pulled the door open for Mia. She passed by so close that her shoulder brushed his chest. He found himself inhaling deeply. Her scent was sweet and fresh, almost like baby powder, although he didn't think it came from any perfume or shampoo. "If you could ever use another person to bounce things off of, let me know."

She turned back to him. A smile flitted across her face. "I might just take you up on that."

"How about this weekend? Brunch on Saturday or after church on Sunday?"

Her mouth twisted, and he was sure she was going to say no.

"Okay. Maybe Sunday. Unless things get too crazy. I'll text you."

When Eli walked into class, he knew he was grinning like a fool, but he couldn't help it.

"One of the hardest parts of the cross is getting the tone right," Eli told the class. "And that tone is going to change for every person sitting in the witness chair. If it's a police officer, you take one tack. And a different one with a criminal. You'll use one tone for a child and another for a neutral witness. Even if the witness is hostile, don't let yourself look like a jerk. Of course, you still need to make it clear that you are in charge, and you need to make sure your questions are answered, but don't go overboard. I know Titus said you were the star on cross, and that's true, but don't let it go to your head. If you're too sarcastic or too rough or too theatrical, you're going to lose points."

A student in the back raised his hand, and Eli nodded at him.

"But how do you know how far is too far?"

"Partly, it's a matter of experience. One trick is to watch the jurors much more during cross-exam than on direct examination. Are they smiling or are they shaking their heads? And if so, who is that directed at? Watch them to see how much they are absorbing and how they are reacting. If they don't meet your eyes, that's a pretty big tell that you've gone too far."

For a second Eli remembered all the times Lydia had accused him of treating her like a hostile witness, turning normal conversations into cross-examinations. And it was true that there were occasions when he had slipped and said things like "Answer the question: yes or no," or "It's a simple question. I think you can give me a simple answer."

And finally Lydia had given him a simple answer. She had told him she wanted a divorce.

CHAPTER 35

Upstairs, Mia tried to let the shower wash her clean, unkink the muscles in her shoulders, make her relax. She moved carefully, as if she had been broken and put back together with glue that hadn't yet set.

She thought about what she and Charlie had learned today, not just about the boys who had dropped the shopping cart, but also about Scott. His falsehoods hadn't begun or ended with Mia, not when he had clearly planned to pass off a fake ring as the real thing. And now Betty, the girl Scott had planned to leave her for, was missing. What did that mean?

The more she learned about Scott, the more she felt a fool. She and the kids were better off without him. He had been going to leave them one way or another. At least this way the break had been clean. Did she really want to be sending the kids to visit their dad and their new college-aged stepmother?

Mia went to bed but found it impossible to sleep. For the first two months after Scott died, she had slept with an old suitcase on his side. The weight had made her feel less alone, had sometimes allowed her to pretend that she wasn't. Now she moved over to the center and spread out her arms and legs.

She thought she heard a car pull up outside, but she paid it no mind. No mind until she heard the front door open and close.

Was Gabe sneaking out with friends? Anger ran hot through her veins. She threw back the covers and ran down the stairs, trying to catch him before the car pulled away—and rounded the corner just as Gabe came back in the front door. He jumped at the sight of her.

"You scared me, Mom. I didn't know you were up."

"What were you doing?"

He paused, and in that pause she felt him constructing a lie. It was a mother's sixth sense.

"I accidentally picked up Eldon's math book at school and he came by to get it."

Gabe and Eldon were both on the JV football team. But Eldon was a year older, so they weren't even in the same grade. "At almost midnight?"

He didn't meet Mia's eyes. "He stays up late."

She looked at Gabe and she couldn't help but see all the boys she and Charlie had talked about this week. Manny, who had tried to do the right thing but failed. Dylan, who came from a home with no hope, no help, no room, not even warmth or light. Jackson, raised by a child, his only role model a man who sold weed. And Luke, lost in a huge house, with a disconnected father and a mother in a coma.

"Gabe, I need you to tell me the truth," Mia said, and braced herself. Was he buying pot—or something even worse? If she searched his pockets now, what would she find?

"Promise you won't be mad?"

Her heart fell. At that moment, she realized he was looking at her. Not up. They were eye to eye.

"I promise," she said. What else could she say?

"I've been giving Eldon a few things."

"Things?" Of all the answers she had been expecting, this wasn't one of them. "What kind of things?"

"Like mac and cheese. Blankets. And toilet paper."

"We're talking about the same Eldon, right? From the football team?" Had Eldon been kicked out of his house? He was a big kid, 220 pounds easy. He had sleepy eyes and creamy brown skin. He was Samoan? Hawaiian?

"His mom has cancer. She lost her job and they can't afford their apartment anymore. So they've been living in Danny's garage."

"What?" Mia's tired brain was still trying to recalibrate.

"You know, Danny. We went to middle school together. The skater dude with the long hair?"

"And Eldon and his mother are living in Danny's garage?" She tried to imagine what that would be like. "Where do they sleep? Do they have heat?"

"No, there isn't any heat, but it was either that or the shelter, I guess, and then they would probably be separated, since Eldon's sixteen. And his mom's car isn't big enough that they could sleep in it. She sleeps on a cot and Eldon's been sleeping on an old beanbag chair. I brought over my sleeping bag and some of our blankets. And I've been bringing them some of our food. They get food stamps, but I guess they don't go very far."

Well, that explained the gaps in their cupboards.

"I should have told you." Gabe heaved a sigh. "But I was afraid you would be mad."

Something inside her melted. "I'm not mad, Gabe. Of course I'm not mad." She wrapped her arms around his wiry shoulders and tried to pull him close.

He went rigid then squirmed away.

"Even if you're nearly a grown man, you're still my son. And sometimes I just need to hug you."

"Mom. Please. You've got a four-year-old. You don't need to treat me like one."

Normally his words would have stung. But tonight all Mia could think was how proud she was of him.

CHAPTER 36

To do a job right, you didn't learn just about the guy you were being paid to kill. No, you learned about other people in his circle. People he might have let something slip to. Or engaged in a little pillow talk with.

Like the wife.

Or the mistress.

Vin had spread enough money around that when someone started asking about Scott Quinn's death, he heard about it.

So what did Mia Quinn know? Had she found something that Vin had missed? He had tossed her dead husband's office only an hour after he died, come away with anything that might be incriminating.

All the secrets Scott had uncovered should have died with him.

So why was Mia Quinn now sticking her nose where it didn't belong?

CHAPTER 37

THURSDAY

Mia's cell phone rang just as she was gobbling a piece of toast and shepherding Brooke out of the house. Trying to persuade her daughter that they had to leave now, not in five minutes, not in five hours.

Gabe had taken the bus today. They hadn't talked any more about Eldon and his mom, but their situation had contributed to Mia's nearly sleepless night. Some part of her, though, had welcomed worrying about them, because it took her mind off of Scott's betrayal.

She jammed the last bite of toast into her mouth as she said hello.

It was Frank, his voice so tight with anger that at first Mia didn't recognize it. "Are you listening to the radio?"

"No." She felt oddly guilty. Lately her life seemed to be a series of things she should have been doing.

"Turn on KNWS. Raines is holding a press conference about the shopping cart case."

"What?"

"Just turn it on. And call me back when it's over."

Before lifting Brooke into her booster seat, Mia stuck the keys in the car's ignition and switched on the radio. She ignored the car's *beep-beep-beep* warning signaling an open door, mentally crossing her fingers that none of the neighbors was trying to sleep in.

In his instantly recognizable gravelly voice, Dominic Raines was saying, ". . . don't feel safe walking downtown anymore. There's a sense of lawlessness in Seattle. As we have all seen, these kids feel like they can get away with anything and get nothing but a slap on the wrist. If the criminals think they won't really be punished, then what won't they do? These two teens are animals, not like the young man who risked his own life to save this poor woman."

Mia frowned a little bit at the hyperbole. Manny had tried to stop it, sure, but he hadn't risked his life.

As Mia buckled Brooke in, Raines continued, his voice dripping with sarcasm. "But the King County prosecutor's office still hasn't decided whether to charge these violent offenders as adults. So once again we're left wondering if Frank D'Amato and his cronies will allow criminals to walk away scot-free. This is just one more example of why the King County prosecutor's office needs to be overhauled, so that more people like Tamsin Merritt aren't victimized. My opponent is overseeing a department that literally lets people get away with murder. When I'm elected, you can be sure that I will hire prosecutors who will work diligently to ensure justice is done."

As opposed to prosecutors who slack off and who don't care about justice? Mia asked Raines in her head. When she started the car and pulled out of the driveway, it was all she could do to drive at a moderate speed.

"As district attorney, I will restore integrity and professionalism to the office," he continued. "I want to bring in experienced prosecutors who have a passion for justice. Not litigators who make excuse after excuse for criminals who are violent predators. Some of these folks need to think about getting their resumes ready."

Great. Not only did she have to worry about what was justice for the victim and what was right for these boys and what was best for society and what Frank wanted, now Mia had to worry that if Frank lost she might be forced out of her job.

A female voice said, "I'm Catherine Belsen, reporting live from a press conference called by Dominic Raines, who is challenging Frank D'Amato for the position of King County prosecutor. Raines was reacting to video footage of the suspects in that horrific incident where a shopping cart was dropped four stories onto a woman's head, as well as news that one of the suspects has a lengthy juvenile record. That record includes charges of second-degree murder that were ultimately dropped by the King County prosecutor's office."

What? That charge hadn't been in the paperwork she had gotten. Mia pulled into the parking lot for Brooke's school, but she didn't get out.

Belsen continued, "Raines contends that if these juveniles had been prosecuted correctly, Tamsin would not be in the hospital today."

"And what is Tamsin's condition?" the male announcer asked. Mia noted that it was just Tamsin for everyone now.

"We understand that she is still in a coma," Belsen said. "Doctors say it's too soon to predict whether she will ever awaken. We also reached out to current prosecutor Frank D'Amato for a comment, but we were told he was unavailable."

"In other news—" the announcer said, and Mia snapped off the radio.

As she got out of the car and unbuckled Brooke, she dialed Frank's number. But it was Judy who answered. "Just a minute, Mia. He's on another line."

With one hip Mia nudged open the door of the preschool and then led Brooke in by the hand. Of course she chose that moment to grab Mia's legs and start crying. "Don't leave me here, Mommy!"

Frank came on the line. "So at what point did you start listening?" he demanded.

"People don't feel safe, the city is lawless . . ." Mia tried to peel Brooke's fingers loose and hoped Frank could still hear her over Brooke's cries. "Somewhere around there."

"Then you missed what he said earlier."

Mia's stomach clenched as if it were deciding whether to reject the toast all together. One of the workers, a young woman named Sarah, swept Brooke into her arms, trying to distract her.

"And what was that?" Mia smiled her thanks at Sarah and gave a little wave as she hurried out the door, trying not to listen to Brooke's wails. She told herself that Brooke would be fine, that her daughter always had a hard time with transitions. Still, she wished she had had a few minutes to play with her, maybe to build a block tower or gallop a Playmobil cowboy on his plastic horse, something to make the switch from home to preschool a little easier.

"It turns out there's more video footage from the shopping mall. Fifteen minutes before they dropped the cart, it shows all three boys leaning over the walkway, dropping cans of Mountain Dew and watching them explode. Raines said that meant they knew exactly what would happen when they dropped a shopping cart onto a woman's head." He sucked in a breath. "I don't like having to learn things from my opponent's press conference, Mia."

"Neither do I." Mia mentally kicked herself. Why hadn't she made sure she had all of the video?

Maybe Frank felt somewhat to blame, because he didn't continue to excoriate her for missing it. Instead, he launched into a series of questions. "Who's leaking?" he demanded. "How come they seem to know more than we do? What have you done so far on this case?"

The honest answers would be *I don't know, I don't know,* and *I have conducted a bunch of interviews but am finding more questions than answers.* But Frank didn't want honesty. He wanted her to fix this.

"It doesn't have to be a leak from our office," she reminded him as she took the freeway on-ramp. "Raines could have gotten the footage from someone in security at the shopping mall. Now that it's all on a computer instead of an actual tape, it's easy for anyone with a jump drive in his pocket to make a copy. And the other information about the second-degree murder charge could have come from a friend, a family member, even a different victim. The thing that concerns me is that if it's true, it wasn't in any of the paperwork I saw. I need to talk to Tracy." Tracy Lowe was head of the Juvenile Unit.

"If they really were dropping cans of Mountain Dew, I think it's pretty clear that they knew what they were doing. In a way, that would just make your job easier."

Did their action show intent? How close was a Mountain Dew can hitting the pavement to a shopping cart hitting a woman's head?

"We can't rush to judgment, Frank. Were they really capable of understanding the results of what they did? You've got kids. You know that sometimes they make stupid, impulsive decisions." She thought of Gabe trying to help his friend. And sometimes they made sweet, impulsive decisions.

"Yes, they do. And sometimes they have to pay for the consequences of those decisions. A woman is near death, Mia. We can't overlook that. We can't say that these were just kids horsing around. Not when the results were so grave." He took a deep breath, and she could almost see his shoulders straighten. "You know that you only have a day to make your decision, Mia. And the longer this drags out, the worse it looks."

And Frank needed it to be her decision. Not just to provide him with some political cover. But also, Mia thought, to provide himself with some psychic cover. That way Frank could tell himself he hadn't let the upcoming election pressure him into it. He had let her investigate and make a fully reasoned decision.

"I still need to talk to Manny, but his psychiatrist has not given us the all clear. Not only can Manny tell me what they were talking about beforehand and shed light on the other boys' states of mind, but we also need him as a witness. Without him, all we're left with is a blurry videotape."

"Do we really need him now?" Frank said bluntly. "Think about it, Mia. We only have to charge these kids as adults, then everyone is satisfied. No more crying about how Seattle is letting these kids run around like packs of wild dogs. And if the charges later get dropped or moved to juvenile court, well, people will have moved on by then. They won't be so focused. They'll have some new obsession and they will barely remember this case."

Mia couldn't censor herself any longer. "You mean they will have voted by then."

"Well, there is that."

For a second she loved Frank for his unexpected honesty.

"But that's not the only reason you should seriously consider charging them as adults. If we want to send a message to youth, then we need an example. And these two are perfect."

"They're perfect because they have zero advantages. Bad home lives, bad neighborhoods, bad schools. There is no one to speak for them except for maybe a teacher or two and whatever public defender they draw. I'm moving as fast as I can, Frank, but if we move too fast we can get ahead of the facts."

"I know that. And I trust you to get this right. That's why I assigned it to you. But I still need your decision as soon as possible."

Mia stifled a sigh. "Sure. Can you put me through to Judy?" As she waited, she reflected on how hard it was for an elected official to balance doing a good job with campaigning. How could you effectively govern when you were dealing with a media that was so quick to pursue the most sensational aspects of a story, with a public that all too often only skimmed the surface?

This morning she had read that so far only sixteen percent of King County residents had turned in their vote-by-mail ballots. In the polls, Raines was behind Frank by four points. That was the good news. The bad news was that the margin of error was plus or minus four points. Basically, the two men were tied. All it would take was one mistake, one wrong word, one revelation to tip the balance. And Raines was clearly determined to make this case be that one thing.

Finally she heard Judy's voice. "Mia?"

"Can you schedule a meeting for Tracy and me as soon as possible this morning?"

"I'll see what I can do."

Mia was starting to say good-bye when Judy added, "And you should know that the public defender's office just called. The lawyers for the two boys charged in the shopping cart case have both indicated they are willing to talk to you with their clients today."

"What lawyers have they been assigned?"

There was a pause as Judy found the information. "Naomi Fairchild and Eli Hall."

Eli. Mia blinked. She had wondered when this day would come.

CHAPTER 38

li, Mia thought as she took the elevator to her office. Representing one of the teens Frank wanted her to charge as an adult. She hadn't seen that coming.

Oh sure, she had figured that someday they would work opposing sides of the same case, but she had always pictured it involving an adult. She was in Violent Crimes, after all, not the Juvenile Unit. But the public defender's office didn't have the budget for their lawyers to specialize.

Before she met with Tracy Lowe, the head of the Juvenile Unit, Mia tracked down the footage of the kids dropping the cans of Mountain Dew. All three kids had leaned over the railing and tried it. Manny had dropped one, and Dylan and Jackson had each dropped two. The remaining can they had passed back and forth to drink. Two of the cans had been dropped when people were passing by, although neither had hit anyone. One man had been sprayed, judging by the way he had swiped at his pants and then shaken his fist at the three laughing boys.

After she had watched it twice, Mia headed for Tracy's office.

"Hey, Mia." Tracy looked up from her computer. Her thick,

straight golden-brown hair fell to her shoulders. Looking at it always made Mia think of wheat fields, a comparison that didn't really factor in Tracy's brightly painted nails and face.

"Tracy, I thought I had all three boys' records, but then I heard Raines on the radio this morning. What's this about a second-degree murder charge that was dropped? Frank isn't happy he didn't know about that, but it wasn't in any of the paperwork I got."

Tracy made a face. "Raines was exaggerating. Dylan broke into a neighbor's house. And that is in the records you got. What isn't is that when the guy came home and found Dylan sitting at his kitchen table, eating his leftover chicken out of his refrigerator, he had a heart attack. He died two days later."

Mia nodded. She shouldn't be surprised that Raines's story had a backstory.

"And this guy was pushing eighty, extremely obese, and on a million meds for high blood pressure, diabetes, and cholesterol." Tracy ticked off her points on her red fingernails. "The medical examiner who did the autopsy said he was a heart attack waiting to happen—and that certainly wasn't Dylan's fault."

"But why was he charged with second-degree murder at all?"

"The preliminary complaint did have that charge, but it was to encourage Dylan to plead guilty and get the help he needed. He was never formally charged with it, just with the B&E. Dylan never raised a hand to the man and actually never stole anything. All he did was eat some leftover chicken."

Mia thought of Dylan's dark, malodorous apartment. "Charlie Carlson and I were over there yesterday to talk to the mom, and afterward I ended up asking Children's Services to check on the other kids. As far as I could tell, they had no electricity."

Tracy made a tsk-tsking sound as they raised their eyebrows at each other and shook their heads. "Poverty's no crime," she said, "but Dylan's mom is not equipped to deal with it. She's not really raising those kids. They're raising themselves—and falling through the cracks. In fact"—she steepled her fingers—"I have to tell you, Mia, that neither of these two kids who dropped the shopping cart seems to me to rise to the level of someone who should be tried in an adult court. If Dylan's anything, he's a victim of a system that hasn't intervened enough for him. And while Jackson may be more culpable, he's still only fifteen. The frontal lobe of a fifteen-year-old's brain is simply not capable of foreseeing the possible consequences of their behavior. They're impulsive and they don't consider the future. I'm not even talking about the results of poor parenting or abuse, although those things certainly don't help. It's simply because they're too young. Trying these kids as adults is like punishing a baby for not being able to walk yet."

"But these are particularly serious offenses." Mia made the arguments Frank would. "And both kids have juvenile records. And you can't tell me that they couldn't foresee the consequences of their actions, especially given that they were dropping cans of soda right beforehand."

"And I heard you spent yesterday interviewing people who know these two boys." Tracy's voice underlined the word *boys*. "Then you must know that these are kids who truly come from nothing. If you put them into adult prison, you'll make them into criminals. You'll ruin their lives, and for what? It won't undo what's been done. I chose to work with juveniles because I sometimes have a chance to help these kids turn their lives around before it's too late." She shot Mia a pointed look. "You yourself know how important that is."

When Gabe had agreed to give up the names of the other kids in the flash mob, Tracy hadn't prosecuted him.

"No decision has been made," Mia said. "We're still investigating. We're talking with both boys and their attorneys today. One of them may be guiltier than the other. And if the other one agrees to cooperate, he might have a very different outcome."

Tracy shook her head. "Just don't let Raines—or Frank, for that matter—get in the way of doing the right thing. We can't run this office based on politics. We have to run it based on what's right, and let the chips fall where they may."

———————

When Mia went back to her office, Frank had sent her a draft of a statement he was planning to release to answer Raines's charges.

Sadly, my opponent is trying to score political points by capitalizing on the tragedy that has left Tamsin Merritt gravely injured. But this case will not be tried in the press.

Instead, it is the prosecutor, and the prosecutor alone, who is officially charged with the duty of seeking the truth and pursuing justice in this case. The prosecutor is in the best position to know the gravity of the crime, the evidence that supports the filing of charges, the criminal history of the accused, and the impact of the crime upon the victim.

Thus the prosecutor has the best reference point from which to make the critical decisions that will affect the victim as well as the offenders. I trust Mia Quinn, a prosecutor in the Violent Crimes division, to carefully weigh all sides in this case before making her decision on how to proceed.

CHAPTER 39

Charlie and Mia discussed strategy as he drove them to the Youth Service Center, where both Jackson and Dylan were being housed.

"How many hours left in your forty-eight before you have to charge them?" Charlie asked.

Mia looked at her watch. "Less than twenty-two."

"I'm sure Frank took Raines's press conference this morning well." Charlie's face was innocent.

"Yeah, right." Mia's mouth twisted. "He's still telling me it's my choice, and he's even putting out a press release saying that, and emphasizing that the case shouldn't be tried in the media. But if I decline to charge these two as adults, you can be sure that Dominic Raines will claim it's even more proof that our office doesn't take crime seriously."

"There's another option," Charlie offered. "Charge them as adults in the preliminary complaint. You can always amend it later. But right now it would get Raines off your back. And if it turns out he's your new boss, then you can decide what's best for everyone all the way around."

It was what Frank had hinted at, a variation of what had originally been done with Dylan. Except instead of pressuring a boy to get help, it would provide Frank with political cover. It might even protect her job if Raines ended up being elected. But should Mia play politics when she wasn't a political appointee?

"I'm just hoping things will be a lot clearer when we're done here," she said as they pulled into the parking garage next to Youth Services.

"If wishes were horses"—Charlie held his hand up to his chin— "we'd all be up to here in horse . . . poop. So how do you want to play this?" he asked as they got out of the car. "Good cop, bad cop?"

"Don't you think that's a little obvious? I mean, look at you and look at me. It's almost typecasting."

"I'll let you be bad cop if you want." Charlie offered one of his lopsided grins.

At the thought of herself leaning into the boys' faces and making threats while Charlie solicitously offered to get them soft drinks and snacks, Mia had to smile. "I'm guessing both of these kids have spent a lot of time parked in front of TVs. They'd realize what was going on within the first thirty seconds, no matter which one of us plays bad cop. Let's just do this without any games."

"None?" He raised an eyebrow.

"Of course we'll still start with softball questions and see if we can get them to open up. Or let down their guard."

"And we might want to make it worth their while for one of them to roll over on their buddy."

"Okay, Charlie, you win. We'll play games. Just not good cop, bad cop."

First they met with Dylan's lawyer, Naomi Fairchild. Naomi had sleek brown hair cut in an angled bob. Only a few years out of law school, she was the youngest lawyer in the public defender's office. Despite her low salary she was dressed in a striking red cashmere jacket that Mia guessed had cost as much as one of Mia's house payments. Naomi's father had made a fortune as a software developer.

Rumor had it that his money allowed her to pursue her passion for defending the downtrodden.

"Okay," Naomi said as soon as Mia had introduced Charlie and they had sat down at the battered square conference table. "We want all the records you have on file for Dylan, as well as his mother, his stepfathers past and present, and his nine siblings."

"What?" Mia was shocked. "That's immaterial. It has nothing to do with the charges your client is facing."

"Oh yes it does. We will be raising the issue of child abuse. Dylan is a victim as much as Tamsin Merritt is, if not more. His abuse has lasted for years. It's left him brain-damaged and mentally incompetent. He doesn't even understand what happened that day. He operates on the level of a ten-year-old. And that's being generous. We're still having him evaluated."

"The very fact that Dylan ran away afterward proves he knew what he did was wrong," Mia pointed out.

Naomi was undeterred. "We intend to show a systematic pattern that led to Dylan's not being responsible for his actions. I've made a list of everything we need." She slid a printout across to Mia, and Charlie leaned in to look.

For Dylan and all his family members, Naomi was requesting every conceivable record. Medical screenings and treatment. Counseling. Drug rehabilitation. Alcohol rehab. Results from psychological tests. Any and all results from any standardized tests, including school records. Every family member's offense history, referrals for placements, disciplinary actions, and any other records held by any department of King County or its affiliates.

With a shake of her head, Mia slid the paper back toward Naomi. "Any records kept on these other individuals are confidential and not material to Dylan's case. If you try to subpoena them, I'll tell the judge this is nothing but a fishing expedition." She managed a smile. "I'm surprised you didn't go looking for records of violent video game purchases."

Mia was being sarcastic, but Naomi nodded thoughtfully and scribbled in the corner of the paper. Then she looked up and said, "And before you speak to my client, I want to set some ground rules. I will be in the room with you two and Dylan at all times. And I want the right to be able to pull the plug at any time."

Even though she planned on agreeing, Mia didn't say anything. She was still ticked at Naomi's demands.

"And I want immunity for anything Dylan says."

Immunity meant that Mia wouldn't be able to use anything she learned from Dylan against him at trial.

"No." Naomi started to interrupt, but Mia raised her hand. "However, we are prepared to offer a plea bargain if Dylan will freely admit that he and Jackson both participated in this crime, both today and at trial."

Naomi's eyes narrowed. "What kind of plea bargain?"

"If he completely cooperates with us, then I am prepared to agree to some type of intensive treatment. Perhaps another stay in a therapeutic foster home."

Naomi just made a humming noise, then went outside to tell them that they were ready for Dylan to be brought in. When he came into the room, his head hung so low that he was curled over like a comma. He kept his eyes on his black shower shoes scuffing over the worn tiles. His brown hair was cut short enough that his scalp was visible between the bristles.

"Can you tell us your name, please?" Mia didn't say *honey*, but it was in the tone of her voice.

"Dylan."

"And, Dylan, how old are you?"

"Fifteen."

"What grade are you in?"

"Tenth." His voice was so soft that Mia had to strain to hear it.

"Do you have any siblings?" Mia asked.

"She means brothers and sisters," Charlie leaned in to explain.

Maybe it wasn't exactly good cop/bad cop, but he was still trying to find an angle.

"There's ten of us." Dylan looked up for half a second. His face was blotched with red. "Plus my mom."

"Things must get kind of crowded at your house," Charlie said. "Do you ever go out and do stuff with your friends?"

"Sometimes." He was speaking to his shower shoes again.

"Who do you hang out with?"

"Jackson mostly. And sometimes Manny."

"And how do you know them?" Mia asked.

"From school."

"Are you guys good friends?" Charlie said.

Dylan glanced up at them again, and Mia had the sad thought that the two boys were his only friends. "Yeah."

It was time to cut to the chase. "Dylan, were you with Jackson and Manny on Saturday?"

"Yeah."

"Where did you go?"

He picked at a cuticle, which was already raw. "We took a bus. To a mall."

"And what did you do there?"

His answer was slower now. "Fooled around."

"Could you be more specific?"

"We dropped some things over the bridge."

"What did you drop?"

"Cans. At first."

"Whose idea was that?"

He shrugged. "I don't remember."

"What about the shopping cart?" Mia said. "You were playing with it, right? Giving each other rides?"

He nodded.

"And then you picked it up and balanced it on the railing. Do you remember whose idea that was?"

He was perfectly still.

"Did you try to hold on, Dylan?" Mia offered him an out. "Did it just slip?"

He continued to be silent.

"Look, Dylan, if you can help us, we can help you. If you are willing to testify—"

"To say in court," Charlie interjected.

"Say in court that this was really someone else's idea, then things could go much better for you."

He shook his head. "But they're my friends."

"This woman was very badly hurt, Dylan. She didn't do anything wrong, and now she's in the hospital."

"So?" His head jerked up and his eyes were blazing. "I don't care."

Mia was shocked. "But what happened hurt her. Hurt her badly."

"I don't care," he repeated.

"She might die," Mia stammered.

In a warning tone, Naomi said, "Dylan! Stop talking! Now!" She grabbed his arm.

He ignored her. "So? Some rich lady in her clip-clop shoes? Someone like that doesn't matter to me! Who cares? Who cares about her?"

But Mia heard another sentence beneath his words. *Who cares about her when no one cares about me?*

"That's it," Naomi said, standing up so fast her chair flew back and nearly tipped over. "We're done here."

CHAPTER 40

Mia's mind was still whirling when Eli walked into the room. Had Dylan played more of a role than she had thought? Had he targeted Tamsin deliberately?

She thought back to how Tamsin had been dressed when she was hurt. She was pretty sure the woman had been wearing heels, or "clip-clop shoes" as Dylan had termed them. Had he spotted Tamsin and decided to punish her for being a woman who could afford nice things? For being the kind of woman who looked like she ran the world?

Eli's greeting was professional, nothing more. Yesterday he might have asked her to brunch, but today they were colleagues on opposite sides of the table. Even if they were seriously dating, however, the law didn't preclude them acting as prosecutor and defense on the same case. The only rule was that the potential conflict of interest had to be disclosed to the client.

"Eli, do you remember Charlie Carlson?" The two men had met at one of Gabe's football games. "He's a detective with the Seattle PD. And Eli Hall is with the public defender."

Charlie stood up, and unsmiling, the two men shook hands. Mia couldn't help but contrast them. Charlie with his black tousled hair that nearly brushed the back of his collar. Eli with blond hair cut short as fur. Charlie took his seat again, resuming his customary slouch.

Eli sat with his back ruler-straight, both feet on the floor. He narrowed his eyes. "Aren't you in the homicide department, Detective?"

Charlie nodded. "That's right."

He turned to Mia. "Don't you think it's a little prejudicial, having a homicide detective conduct the investigation?"

She blinked, suddenly wishing it had been Eli doing the cross-examination in class Tuesday. Maybe then this side of him wouldn't have been such a surprise. "This is a preliminary investigation, and Charlie's working for me. He's been identifying himself as I did just now, strictly as a member of the Seattle PD. Besides, no one knows yet whether Tamsin will live." Mia crossed her arms and leaned back. Eli wasn't the only one who could come out swinging. "To be honest, I'd be more worried about your client, Counselor. He's got a lengthy juvenile record. He's charged with a serious offense. And obviously past rehabilitation has been unsuccessful. Everything argues for him being tried as an adult."

Eli's mouth tightened. "First of all, there is no proof of intent. None. These were kids just fooling around. The cart slipped from their hands. Jackson had no intention of dropping it on this woman. But it weighs fifty pounds. Once it reached a tipping point, they both lost their grip on it, and then it was too late."

Charlie sat forward. "You're trying to tell me that after they watched five cans of Mountain Dew explode on the concrete they had no idea of what that shopping cart—and as you say, it weighs fifty pounds—would do to a woman's skull?" A muscle in his jaw flickered.

"I'm saying that there is no proof they intended to hurt anyone. If they did, why didn't they drop those cans on people? They were leaning over the railing, watching what was happening underneath them. They could easily have targeted someone. But they didn't."

Eli was painting things in a flattering light.

"They came pretty close, though, didn't they?" Mia pointed out. "Especially Jackson."

"That can was still at least ten feet away from anyone. And there was no more malice in what he did than in a kid who puts Mentos in a Diet Coke and tries to make a fountain. These are just kids, Mia. They were giving each other rides in the shopping cart before they lifted it up. They weren't planning anything. At their age and their stage of social development, they're not really capable of planning." He took a breath. "Look, can I be honest with you?"

Charlie looked dubious, but Mia nodded.

"With a kid like Jackson, a kid who is only fifteen and looks younger, if you put him in an adult facility, he'll be like a guppy in the ocean. The first time he's in gen pop, he'll be assaulted physically or sexually. Or both. After that he'll be placed in isolation for his own protection. That means he'll spend twenty-three and a half hours of every day alone. If Jackson isn't mentally ill right now, which he may very well be, he's going to be mentally ill pretty darn soon once he spends twenty-three and a half hours every day in absolute isolation. Check out the statistics. Youth housed in adult jails are thirty-six times more likely to commit suicide than those who go to juvenile detention facilities."

Imagining Gabe in the same situation, Mia started to weaken.

But Charlie didn't. "These punks left a woman with her head stove in on the sidewalk." He put his hands flat on the table and leaned forward. "She was out there minding her own business, running errands with her kid, and they left her to die. Left her facedown on the sidewalk with her skull fractured, lying in a pool of her own blood. Right in front of her kid. And she might still die. Even if she lives, she'll never be the same again."

"Jackson took part in this, Eli," Mia said. "He's already sentenced a woman to what is more than likely a broken life. And that's if she's lucky."

"Two wrongs don't make a right," Eli said. "I'm not saying these boys are sweet or innocent. I'm saying that we as a society failed them. And now we're going to blame them for acting on those failures."

Charlie rolled his eyes. "There're kids who go to school every day who face the same problems, maybe even worse, and they're not out assaulting people."

"I'm not saying he shouldn't be punished. I'm saying there are a whole range of options that are open to him as a juvenile that aren't to an adult. Treatment programs, probation, detention, even incarceration. But if you put Jackson in an adult court, anything could happen. He could even be sentenced to life. Would it really be fair if he spent the next sixty-five years in prison?"

The question hung in the air.

Finally Mia said, "I appreciate your input, Eli. But before I can decide anything, I need to talk to your client."

Jackson was a beautiful boy, with the darker skin of his mother and tip-tilted long-lashed eyes that must have belonged to his father.

Mia began as she had with Dylan, circling around the facts of his life, starting with his family and then eventually moving on to his record. Without hesitation he admitted to his long list of criminal activities. Then she brought him up to the event. "Why did you do it, Jackson?"

"I didn't think. We were just fooling around. Then Dylan or Manny said maybe it would be fun to tip it over." He spoke more and more slowly. "We lifted it up, but nobody really meant to do anything after that. But all of a sudden it was falling. I never thought there would be a lady underneath it." He took a ragged breath. "I never thought at all."

Mia's phone buzzed, but she pressed the button to silence it.

"Bull!" Charlie slammed his hands down on the table. He might look like he was playing bad cop, but Mia was certain this was no role. "You had already been looking down from that walkway. You knew how busy it was. I've seen the videotape. It shows you guys waiting to drop those cans until it was clear, so that no one would stop you or complain. But that means you knew exactly how good the chance was that you would hit someone."

"You don't know how sorry I am." Jackson blinked. His eyes looked wet.

That was the exact truth, Mia thought. She had no idea how sorry he was.

CHAPTER 41

"Talking to those two boys didn't make it any easier," Mia told Charlie as they left the Youth Service Center.

He nodded in agreement as he scrolled back through his phone.

Before talking to Jackson, she had been sure that he was most at fault. Now she didn't know what to think. Had those been crocodile tears he was crying, or was he genuinely upset? She remembered what Tracy and Eli had said. If Mia charged either of these boys as adults, then she was basically writing them off. It would be impossible to put them through the adult system, even for a few years, and have them not come out on the other side irreparably broken.

When Mia finally checked her own phone, she found a message from Willow Grove, the children's inpatient mental hospital. It was from a Dr. Sandstrom, who said that Manny Flores was asking to talk to them.

When Mia called back, the woman said in a clipped voice, "Manny insists that he has to talk to you. I want you to understand that this goes against my medical advice. I don't think he's ready.

Especially not after trying to harm himself. But he says it's important and that he won't be at peace until he talks to you."

"I appreciate your concern for his well-being, but it is important," Mia said. "This was no accident. At the very least, the other boys showed callous disregard for human lives. They could be charged as adults, possibly with attempted second-degree murder. The victim is in intensive care, and if she dies the charges will be even more serious. Manny is key to our understanding what happened to put her there. There's a lot about this situation that is still unclear, and he is the only witness." She looked at her watch. "We can be there in half an hour."

"Visiting hours are from six to seven p.m."

Which was when Mia and Charlie were going to be at the Jade Kitchen in Coho City. "But we're not visitors." Mia kept her words as clipped as the doctor's. "We're law enforcement. And we will need someplace private where we can talk."

A heavy sigh. "We could arrange something at four p.m. All his group and individual therapies will be finished by then. Will that work for you?"

"Four o'clock today?" Mia echoed, looking at Charlie. When he nodded to show he was free, she said, "We'll see you then."

"You need to be aware that you cannot bring in food, drinks, cigarettes, writing instruments, cell phones, wallets, or purses." From the tone of Dr. Sandstrom's voice, the full list was even longer and she was only hitting the highlights. "Or, of course, weapons of any type. Basically, all you're allowed into the facility with are your keys and a photo ID."

"What about a tape recorder?"

"No. Manny is too fragile. Whether it's logical or not, he's feeling a lot of guilt about what occurred. Just seeing a tape recorder might put him back in the place where it will be necessary to check him every fifteen minutes to make sure he hasn't succeeded in killing himself."

Mia winced. She couldn't imagine such torment. "Okay. No tape recorder." Besides, Charlie had near-perfect recall for conversations.

At five minutes to four they walked up to the front door of Willow Grove. The grounds were perfectly manicured, the grass as even and green as artificial turf. The large windows were all covered by blinds, making the two-story building look oddly blank, as if it were sleeping.

Charlie pressed the buzzer, and the two of them looked up into the lens of the camera mounted over the door.

The security guard who answered was a heavy-set man in a blue uniform. He checked their IDs, then asked if they had brought any of the contraband items in with them. When he let them into the foyer, a clerk with a tight gray perm asked them to sign in at her desk. She wrote their names and the date on paper badges, as well as Manny's name. Charlie slapped his on his suit jacket. Mia did the same, but lightly, mentally crossing her fingers that it wouldn't leave a mark on the silk.

With the security guard escorting them, they went through four more locked doors. Each time the guard scanned the plastic badge he wore around his neck and then punched a number into the key-pad. He then let Mia and Charlie through and made sure the door was closed tight before making his way to the next door.

"This is better security than they got over at the prison," Charlie stage-whispered to Mia.

"In this case we're not keeping the world safe from the people inside," the guard said as he waved his badge in front of yet another door. "We're keeping these kids safe from the outside world."

Finally they reached the ward. All the doors to the rooms were closed. The walls were painted blue. The pictures on them had been bolted down on all four corners, and when Mia tapped one with a knuckle in passing, she found it was covered in plastic, not glass.

"I need your keys." The dark-skinned nurse at the nurses' station put out her hand. She put each set in a plastic bag, which she zipped closed and then dropped into a blue plastic bucket that she put by her feet. "I'll take you to the visitors' room now," she said. "Dr. Sandstrom is waiting for you."

Even getting into the visiting room required the same routine with a badge and a keypad. The room was empty except for a jumble of overstuffed couches and chairs, as well as a card table topped with a half-finished jigsaw puzzle of a kitten.

Dr. Sandstrom was a petite woman with thick blond hair twisted back into a bun and a face bare of makeup. She tucked a clipboard under her arm and then shook their hands.

"I appreciate you letting us talk to Manny," Mia said after they had introduced themselves.

"Manny has posttraumatic stress disorder from witnessing the accident, as well as previously undiagnosed depression and anxiety. I need to warn you that those things might compromise his ability to answer your questions."

"Any information he can provide us with would be very useful," Mia said. "Tomorrow morning is the deadline for charging the perpetrators in this case. Manny is the only one who can tell us what really happened."

"He was very insistent, but I'm still afraid the stress of being questioned by you may harm him." Dr. Sandstrom drew herself up to her full height, which couldn't have been more than five foot one. "I will stop the interview if I feel his physical or mental condition is changing for the worse."

"Of course," Mia said as Charlie nodded.

"Because Manny is on suicide watch, I will be within arm's reach at all times. And if I feel that things are getting out of hand, that he is being adversely affected, then I will end the visit."

Mia didn't want this woman there. It was going to be hard enough to establish trust with three of them. But four?

"Because this is an active law enforcement case," Mia said, "what Manny says to us needs to stay confidential."

She frowned. "I'm a psychiatrist. Confidentiality is my stock in trade."

Mia had to remember they were both professionals, albeit with different goals. "Would it be possible for you to sit behind him so you're not in his line of vision?" she asked. "I don't want his attention to be divided."

Dr. Sandstrom pursed her lips, thinking, then nodded.

Mia and Charlie pushed the furniture around until it was in the configuration they wanted—a couch for the two of them, with a chair facing it. The second chair for the doctor was set behind Manny's. Dr. Sandstrom then left through a different door and came back with Manny.

He was a slight boy, with dark lank hair hanging over his eyes. The white bandage on his left wrist made Mia feel sick.

As they sat down she said, "Manny, I'm Mia, and this is Charlie."

"Hi." He spoke to his hands, twisting in his lap.

"First of all, Manny, I want you to understand that you are not in trouble. We've both watched the videotape, and we know you tried to stop the cart from falling over."

"You do?" He jerked his head up, his eyes wide.

"Yes."

Charlie leaned forward, his elbows on his knees. "But, buddy, the only one who can really tell us what Dylan and Jackson were thinking about, talking about, before that is you. So can you tell us how you all ended up at the mall?"

"Me and Dylan and Jackson, we were just bored, you know? So we took the bus to that mall. It was kind of far away. And we really didn't have much money."

"So what did you do?"

"We got a six-pack of Mountain Dew at a store. And we were up on the sky bridge, just watching everyone go by."

"Whose idea was it to drop the cans of soda over the railing?"

"Mine," Manny said. "I wanted to see what would happen."

"What did happen?" Charlie asked, as if he had not seen it on the videotape.

Manny's head came up and his face was animated. "It was cool! It, like, exploded." He put his fists together and pulled them apart, spreading his fingers to mime the explosion.

"Did you talk about what would happen if a can hit a person?"

"No. But nobody tried to drop 'em on anybody. And then we ran out of cans."

"What did you do then?" Mia asked softly.

He dropped his head. "We started giving each other rides in a shopping cart, seeing how fast we could make it go." As he spoke, his words came slower and slower.

"And then what happened?" Charlie prompted.

Manny rested his fingertips on his forehead, hiding from them even further. "If they didn't mean for it to happen, how much trouble will they get into?"

"Are you saying they didn't mean for it to happen?" Charlie asked. "Did they know that lady was down there when they dropped the cart?"

"What if they didn't know? What if the cart just slipped out of their hands?"

"Well, they should still have foreseen that something bad would happen," Mia said. "So I don't think they would get off without any consequences at all. But it would certainly be a different story than if they meant to do it."

Manny was silent for so long that Mia thought about prompting him. Then he said in a voice so soft Mia could barely hear it, "It's all my fault."

Her heart contracted. "No, it's not, Manny. We saw you struggling with them. You tried to stop it, Manny. It's not your fault you couldn't."

"It's more than that," he said and then fell silent.

Mia opened her mouth to ask him what he meant, but Charlie laid his hand on her knee and shook his head. All three of them—Mia, Charlie, and Dr. Sandstrom—waited for him to speak.

"It is my fault, it is. Even after they lifted it up, I knew they were teasing, they really wouldn't let go, but I still grabbed the cart. I grabbed the cart and yanked, but instead of pulling it back, I made them let go. I made them drop it." Manny's breathing was heavy with repressed tears. "It's my fault," he repeated. "It's my fault that lady is going to die."

CHAPTER 42

Mia didn't say much to Charlie for the first part of the drive to Coho City. Finally he broke down and asked, "So whatcha think about what Manny said?"

"You heard Dr. Sandstrom," Mia answered. "Just because Manny believes it happened doesn't mean that it did."

"But his story makes sense." Charlie thought about the videotape. "I can see it happening the way he said."

"But what about Dylan and his clip-clop shoes? Or Luke saying he heard the boys laughing?"

"I'm not sure that adds up to criminal intent," Charlie said. "Plus, those carts weigh a lot. And once the balance was tipped over the railing, it would have been very hard for them to bring it back. Even if Manny hadn't grabbed it, they still could have just been playing around with it and lost control."

"I still have about twelve hours to decide. Meanwhile, we're going to be at the Jade Kitchen pretty soon, right?"

He glanced at the clock on the dash. "In about twenty minutes. So I've been thinking a lot about what might have happened. Scott used to work for a big firm, right?"

"Right. And then before Brooke was born he went out on his own."

"So big accounting firms deal with other big companies. Companies that have compliance officers and are maybe publicly traded and have their books regularly audited. But when you're a one-man shop, you're gonna have smaller clients. And once the economy started to tank, businesses started going down the tube, meaning there was less demand for accountants and more newly laid-off accountants competing for the same work. If you wanted to get and keep clients, I'd imagine the best thing would be not to ask too many questions or look too closely."

He saw Mia shake her head.

"I remember Scott giving a cashier back a five-dollar bill because she gave him too much change."

"That's a person, Mia. A person who might get in trouble if her till didn't balance."

Maybe because she was a prosecutor, Mia tended to see things in black and white. In Charlie's world, there were a million shades of gray.

"But when you cheat on your taxes, it's cheating a big, faceless government that wastes hundreds of thousands of dollars. It's way easier to cheat if you think it's not really hurting anyone. And I'm not saying Scott actively cheated. He may simply have not asked many questions."

Although as far as Charlie was concerned, the note they had found to Kenny Zhong, the restaurant owner, was more than that. The note to Zhong was a warning.

"So you're saying there might have been some 'don't ask, don't tell' situations?" Mia said.

"Exactly. I'm guessing it's just easier to take the information they give you and prepare the books and the returns from that. And if they don't give you everything, well, that's on them."

———

Kenny Zhong, owner of the four Jade Kitchen restaurants, turned out to be no bigger than Mia's son, Gabe. In fact, Charlie thought as he shook the other man's hand, staring down at the top of his head, he might even be smaller.

"I really appreciate you coming out here to meet with me and my friend Charlie," Mia told Zhong. They were standing in the lobby. The restaurant was crowded. Only a few of the customers were Asian.

"I am honored." Zhong clasped his hands and made a little bow. If he was wondering who Charlie was, his face did not betray it. "Have you eaten?"

When Mia hesitated, he said, "Please, please, you must eat." He barked an order in Chinese at a young waitress in a high-collared silver blouse. She wore her long hair pinned up, her bangs falling slantwise over her eyes.

She led them to a table in the back. Charlie automatically took a seat on the banquette so that he faced the door. His cop habits were so ingrained in him that they were second nature. Whenever he encountered someone he looked at their hands first even before he looked at their faces. His first partner had drilled it into his head, saying over and over, "They can only hurt you with their hands."

Mia sat on the other end of the upholstered bench, and Zhong took a chair opposite. The waitress scurried over with three menus, but he waved them away. "I order for you, okay? Specialties of the house."

After they both nodded, he rattled off orders in rapid-fire Chinese. Then he turned back to them. "America is a great country. I came here seven years ago with nothing, and now I own four restaurants."

Hard work would get you a lot of things, but would it really get you four restaurants in seven years? Was Zhong in debt? Or was he cheating the tax man, as Scott's letter had suggested, and plowing it back into his business? Or maybe the Chinese community had all pulled together to make one of their own successful.

"Is the food you serve here like what you ate at home?" Mia asked.

"No." His tone was amused. "Not at all. I am from the Guangdong Province. Here they call it Canton. Everything at home is so fresh. You walk into a restaurant, you pick out what you want to eat from a cage or tank or bucket."

Charlie did not want to think about what might be kept in a bucket.

"You mean it's still alive?" Mia asked, wrinkling her nose.

Zhong laughed. "The rest of China say we will eat anything with legs that is not a table and anything with wings that is not a plane. No one here really wants to eat like that. Americans won't eat snake, except as a joke, and they would never eat dog or rat. Even if they say they appreciate authentic cuisine. Even though eating snake make you stronger and rat keep you from going bald." He must have seen their expressions. "No worries. Chicken, beef, pork, shrimp—that's all we have on the menu here."

Charlie was pretty sure that only shrimp looked like shrimp. He resolved to stick with that.

Mia cut to the chase. "I should have come to you earlier," she said, "but I only recently learned that this restaurant is where Scott ate his last meal. But I don't know who he was with. Did he eat here with you that night?"

"Oh no, no." Zhong frowned and shook his head. "We meet many times in our main restaurant, which is on Queen Anne in Seattle. And of course we always eat there. But I never met him here."

"Do you have any surveillance tapes we could look at?" Charlie asked. "To maybe see who he was with that night?" After seven months it was a long shot, but sometimes if you took enough of them, one hit a target.

"No, I don't," Zhong said. "Sorry."

"Would you mind if we asked the staff after we talk?" Mia asked. "Just in case one of them remembers who he was with that night?"

"Of course," the other man said. With his unlined face, it was impossible to guess how old Kenny Zhong was. He might be thirty, he might be fifty. The only thing Charlie was sure of was that his name probably wasn't Kenny. "That is not a problem."

The waitress came up with three tall glasses filled with a pale yellow frothy concoction. She set them down, and Charlie saw that faint marks braceleted her right wrist. They were the size and shape of fingerprints. He was careful not to stare.

"This was Scott's favorite drink when we met in Seattle," Zhong told them. "Our honey ginger latte. All high quality—the best ginger and honey, and a superior grade of creamer." He lifted his glass to them.

It was sweet and smooth, rich and creamy, with an underlying bite from the ginger. It was strange to think that Scott might have sat at this very table about seven months ago, drinking this same drink, not knowing he only had an hour or so to live.

"Did you ever see him drink alcohol?" Mia asked in a steady voice.

Zhong furrowed his brow. "Your husband did not drink. He was very clear about that."

Charlie wondered what was more important to Kenny: to tell a widow the truth, or to keep the secrets of his dead friend?

Next came a selection of dim sum. One came with a dipping sauce that tasted of soy and honey, ginger and garlic. Charlie resisted the urge to double-dip. He also tried to get a second look at the waitress's wrist, but she moved too fast. When the main courses came, some of the dishes were spicy and some were sweet, but whatever they were, it was all good. Charlie flung caution to the wind and even ate some smooth white meat that looked like chicken and some of the pale and more fibrous meat that certainly seemed to be pork.

As he chewed, he tried very hard not to think about what rat would look like.

"The other thing I wanted to ask you about was my husband's

services as your accountant. I, um, found a note that he wrote you about your business." Mia lowered her eyes to her lap, as if overcome by shyness, but Charlie kept his eyes on Zhong.

Who didn't blink.

"Scott is always working with me, explaining how it is not like China here."

"How is it different?" Charlie said.

"In China, we have *guanxi*." He pronounced it gwan-she. "You want to get anything done in China, you need guanxi. It's all about relationships. We have a saying, 'No guanxi? No good!'"

"What is guanxi exactly?" Mia asked.

"In China, guanxi means you should give your customers a box of moon cakes during the Mid-August Festival. It's just something nice you do, to be friendly. Or maybe it is a meal or a spa treatment or a ticket to a basketball game. It smooths the way." He flattened the air with his hands. "It is absolutely key to getting things done in China."

Mia said carefully, "In some cases in the United States, we would call that a bribe."

He reared back. "It is not a bribe. It is a relationship. For example, Scott introduced me to Oleg Popov. And now I buy the jewelry I use for gifts from him. To thank Scott, I gave him free meals at our restaurant."

"One hand washes the other," Charlie said blandly.

He nodded at Charlie. "Yes. Exactly."

"I found a note where Scott told you that you didn't have enough cash receipts," Mia persisted. "What happened after he told you that?"

"Scott knew how to give face," Zhong said. "He never embarrassed me. He never made me feel like a stupid person who did not understand numbers. It made me take a closer look at how my business was being run. To make sure everything accurate, everything matching up." He brought the fingers of his two hands together.

Charlie was willing to bet that he had just gotten better at hiding things. And that Scott had probably helped.

Mia asked one last question. "Did you know Betty Eastman?"

Now it was her face that was blank and Zhong who looked away. Looking at him, Charlie was sure Zhong knew the truth.

"She came with him to the other restaurant a few times. She helped him with his business, I believe. I did not know her well."

When their meal was over, both Charlie and Mia took out their wallets. But Zhong refused to accept any payment, saying he owed it to Scott's memory. Charlie whispered into Mia's ear, "It looks like we've got a Mexican standoff," but she didn't smile. She also didn't succeed in paying.

Then Zhong gathered the five waitresses and two busboys that he thought might have been working that night and spoke to them in Chinese. They all nodded, and then Mia found a photo of Scott on her phone and handed it to the nearest one. Charlie found himself wondering how often Mia looked at that photo and what she thought when she did.

The first girl took a quick look at Mia's phone and then passed it to the waitress next to her. And so it went, hand to hand. Charlie watched closely, but no one's expression changed.

When they were finished, Zhong barked a question. They all shook their heads. "I am so sorry," he said, turning to them. "No one remembers Scott being here. Of course, why should they remember one person out of many seven months ago?"

The thing was, the waitress with the bruised wrist—Charlie thought he had seen the faintest shiver run through her.

CHAPTER 43

As Charlie walked briskly back to the car, Mia trailed a bit behind him. She was in no hurry to go to the place where Scott had drawn his last breath. She didn't believe in ghosts, but it still seemed like it might hold an echo of his last desperate struggle.

She just hoped he had been unconscious when the blows had come.

"Lady!" An urgent whisper broke the silence.

She turned.

"Lady!" It was an Asian man dressed in a stained and wrinkled white uniform. Standing between a side door and two big black trash receptacles, he beckoned her closer.

Mia turned back to look for Charlie, but he had his back to her. He was talking on his cell phone, one foot up on the frame of the open door of his car.

"Lady!" Cringing, the man beckoned her with both hands.

She did not want to venture into that shadowed space with a stranger. Shaking her head, Mia motioned for him to come to her.

He shook his head even more violently than she had. Then he pointed at a spot high above the entrance doors. She followed his finger to something tucked up in the eaves.

It was painted the same color as the restaurant's exterior, but it looked like a small video camera. A video camera that must have a good view of most of the parking lot.

But hadn't Kenny Zhong just told them that he didn't have any video footage? Or maybe he had thought Mia meant just of the inside of the restaurant? Or just of that night, months earlier?

She tore her eyes away. If someone was currently monitoring or later reviewed this tape and saw her stare, they might also realize who had shown it to her. If this cowering man was so afraid, she didn't want to get him into trouble.

Mia hurried over to him. He was dancing on his tiptoes, looking ready to break into a run. The air stank of fryer grease that had been used and reused and re-reused. She thought of the pot stickers that had begun the meal and her stomach roiled.

"You Mrs. Scott?" he asked.

"Yes?" This guy wasn't one of the people who had looked at Scott's photo. He must work in the back of the restaurant. Judging by his damp, dirty apron, Mia thought it likely that he was a dish-washer rather than a cook. At least she hoped he wasn't a cook.

"He . . . he . . ."

As the man searched for a word, Mia found herself wanting to fill in the blank. Only she had no idea what it was.

Finally his face lightened as he found what he was looking for. "He help." He nodded, watching her expectantly.

"Help who? With what?" Mia didn't understand what this man was trying to say, but she did understand his body language, his nervous darting glances. He was afraid someone would see them together. Terrified.

His mouth opened, but then he suddenly jerked his head to look over his shoulder. His head whipped back to her. "Go," he whispered urgently, his hands now flapping at her to get away. "Go!"

His fear was now hers. She turned and hurried back toward Charlie. When she looked back, the man had disappeared.

Charlie was still holding his phone, but he wasn't talking on it anymore. Instead, he was watching her. "Who were you talking to?"

"I don't know. A dishwasher, I guess. And I don't know if *talking*'s the right word. All he did was ask me if I was Mrs. Scott. And when I said I was, he told me, and I quote, 'He help.' He seemed to think that was enough for me to understand."

"Do you think he meant Scott was helping someone? Helping him? Helping someone to do what?"

"I started to ask those questions, but he must have heard somebody coming. He freaked out and told me to go, and then he went back inside."

"So much for no one knowing anything about Scott."

Something more than old fryer grease smelled bad here. But even though Mia was angry, she also had to think things through.

"Yeah, but if I go storming back in the door and demand to speak to that guy, whoever he is, I'll bet that he would pretend to speak even less English than he does. Plus, by the way he was acting, he was worried about getting caught. So it wouldn't do me any good, but it might end up costing him his job." She remembered what he had shown her. "Oh, and you'll love this, Charlie."

"What?"

"He pointed at something, and I'm pretty sure it's a video camera mounted up in the eaves. I'd say it has a good view of the entrance and most of the parking lot."

Charlie snorted. "So that's another thing Kenny lied to us about."

"Well, it might not be a lie, but it's not all the truth either. He didn't say they didn't have a video camera. He just said they didn't have footage from that night."

"Something about this place bugs me." With narrowed eyes Charlie looked past Mia and at the restaurant. "Did you notice our waitress's wrists?"

Mia was embarrassed to think she had only had eyes for the food. "No. What about them?"

"They were bruised." He circled one wrist with the other hand. "And the bruises were shaped like fingerprints."

"That doesn't mean she got them here," Mia pointed out. "She could be being abused at home."

"Maybe." Charlie looked dubious. "And maybe not. I wish I spoke Cantonese or whatever Kenny was speaking. I'd really like to know what he told them about Scott's photo. Maybe he didn't ask if anyone had seen him. Maybe he told them all they would be up the creek without a paddle if they admitted to knowing him."

"So do you think Kenny did meet Scott here that night?"

"I'm not sure what's true and what's not." He shook his head. "All I can tell you is this: I am sure that at least some of what he told us tonight was lies."

CHAPTER 44

As Charlie started the car, Mia kept thinking about the frightened man and what he had said—or tried to say—to her. How desperate he had been to communicate. If Kenny figured out they'd been talking, would the poor guy end up losing his job—or worse?

The sky was growing dark. She wished they didn't have to go to the accident site. Wished Charlie had asked to meet Alvin Turner some other place.

"Okay, we already know that Scott warned Kenny that he was not showing enough income," Charlie said. "Maybe Kenny killed Scott because he was threatening to turn him in to the IRS?"

"Would Scott really put himself on the side of the angels like that? He didn't say one word about the IRS in that note," Mia pointed out. These days it was easy to believe that Scott had been capable of anything. "Maybe it's more likely that Scott was blackmailing him. Only maybe he called it guanxi."

"Either way it would give Kenny a reason to want him dead." Charlie began to construct a scenario out loud. "So say Scott came out here that night, met with Kenny, had a few drinks, they argued, he left, and Kenny followed him. Maybe the reason that guy saw

Scott speeding was because Kenny was chasing him. Then Scott crashed the car and Kenny thought, *Aha, here's my chance. I'll finish him off.* And he got a golf club or something out of his car."

Mia's shoulders hunched as she wondered how close they were to the accident site. She made herself think back to the report Charlie had given her. "Yeah, but the witness only reported one car passing him at a high rate of speed. Not two."

"That doesn't necessarily mean anything," Charlie said. "Probably the patrol officer only asked about Scott's car. It's not like he had any reason to believe this was anything but what it seemed—a one-car accident. Too bad Scott was in a loaner and not the Suburban. I checked on the make and model he was driving. It didn't have a black box. If it did, we'd know exactly how fast he was going, whether he braked, and whether he was wearing a seat belt. Plus any vehicle fault codes."

With each passing second Mia's tension grew. By the time Charlie turned onto Vollhanger Road, her left leg was jiggling and her hands were twisting together.

The road rose ahead of them, curving sharply to the left. A line of evergreens bordered the right side. That must be the place. Mia's stomach bottomed out.

Charlie nosed the car onto the narrow shoulder. Just ahead of them, one of the trees bore a white scar, an ugly slash about knee-high. Or bumper high. It no longer bled sap, but the bark hadn't grown back either. It was like Mia. The wound was still there, it still gaped, but it no longer hemorrhaged.

"Breathe, Mia." Charlie's voice interrupted her thoughts.

"What?" She didn't turn her head, her eyes still fastened on the scar.

"Don't forget to breathe. Breathe deep."

She did. For a moment she saw stars, but then they flickered and faded.

Mia pushed open her door. It was absolutely silent. The sun was setting. There was still enough light to see, but the colors were shifting and darkness waited on the edges. They had stopped at the pivot point of the curve. She looked back the way they had come, then ahead to where Scott should have gone if he hadn't been drinking, if he hadn't been speeding. There wasn't much to see around them. Just land. Some of it farmed, some of it filled with nothing in particular, as far as she could tell. No houses holding potential witnesses. Theirs was the only car in sight.

"No skid marks," she observed. She felt brittle and light, as if she weren't really there at all. "Although I guess it has been nearly seven months. Maybe they just got worn away."

"It was wet that night," Charlie said, "which takes away most of the friction. There wouldn't have been enough heat to melt the rubber."

She leaned down to look closer at the gravel. Mixed in among the small gray stones were shards of plastic—some clear and some yellow, as well as little pebbles of blue safety glass from the windshield. If someone had really hit Scott, seven months ago there would have been cast-off blood spatter every time they drew back to hit him again. If Charlie and Mia stayed until it was fully dark and he sprayed Luminol, would the gravel and these tree trunks light up like the night sky? Or had all the rain in between washed everything away?

"Mia, breathe," Charlie reminded her again.

She forced herself to take a slow breath. Was it possible that one of the molecules now entering her lungs had been part of Scott's dying breath?

She put her hand on the trunk of the tree and closed her eyes. *Scott*, she thought, *I'm sorry I didn't help you. I'm sorry I knew something was wrong and didn't push when you told me that it was nothing. I'm sorry I didn't fight hard enough for our marriage.*

"Are you okay?" Charlie asked.

"I knew for a while that things were wrong," she said without opening her eyes. "I asked, but only a few times, and when he said he didn't want to talk about it, I stopped. I was afraid he was thinking of leaving me, and if I pushed him that was exactly what he'd do. Maybe I could have changed things if I had spoken up right when things went off track."

He rested his hand on her shoulder and then took it away. Mia opened her eyes and turned to face him. "You never met Scott, did you?" Of course he hadn't. Charlie mostly belonged to her new life, Scott to her old. She and Charlie had worked exactly one case together before she quit the DA's office and became a stay-at-home mom. And even that one case had fallen apart when Charlie's unique approach caused the whole thing to get thrown out.

Now she saw him with different eyes. She knew his heart, both how reckless it was and how brave.

Or maybe she only thought she knew Charlie. After all, she had thought she knew Scott. And learning the truth wouldn't bring him back, wouldn't change what had happened. Maybe it was better to live with the falsehoods she had told herself, her selective memories.

"Somebody's coming," Charlie said, pointing. Two headlights pushed toward them through the gathering darkness.

CHAPTER 45

An old blue Taurus drove slowly past them. The white-haired man at the wheel had his hands at ten and two. He favored them with a nod, then carefully maneuvered off the road until he was parked about thirty yards past Charlie's car.

He got out and walked toward them. He was dressed in a black Windbreaker and dark jeans that were a little too short. Under a shock of pure white hair, his face was ruddy. As he got closer, Mia saw that it was pitted with old acne scars, scars layered on top of scars. He gave them both another nod and a tentative smile.

It was the kind of face that probably wasn't being made anymore. Today the jumble of crooked teeth would have been straightened long ago with an Invisalign, the skin smoothed with Accutane. The senior citizens of the future were going to be a much more homogenous lot.

"I'm Charlie," Charlie said, holding out his hand. "And this is Mia. Scott Quinn's widow."

Mia hated the word *widow*. It conjured up the image of a weeping old woman dressed in all black. It simply seemed impossible to be a widow while you were still in your thirties.

Alvin's rheumy eyes were at the same level as Mia's. "I am so, so sorry," he said as he shook her hand. His grip was soft, as if he was afraid of injuring her further.

"Thank you." It was what Mia always said, but it never sounded quite right. What was she thanking people for? Their apologies were just awkward words or easy platitudes, and her hurt was so deep, far past the level that a word or two could reach. "And what do you do? I don't think the accident report said."

"Me?" He gave a little laugh, as if it had been some time since anyone inquired. "Oh, I'm retired. I used to work in hardware."

"We really appreciate your coming out tonight to talk to us," Charlie said.

Alvin waved his hand. "It's no trouble at all."

"Like Mia said, we've both seen the accident report," Charlie said. "But it doesn't go into many details. What we'd like is to hear from you in your own words what happened that night."

"Well." Alvin took a deep, sighing breath. "That night I had been visiting my granddaughter. We were having such a good time—she's nine—that I left later than I intended. I was driving back to Seattle when I saw headlights coming up fast in my rearview mirror. This guy got on my tail"—he flashed an apologetic look at Mia—"excuse my French—and started flashing his brights. He was driving way too fast, especially since the road was wet. I was doing thirty. That's the speed limit, and even that might have been a little speedy for the conditions. He was riding my bumper so close I couldn't even see his license plate. Finally I pulled over in my lane as far as I could, and I rolled down my window and waved to let him pass. Maybe he thought I was doing something else, because he made a, um, gesture." Another shamed glance at Mia. "And then he passed me."

Scott? That didn't sound like Scott. Then again, how well had Mia known him, given the drinking, the debts, and the dame?

"When I got on Vollhanger and was going around this corner, I saw headlights shining in the wrong direction. There was a blue car off the road. I realized it was the same car that had passed me, only now it was skewed around. It had run into that tree right there." He indicated the spot with his chin. "I turned on my hazard lights and pulled over. I parked about where I am now, maybe a little farther down. I didn't want to cause another accident."

Mia wanted to scream at how he was taking things step by step.

Alvin pressed his lips together. "I'll admit it took me a minute before I got out and went over there. I was trying to get my heart to slow down." He put his hand on his sternum, flattening out his jacket. He was stockier than Mia had first thought, with a barrel chest. "It felt like it would beat right out of my chest. I was afraid. A man like that, one who had nearly forced someone off the road—what if he had a gun?" He shot her another glance. "I'm sorry I thought that. I heard later he'd been drinking. I'm sure he wasn't really like that when he was sober. But when you're on a lonely road like this in the dark, you start thinking all kinds of things. At the same time, I knew if I didn't stop to help then he might not be found until morning."

Mia managed a nod, as if offering him absolution.

"When I got to the car the engine was still going, so I reached in and turned it off. Your husband was lying across the seat. I think he may have been alive when I got there."

"Really?" She tried to suck in a breath, but it wouldn't go down.

"After I turned off the engine, I thought I heard these sounds, kind of like a cross between a gurgle and a breath. I leaned in but I was afraid to touch him. His face was all messed up. Broken. And I don't have any training in CPR. It took a little while to even think to call 911." His eyes flashed to her and then away. "But I don't believe it would have made any difference even if I had called right away."

They would never know, would they? Mia knew what it was like to live with that question every day. To ask, if you had just done something a bit differently, would it have been enough to change everything?

"I told him that help was on the way, but I don't know if he could hear me. The sounds had pretty much stopped by then. I took his wrist and I tried to find his pulse, but either I did it wrong or he was gone."

"Did you unbuckle him?" Charlie asked.

"No. He wasn't wearing a seat belt."

"While you were pulled over on the side of the road, did any other cars pass you?"

"I don't know." He squinted up at the sky, now midnight blue, trying to remember. "I think there might have been a couple." His gaze shifted from Charlie to Mia.

"Did you see any other cars at the accident site?" Charlie asked.

Alvin cocked his head. "But it was a one-car accident. He went off the road and he hit a tree."

"It's possible that someone stopped before you, not to help him, but to hurt him." Charlie leaned in. "So did you see another car at the accident site?"

"Dear Lord." Alvin blinked rapidly, then pinched his lips with his thumb and first knuckle. After a long pause he said, "You know, I think I *do* remember seeing taillights right as I was coming up. But whoever it was, they were just driving off as I got there."

CHAPTER 46

Penny for your thoughts," Charlie said as he drove them back toward Seattle.

Mia tried to untangle her thoughts enough to express them. "Talking to Kenny and Alvin made me feel like I did after interviewing the kids this morning. We might have more information, but we don't have any more answers. We've got a witness who thinks he saw another car leaving the scene of Scott's accident. Not that he knows anything else useful about the vehicle. Or is even all that certain that he saw one. We've got a restaurant owner who may or may not be cheating the IRS and who thinks bribes and kickbacks are just how business gets done, but who says he had no problem with Scott correcting him."

"And then there's your dishwasher," Charlie added.

"And then there's my dishwasher." Mia felt a twist of frustration. "I want to find a way to talk to him without getting him in trouble. I just don't know how to arrange that." The man had been so jumpy. "His English was pretty much nonexistent, so if he ended up getting fired for talking to me, he'd have a hard time finding another job."

And there was the matter of what he had said. "He *help*?" How had Scott helped? Who had he helped? And was it a sad sign of just how low Mia's opinion of Scott had fallen that those two small words had lit a tiny flame of hope within her?

Charlie's eyes slid sideways and then back to the road. "Whatcha thinking you're gonna do about those boys in the shopping cart case?"

"That's what they are, aren't they? Boys. Kids. They're definitely not adults. And Eli's right. If I charge them as adults, their lives will be ruined. They'll either get broken or hardened. Either way, past all repair." She sighed. "Nothing's ever clear, is it? Manny thinks it's his fault, but he could be imagining it. And when we interviewed the boys, I went in thinking Jackson was the guilty one, but then it seemed like Dylan was the one who did it on purpose. And Jackson was the one who fell apart when he talked about what had happened."

"People cry for all kinds of reasons," Charlie observed. "Including being sorry that they got caught."

"I'm not saying they don't deserve to deal with the consequences of what they did. I'm just saying it's not right to destroy them. I have until tomorrow morning to file. I think I'm going to run the clock out. That will give Raines less time to turn it to his advantage." Not that that would really slow him down.

"Nobody's got too much sympathy for those two," Charlie said. "Everywhere I go, people are talking about that video."

"I'd bet if we could trace back how that leaked to the media, we'd find Raines's fingerprints all over it."

He shrugged. "It doesn't make what it shows any less true."

"Do you think I'm making the wrong decision?" Mia asked. Once her mind was made up, it was rare for her to ask for someone else's opinion. But Charlie had seen the same things she had, heard the same explanations and stories. The only thing he hadn't experienced for himself was seeing just how shattered Tamsin was.

"No," he said slowly, "I don't. But I might be in the minority."

"But we both know that a blurry black-and-white video doesn't tell you what the kids were thinking when they did it. It doesn't tell you if they meant to hurt someone or if the cart just slipped. I'd have to be absolutely certain it was the right thing to do to charge them as adults, and I'm not. It's kind of like what's happening with Scott. I feel like there are pieces we're missing."

Charlie shifted in his seat. "Speaking of Scott, what's next on that front?"

"I'm going to call the IRS agent tomorrow, see if they really did close the investigation. And I'm going to try to figure out a way to talk to that dishwasher."

It was a little after eight when Mia showed her badge to the security guard at the courthouse. She took the elevator up to the office to grab files to refresh her memory for an upcoming court case. All of her time was being eaten up by the shopping cart case as well as trying to unravel the mystery of Scott's murder, but she couldn't neglect her other work.

The offices were deserted, most of the space dark. As she walked past Judy's desk, Mia heard a whirring. Judy's personal fan was still on. She must have been in the middle of a hot flash when she left for the day and forgot to turn it off. Mia felt around the base but couldn't find the switch. She tugged on the cord where it disappeared under Judy's desk, but the fan kept on spinning.

Mia was down on her hands and knees, tracing the cord back to its plug, when she heard a voice. She started, hitting her head on the underside of the desk drawer. Her hair muffled the thump, and the footsteps didn't pause.

"I love you too, honey."

Just Frank talking to his wife. Mia found the place where the plug went into the socket.

"What does Diann have to do with any of this?" Frank said. His voice sounded like he was only a few feet away.

Diann was his wife. Which meant that whoever Frank was talking to was not. But it was someone he loved, or said he loved, two things that, for Frank, might not be quite the same thing.

It sounded like Frank was having an affair.

Now what? Should Mia just stay hidden and hope he didn't see her? Pop out and pretend to have heard nothing?

Meanwhile, her hand continued mindlessly on the task she had set it: pulling on the plug. At that moment it came free—just as her thumb slipped between the two prongs while they were still conducting electric current.

The next thing Mia knew she was no longer under the desk, but sitting on the floor next to Judy's chair. Her skirt was rucked up and tears were running down her face. It felt like someone had stuck a thousand needles in her thumb and then the pain had blasted through her whole body.

"Mia!" Frank was leaning over her. How long had he been there? Feeling like a rag doll, she lifted her head.

"What are you doing on the floor?"

What was she doing on the floor? What had just happened? It felt so cataclysmic that it seemed like Frank should be shaking and crying too, but instead his face was screwed up with concern. Concern and confusion.

"I, um, came up to get some files. Judy left her fan on. I couldn't find the switch, so I was trying to unplug it. I think I might have gotten shocked." Gingerly she touched the thumb with her fingers. There was no wound, but the ball seemed oddly smooth, as if it had melted. She straightened her skirt, then, using Judy's desk and chair for balance, she pushed herself to her feet. Frank hovered over her, hands outstretched.

"You certainly shocked me. I didn't even know you were here, and the next minute you come flying back from under Judy's desk, screaming." If Frank was concerned about whether she had overheard him, his face didn't show it. Instead, he said, "I'm a little worried about you, Mia. After all, somebody tried to kill you Monday. Maybe once this shopping cart case is put to bed, you should take some time off. You can't just keep going like the Energizer bunny and not expect it to catch up with you."

"About the shopping cart case . . . ," Mia began. She had to tell Frank, but at the same time she was reluctant to.

"Yes? Have you decided?"

"I'm going to call Tracy Lowe tonight and tell her I'm not going to be charging them as adults." She would give Tracy all her notes, and then Tracy would file the charges. Tomorrow there would be a bond hearing to see if the two boys would remain in custody. If Mia were Tracy, she would argue for their being held. But she wasn't Tracy, and in a few hours this wouldn't be her case.

Frank narrowed his eyes but kept quiet.

"Look, Frank, I can't justify charging them as adults. A few hours ago Charlie and I were finally able to interview Manny Flores. He says it's his fault the cart tipped over. That he was trying to grab it from them, and instead he made them lose their grip."

"And you believed him? Maybe he was just trying to cover for his friends. Friends with criminal records."

"Jackson has a criminal record, but it's not particularly violent. And Dylan is borderline crazy. Frank, I am telling you, it would not serve justice to try them as adults. I'm sorry. I even thought about charging them as adults in a preliminary complaint, then filing an amended complaint after the election is over." She phrased it as if Frank hadn't suggested that very move. "But I just can't do it. You told me to make the best choice, and this is it. But I know Raines will rake you over the coals for it."

After a long moment he shrugged. "If that's what you say should be done, then that's what should be done. And Raines is going to rake me over the coals either way."

For a moment Mia wanted to hug him. Then she remembered his phone conversation and the impulse faded. "How are things going with the campaign?" she asked instead.

"I'm not even sure I'm allowed to talk about it," he said sarcastically. "Raines will complain that I'm abusing my office." The line was thin and getting thinner the closer they got to the election. These days Frank was perpetually engaged in positive photo ops—visiting hospitals, attending civic events, speaking to Mothers Against Drunk Driving, making upbeat appearances on talk radio. Now when Frank gave a speech, was it as prosecuting attorney or as someone who wanted to be reelected? The answer, of course, was both.

"I got the latest poll numbers two hours ago." Frank blew air out of pursed lips. "We're within a point of each other now."

Which meant Raines was gaining. Had jumped at least a point in the last two days. Mia supposed it was even possible—although she couldn't bring herself to ask Frank—that the two had switched places and Raines was now in the lead.

If so, Mia might have just cost herself a job.

CHAPTER 47

From the shelter of a cedar whose branches touched the ground, Vin watched Mia Quinn as she moved from room to room. He adjusted the focus on his binoculars until he could see every detail, down to the shadows under her eyes. She had a sheaf of mail in one hand. Her little girl, Brooke, was following her, chattering.

Mia was a civilian. And according to his own rules, he never touched a target's kids.

The spouses could be more of a gray area. The wives—and occasionally, the husbands—maybe they had known a few things or had looked the other way. But still, they did not deserve to be punished for the mistakes of their spouses.

Unless they became a problem.

CHAPTER 48

FRIDAY

Mia was exhausted. Her dreams had been a jumble of images: The cart plummeting from the walkway. The white bandages circling Manny's wrist. The anxious face of the dishwasher. The bits of broken glass and plastic marking the spot where Scott's life had ended.

Last night before she left the office she had called Tracy to let her know about her decision. This morning she found herself in no hurry to get into work. Maybe Frank was right. Maybe she should take some time off. She was tired of trying to figure things out, of running through a million possible permutations until the truth seemed as slippery as a silver bead of mercury.

"Love you," she said to Gabe as she dropped him off at school. He grunted in reply and jumped out of the car to greet his friends with a complicated series of fist bumps and backslaps. As she walked Brooke into preschool, Mia thought of Gabe's friends, his choices, his opportunities. Where had Gabe said Eldon was staying again? With Danny?

Gabe and Danny had been tight in grade school. Back in the day, Mia had had a nodding familiarity with Danny's mom, Sandra. She had been to their house on a couple of occasions, although the last time was four or five years ago now. If she remembered right, it was a small brown house on a corner lot.

Instead of turning onto the street that would take her to the freeway, Mia impulsively turned in the other direction. Toward Danny's house. Maybe there was some way she could help Eldon's mom. Loan her a bit of money, bring her something better to eat than chili or mac and cheese, find out what else she needed? By now Eldon would also be at school, so she wouldn't embarrass the other woman by asking in front of her son.

The house was as she had remembered it, a tiny two-bedroom bungalow that had probably been built right after World War I. Mia pulled into the driveway and parked by an old Honda that sagged on its wheels. The single-car garage was closed. After a moment, she knocked on the metal door. It made a hollow sound.

She was ready to knock again when a woman's voice said hesitantly, "Mrs. Conroy isn't home."

"I'm actually looking for Eldon's mom."

"Oh." She sounded even more wary. "Come around to the side door."

Mia navigated the narrow strip between the garage and the neighbor's fence, her heels sinking into the wet grass.

The door opened to reveal a woman who had once been built on the same scale as Eldon. Now her creamy brown skin looked like a deflated balloon. Her head was wrapped in a scarf, and she was dressed in layers of sweaters.

"Hey, I'm sorry to bother you, but are you Eldon's mom?" she said. "I'm Gabe's mom. Mia."

"Oh! Um, come in." The other woman stepped back.

Inside the garage, it felt just as cold and damp as it did outside. The walls were hung with weed trimmers, rakes, and shovels, the corners taken up by recycling bins and plastic storage containers. To this mix had been added a swaybacked cot covered with a sleeping bag and old blankets, a beanbag chair with more blankets (some of which Mia recognized), and cardboard boxes piled nearly to the ceiling. A card table held a couple of pots and a hot plate. Under it sat a box half filled with boxes and cans of food. The hot plate and a small portable heater were both on long orange extension cords that snaked back through the garage and threaded through a door that was barely ajar to the house.

The other woman broke the awkward silence. "I'm Kali. It's so good to finally meet you. I can't thank you enough for all the things you've given us."

"Um, you're welcome." Mia's voice betrayed her, going up on the end like a question mark.

The other woman's face changed. "You didn't know anything about it, did you?"

"Not until two nights ago." Mia laid a hand on Kali's arm. "But don't worry. If I had known, I would have given everything Gabe brought you and more."

Kali bit her lip. "I feel terrible. I didn't mean to encourage your son to take things from you. I want to pay you back."

"For what? Some blankets we weren't using, a few boxes of mac and cheese?" She shrugged. "Don't worry about it. I'm sure you would do the same for me if our positions were reversed."

"And I'm sure you'd feel just as awkward as I do right now," the other woman said softly. "I'd offer you a place to sit down, but as you can see, there isn't anyplace." Her mouth twisted. "You're probably wondering how we ended up like this."

"Gabe said you had cancer?"

"Breast cancer. And I'm not tolerating the chemo very well, to put it mildly. I need to sleep all the time, and I can get pretty nauseated. I was working at Foodstuffs, but no one likes a cashier who's throwing up, so they let me go."

Foodstuffs was an upscale grocery store that catered to people who liked organic vegetables and free-range chickens.

"What?" Anger straightened Mia's spine. It was disgusting to think that a store that trumpeted its fair-trade coffee did not treat its own workers fairly. "That's not my area of legal expertise, but I'm pretty sure they can't fire you for having cancer!"

Kali shrugged. "They didn't put it that way. They just said they didn't see a place for me anymore."

"Look, I don't know if Gabe's told you, but I'm an attorney. I'd be happy to write you a letter pro bono—without any charge—insisting they make accommodations for your illness. Sometimes just a letter signed by a lawyer is enough to make people see the light."

Kali shook her head. "That's okay. Right now my job is to fight this cancer, and that's about the only job I can handle. Besides, by the time I left I had already run through all my sick leave. There are days I barely get out of bed. The other day I was eating breakfast and had to go lie back down again. I ended up falling asleep while I still had a piece of bagel in my mouth. It's a wonder I didn't choke to death." She smiled ruefully. "I wish I could work, because I could use the money. Even though I'm hardly eating, the food stamps we're getting aren't enough. You know my son, you know how big he is."

Mia thought of Gabe, who routinely came back for thirds and fourths. Eldon was twice his size. "And with kids this age," she said, "it's like they can't ever eat enough." They shared a knowing smile, then Mia turned serious again. "Do you have any relatives who could help you?"

Kali's voice rose. "Do you think we would be living in a garage if I did?" She winced and pressed her fingers against her mouth. "I'm sorry. I know I shouldn't shout. But it's horrible. We're here on Sandra's good graces, and I know she likes the money, but I also know it's getting old for her. She can't park her car in the garage and she's got four people using her bathroom instead of just two.

She keeps telling me she hopes I'll have something figured out by Thanksgiving. I don't say anything. What am I supposed to say?"

Mia was surprised. "Wait—you're paying to live here?"

"Eldon's dad pays some child support, so I'm giving Sandra three hundred a month."

"To sleep in an unheated garage?"

"What else can I do? A one-bedroom apartment in this neighborhood is at least twelve hundred. And it's important to me that Eldon stay in the same school. It's a good school. You know that. And he's happy there. So much is changing for him, I don't want that to have to change too."

Mia could only nod. Kali's words echoed her thoughts after Scott died. It was why she was working so hard to hold on to the house, even though it was a stretch to make the mortgage every month. Sometimes she felt like she was walking on a tightrope. One slip and she would plummet to earth.

And Kali had slipped.

The words were out before Mia could think of whether it was a good idea. "What if I gave you the same deal to live with me? Only we actually have the room. There's a guest room you could stay in and bunk beds in Gabe's room."

Kali just looked at her for a long moment. "Why? Why would you do that for me?"

The words came to her. "'I was sick and you visited me, I was hungry and you fed me.'"

"You're a churchgoer?" The other woman narrowed her eyes warily.

Mia had gone to church with her dad a few times lately, trying to find the same solace in it that he had so recently embraced. "Maybe not like I should be. But this feels like what I'm supposed to be doing."

CHAPTER 49

What had she just done? Mia asked herself the question as she drove to work. Turned down to a murmur, the radio provided a backdrop to her anxious thoughts, with stories of bombings in Iraq, threats from North Korea, and a horrific pileup in Texas. How many times had she told Gabe he shouldn't be so impulsive, told Brooke their family didn't have time to care for a pet? Now she had recklessly committed herself to a woman she had just met, offered to upend her own life and her kids' lives to help a stranger.

And if this turned out to be a huge mistake, how would she undo it without making things worse? "Protect us, Lord," she whispered. "Protect us all."

And against all reason, she felt a sense of calm descend on her.

Less than two minutes later, that calm was shattered when she picked out Frank's name from the radio. She turned up the dial.

" . . . two fifteen-year-old suspects alleged to have dropped a shopping cart four stories onto a woman named Tamsin Merritt will be charged as juveniles, not adults. While the prosecutor's office declined to release a statement, Dominic Raines, who is running opposite King County prosecutor Frank D'Amato, said he was shocked by the decision."

Mia heard Raines's voice.

"This is yet another unbelievable mistake made by the prosecutor's office. What have these two young thugs learned? By charging them as juveniles, Frank D'Amato's allowing them to be let off with a slap on the wrist. He's also sending a message to all would-be violent teens out there: 'Come on, go ahead and go wild, hurt people as bad as you want, maybe even kill them, just as long as you're younger than sixteen.' After this decision, I wouldn't be surprised if we see gangs of kids appointing their youngest members to do their dirty work. And what happens when these boys who left Tamsin in a coma find their next victim? Because trust me, they will. Frank D'Amato should be forced to explain his flawed reasoning to those future victims. He should have to explain how he had a chance to make sure these punks didn't hurt anyone again, and he threw that away. You can bet that if this decision had been made under my administration, it would have gone differently."

The announcer cut back in, "The most recent poll shows that Raines now leads D'Amato by a single point. While the race is still too close to call, Raines has jumped three points in just as many days."

———

When Mia walked into the break room to get some coffee, Anne, DeShauna, and Jesse were all talking in low voices. Their faces swung to her. Without speaking, they tossed looks back and forth. Then DeShauna and Jesse left without more than nodding at Mia. Were they thinking the same thing Charlie had suggested—that she should have gamed things by charging the boys as adults in a preliminary complaint?

"Let me guess," Mia said to Anne. She had a feeling she wasn't the only one who had heard Dominic Raines's veiled threat. "You guys were talking about the shopping cart case." Anne worked in Violent Crimes with Mia. DeShauna worked in the Sexually Violent Predator Unit, and Jesse was in Involuntary Treatment. Both worked with offenders, who, if given a second chance, were likely to use it as an opportunity to find more victims. They probably thought she was crazy for not charging the boys as adults.

Anne shrugged one shoulder. "Everyone's a little on edge about the election." Her brown eyes were steady on Mia. "But they also know you must have weighed everything before you made your decision." She rinsed out her coffee cup and left.

Mia followed her out, wondering if she had just helped nudge Frank out the door—and risked her job as well as those of her co-workers.

It was only when she sat back down at her desk that she realized her coffee cup was still empty. She was debating getting up again, risking another gauntlet, when her phone rang. It was Eli.

"Thank you," he said when she answered. "You made the right call."

"I'll see if I agree with you after the election." What should she tell him about Manny? "Just a heads-up that you might want to talk to Manny, or at least try to when he's better. He's got a third version of events, one that could help your client. And that's all I'm going to say."

"Oh. Okay. I appreciate that." He took a deep breath. "Are we still on for brunch on Sunday?"

Did she really want to do this? Have a date? "Sure," she found herself saying.

"Want me to pick you up after church? Our service is usually done around twelve fifteen."

"How about if I just meet you?" If things were weird, she wanted the freedom to vanish. They agreed on a time and place. After Mia hung up, she realized her palms were sweaty. It must be from worrying about her job. Not from talking to Eli.

She used her personal phone for the next call, which was to the IRS. While she waited for the phone to be answered, she double-checked the name on the IRS letter Popov had gotten. James Lobb. But it was a woman who answered.

"May I speak to James Lobb?"

"I'm sorry, Mr. Lobb no longer works here."

Mia blinked. "He doesn't? Where did he go?"

"Oh, he retired. Back in April. The lucky duck. But I took over his caseload, so maybe I can help you."

"I had a question about a tax audit Mr. Lobb was working on. It was of a business called Oleg's Gems and Jewels. My husband was Oleg's accountant, but he died a few months ago. I recently found some of the paperwork related to the audit. I was wondering what happened to the case."

The woman's voice turned formal. "Well, I certainly couldn't tell you anything, even if I knew," she said. "That's sensitive tax-payer data. You should not have anything at all like that in your possession. You need to either return the paperwork directly to the business or shred it."

"Oh. Okay. Thank you for that information." Mia hung up.

What she needed was someone to tell her if it was a coincidence that two of the three people involved in examining Oleg's finances were no longer around to trouble him.

CHAPTER 50

By the time she pulled into her driveway, Mia was so exhausted she could have leaned forward, rested her forehead on top of the steering wheel, and fallen fast asleep. Instead, she needed to get things ready for Kali and Eldon.

As soon as she walked in the door, Gabe hurried out of the family room. His words were as sharp as a slap. "You went to Danny's house this morning?"

"Yeah, I did. Why?"

"How do you think that made Danny feel?" Gabe didn't wait for an answer. "Like you think we're better than him and his mom."

Brooke wandered out into the hall, dragging a doll by one foot. "I'm hungry, Mommy."

Mia took a deep breath and set her purse on the hall table. "Just a second, sweetie. I'm going to order us some pizza." She turned back to her son. "I didn't even talk to Danny or Danny's mom. I only talked to Kali. She's living in a garage and she's got cancer, Gabe. I just wanted to help."

"If there was any extra room, Danny's mom would be letting

them stay in the house. Besides, the garage isn't that bad. I've been in it. Maybe they just have to put on an extra sweater. What's the big deal?"

"I want cheese." Brooke drew out the *eeee* sound. "Not pepperoni. Just cheese."

"Okay, sweetie," Mia said, shrugging out of her coat. She turned back to Gabe. "That garage isn't heated, and Kali's really sick." Why was Gabe so upset? "I don't think it would be healthy for anyone, but she's going through chemotherapy."

"You didn't even tell me you were going to do that. The first I know about is Eldon asking me in front of Danny because his mom texted him." Fists balling, Gabe kicked at the skateboard he had once again left under the hall table. The toe of his Vans caught it and sent it rattling down the hall.

Brooke tugged at her sweater. "Nothing but cheese. Nothing to pick off."

Mia nodded distractedly. "I didn't plan it, Gabe. I just did it. I was driving by the house and I thought I would check in with Eldon's mom." She opened the closet and hung up her coat. Deciding it wasn't worth complaining about the skateboard, she picked it up and put it away. "But when I walked in there, it was clear Kali needed a different place to stay, someplace that's not so cold and damp. Someplace with actual beds. And you've got bunk beds and we've got a guest room. We can make this work."

Gabe refused to be mollified. "How many times have you lectured me that I can't just do things without thinking, that I have to check with you first? But now you just go and make some decision that's going to change all of our lives forever." His tone suggested that Mia was clearly stupid as well as a hypocrite. "And that's not fair to me or Brooke."

Brooke looked from one of them to the other. "What's not fair? Don't get pepperoni! I told you!"

"Don't worry, Brooke, I'm not," she said distractedly. And then to Gabe, "I don't think it's going to make any difference to your sister." Although really she had no idea.

The thing was, Gabe was right. Mia hadn't thought this through. Maybe she shouldn't have been so impulsive. Ever since Scott died, she had worried about the many changes happening in her kids' lives. Scott dead, Mia back at work, Brooke in preschool, and Gabe turned into a live-in babysitter. Now, simply because she had put herself in another person's shoes, had she just added to her kids' burden? But how could she see someone who was hurting even worse than she was and not want to help?

"I'm not a kid anymore," Gabe said through gritted teeth, "but you're still treating me like one. I'm only a kid when you want to tell me what to do and tell me what to eat and when to go to bed and who not to hang out with. Or when you want to make important decisions that affect me without even asking me. The rest of the time you want me to be a grown-up, to clean and cook and watch after Brooke like I'm some kind of stay-at-home dad. But I'm only fourteen. None of my friends have to think about stuff like that."

Why couldn't Gabe see that they were still blessed beyond belief?

"You saw those pictures your grandpa sent from the mission trip he's on in Guatemala. Those kids with no shoes, playing with a soccer ball made of old T-shirts. There are millions of kids in this world who are married off by your age or sewing in sweatshops or working in the fields."

"But we're not in Guatemala, are we? We're in Seattle. And that's not how kids live here."

"You think so? Earlier this week I saw a really little kid changing an even littler kid's diaper. And they were in an apartment with no electricity, which means no light and no heat. I'm not even sure they had food."

"Oh, so why didn't you invite them to come live with us?"

Seven months ago she would never have stood for Gabe talking back to her. But he was no longer a mouthy kid—or not *just* a mouthy kid. He had earned the right to have an opinion, even if Mia had the final say.

"I did call someone to check on them. Honestly, Gabe, I don't understand why this is so upsetting to you. I thought Eldon was one of your best friends. But you're acting like I invited in some homeless guy off the street." She walked into the kitchen, Gabe following. "After all, half of what I saw in that garage seemed to have come from our house." But then the charity had been on his terms, using things Mia had bought. The personal sacrifice had been minimal. This would mean sharing 150 square feet with another person. A boy who weighed a hundred pounds more than he did. She took the Pagliacci menu from the fridge. "What kind of pizza do you want?"

Gabe's mouth twisted. "Pepperoni."

It was true that having to share would impact all of them, Mia thought as she dialed the number and ordered, reciting her address automatically. Nearly twice as many people in the same space. All of them having to negotiate who got to shower first. Would Mia now be responsible for purchasing and preparing food—or at least ordering pizza—for all of them? Would she need to partition off the refrigerator or come up with some system of color coding? What if Eldon did something she didn't approve of? She thought of the times she had seen him with red, sleepy-looking eyes. What if he smoked pot? Or drank?

And then there was Kali. They would all witness Kali getting sicker. Maybe even watch her die.

As she hung up the phone, Gabe echoed her thoughts. "What happens if Eldon's mom dies? Are you saying he'll live with us for always?"

"It's way too early to go there, Gabe. I want to help them. It's the right thing to do. I think you know it too."

"He's going to have to take the bottom bunk."

Gabe slept on the top one anyway. "That's fine," Mia said.

"And what you call the guest room is more like the junk room. I don't see how she can stay in there."

Mia went down the hall and opened the door. Gabe followed. He was right. The sewing machine was set up on a card table heaped with mending that needed to be done. More mending dangled from an Exercycle in the corner that she hadn't used in months. On the bed were clothes she planned to take to the dry cleaner, as well as wrapping paper, ribbons, tax records, and a few of Brooke's stuffed animals.

"You're right. It's a mess. Can you help me clean it out tonight?"

Gabe was not letting go. "This is all because of Grandpa, isn't it? You feel guilty because we don't ever go to church anymore."

The sad thing was, Gabe was the only one of her kids who had memories of going to church regularly at all. Over time, Scott and Mia had gotten to the point that they barely qualified as chreasters—the people who attended only at Christmas and Easter. The last time any of them had been to the church they nominally belonged to was Scott's funeral.

"That's an interesting theory, Gabe. But I don't think I'm doing it out of guilt. I'm doing it because it's the right thing to do, and I was moved to do it."

"Does this have anything to do with Dad?" His voice thickened and caught. "With trying to prove you're better than him?"

Mia's head jerked back. "What? Where did that come from?"

"I heard you guys downstairs on Monday. You and Charlie."

"What did you hear?"

With a wince, Gabe turned away. "Enough."

CHAPTER 51

SATURDAY

The machines were the only things keeping Tamsin alive. Breathing for her. Monitoring her. Putting drugs and saline into her veins. Pumping nutrition through a tube that ran into her nose and down into her stomach. Taking away her waste products.

His wife had once been so beautiful. Now her beauty had fled. Her face was swollen and grotesque, shades of purple and yellow and green. Half her gorgeous hair was gone, her scalp stubbled like a man three days past a shave. Blood and other secretions matted what was left.

But it was the hole at the base of her throat that drew his eye, an obscene second mouth that now held the tracheotomy tube.

As Wade Merritt watched, Tamsin's real lips drew together. Her brow wrinkled. It looked like she was in pain, despite all the drugs they were pumping into her.

And suppose she did wake up? How much more pain would she be in when they started trying to make her relearn the basics? How to feed herself. How to toilet herself, as they termed it. She might not even be able to walk. Or talk. Or even know who she was. It would be like having a toddler again, only one that would probably never grow up. Lingering on and on. For years. Maybe decades.

Before the accident, he had been willing to put up with her recent enthusiasm for helping the poor and downtrodden. People who weren't smart enough not to make bad choices, not to continually fall back into trouble. Look at Tamsin—she had made something of herself, gone to college, married him. So why did she feel this need to turn back, to reach out her hand and drag someone else who was less worthy up to her level?

She had told him she felt guilty, but that certainly didn't make any sense. She said she had been given so much, which was a crock. She hadn't been given anything. They hadn't been given anything. He had worked to make their dreams come true.

And that work meant long hours and frequent travel. Now he would need to hire someone to watch her and take care of her needs. Hire a team of people, not only to care for her, but for the house and for Luke.

As Wade looked down at her, he imagined their future. She would never again greet him to ask about his day, rub his shoulders, bring him a Tanqueray and tonic with a fresh slice of lime. She would probably never see the second floor of their house again. He pictured the wheelchair ramp that would have to be installed, like a mongrel's unfurled black tongue, marring the facade of their beautiful home. Pictured the constant presence of a nurse and probably a housekeeper. There would never be any privacy. Every word overheard, every sight observed, every slight noted. Always someone judging him from behind a professionally blank expression.

But you didn't get to be as successful as Wade was if you weren't willing to break a few eggs. To make the hard decisions. To know when to cut your losses.

Only what would he look like if he divorced her? Even if he put

Tamsin in the most expensive of nursing homes, he already knew the answer. People would whisper about him behind his back. He would be called cold. Callous. Heartless. He would not be seen as someone you could trust. And in his line of work, it was all about trust. Money was even more important than life and death.

But if he were a widower? Everyone would rally around, try to cheer him up, talk about how brave he was to soldier on. They would fall over themselves trying to help.

When you added it all up, wouldn't it be better for all of them if she died? Better even for Tamsin? He was sure she wouldn't want to live like this, lingering in some half-life. And Luke needed a mother who could care for him. Not some crippled thing that would be a drain on all of them. He looked down at the shell on the bed, this poor facsimile of his wife. Tamsin wasn't even here anymore. All he was left with was this grotesque sack of flesh that couldn't even breathe on its own but was still determined to drag him down too. Him and Luke. But Wade wouldn't let it.

His anger fueled him, made it easier to do what needed to be done. Tamsin had changed. He had been willing to overlook that. Willing to take his discreet pleasures elsewhere. Willing to listen to her natter on about the kind of example they were setting for Luke.

But then those kids at the mall had done this thing to her, left her so broken, left Wade with no other choice. They were making him do this.

He had spent enough time by her side, wondering just how long this could go on, that he had learned a little bit about what all the equipment did. Every time the heart monitor sounded an alarm, the nurses would just turn down the volume. So now Wade did it himself. Then he knelt by her bedside, positioning himself so that he was between her and the camera on the wall. The feed from each room's camera was displayed at the nurses' station in one of a series of tiny squares on a monitor.

"Things weren't perfect between us, darling," he said in a low voice. "I'm sorry for that." He unclipped the pulse oximeter from her finger and clipped it onto his own, then glanced up at the monitor. His pulse was a steady 62. Having that home gym installed had paid off.

There were still the five leads glued to her chest, but with the alarm turned down, no one would hear when it sounded.

With his free hand, he pulled the tracheotomy tube loose, as he had seen the nurses do for a few seconds to suction mucous out of her throat.

There. Her chest no longer moved. With no air being pushed into her lungs, she should be gone in a minute or two. He would wait until he was sure, then put the tube back in, return the monitor to her finger, and call for help.

Only she wasn't quite dead yet. The hair rose on the back of his neck as he watched her.

Tamsin opened her mouth wide. The cords in her neck stood out like wires under her skin. All from some futile, primitive effort to breathe.

It was horrible. He did not want to do this. She was making him do this. Her mouth opening and closing like a fish's. Why couldn't she just go quietly? Hiding her face with his upper body, he covered the hole in her throat with his palm. With the other, he pinched her nostrils between his fingers and covered her mouth with his palm.

He was doing her a mercy.

He would want the same if it were him.

CHAPTER 52

Mia slowly turned her head from side to side, trying to ease the kink in her neck. Then she bent over the scratch paper on which she was writing her grocery list. She had spent the morning helping Kali and Eldon pack up and then ferrying their belongings over. Now everyone was more or less settled. Kali was taking a nap, and Gabe had gone out for a run.

Eldon had turned out to be even bigger than Mia remembered. Maybe she should just buy everything she normally did, only at three times the quantity. But she had no idea what he and Kali liked to eat.

She went upstairs. The door to Gabe's room was ajar. She heard voices speaking a language that wasn't English. But she was sure Eldon was alone. Maybe he had called someone and was using the speakerphone. But one voice sounded mechanical. It was reciting a string of syllables. Then Eldon repeated what the first voice had said.

Her curiosity got the better of her. Rapping lightly on the door, she called out, "Eldon?"

"Yeah? Come on in."

Eldon was sitting at Gabe's desk with his cell phone in front of him.

"Oh, sorry, are you on the phone?" Mia was already backing out.

"No, it's okay. I'm practicing talking to my grandma."

Which just raised more questions. Mia settled on the first one. "Why do you have to practice?"

"I talk to her every Sunday. She likes it if I speak Samoan with her, but since I don't speak it that much, I'm not that good. But there's this app I got on my phone. You can speak in English to it and it will say it back in Samoan. I use it to practice stuff I want to say to her, especially if I don't know all the words." He handed her the phone. "Try it."

The phone was in landscape mode. On one side it read *English*, on the other *Samoan*. In the middle was a large pink button.

"Press the button before you start speaking and then when you're done."

Mia pressed the button. "This is cool," she said. "But does it really work?" She pressed the button again.

Detecting language appeared at the top, and then her words showed up on the left-hand side of the screen. After another few seconds more words showed up on the Samoan side. Only now she couldn't read them. A mechanical voice spoke the syllables.

"There're apps for all different kinds of languages," Eldon said.

A light bulb went on for Mia. "What about Chinese?"

"Oh sure, there must be. Probably more than one. Way more people speak Chinese than speak Samoan."

Apps could do so many things. Say where Gabe was. Pick out a good restaurant. Catch her up on the news. Tell what the weather would be tomorrow. And maybe figure out exactly what sort of help Scott had promised the dishwasher at the Jade Kitchen.

After talking to Eldon for a few more minutes, Mia went back downstairs and picked up her own phone. She typed in **Chinese-English translation** in the app search bar. A half dozen choices appeared. **Speak a sentence and hear the translation!** read the first one. **Requires active Internet connection to work.**

After clicking to download it, she went back to her grocery list and added coconut milk, pineapple, and green bananas—all requests she had gotten from Eldon. Her phone rang.

"Guess who's just been charged with attempted murder?" Charlie asked without preamble.

"Who?"

"Wade Merritt."

"Oh no!" Her heart seized. "Did he go after one of the boys?" At least Charlie had said "attempted." So Wade must not have succeeded.

"No. His wife. He tried to kill Tamsin this morning."

The idea made Mia recoil. "What?"

"He's claiming it was supposed to be a mercy killing, that they had had a pact that if either of them was incapacitated, the other would be there to pull the plug. Only in this case it was her ventilator tube. Before he took that out, he disconnected some of her monitors or hooked them up to himself. Unfortunately for him, but fortunately for Tamsin, he didn't realize that the ventilator also has an alarm that has a bit of a delay. The doctor who responded held him until hospital security could get there, and then they called the cops."

"So did he do any damage?"

"As far as they can tell, he didn't do any more damage. She was only without oxygen for a minute or so. Now they're actually beginning to try to bring her out of her coma and wean her off the ventilator. So time will tell."

"What a mess. Poor Luke." Her heart broke for him. "What's going to happen to him?"

"Tamsin's mother was already staying in a motel nearby. I guess she's gonna move in with the kid until things are settled."

How could things ever be settled, with his mother in a hospital bed and his father in jail? Mia was just thankful he had someone else to turn to.

"Speaking of settled, what are you doing tonight, Charlie? Want to take a little field trip with me to settle what Scott was really up to?"

"Where to?"

"Back to the Jade Kitchen in Coho City. I think I've figured out how to talk to the dishwasher."

"You found someone who speaks Chinese?"

"In a way," Mia said. "I downloaded a translation app onto my phone. You can talk into it in English and it says the words in Chinese."

"They have those?"

She felt briefly superior, even if she hadn't known any different herself an hour ago. "Yup."

The smells behind Jade Kitchen's Dumpsters were so strong Mia felt like she could chew them. Overlaying the sweetish stench of rotting food was the reek of oil that had been used a thousand times. Used until it burned, then used some more until it went rancid, and then used until it was a black sludge before finally being discarded.

When the dishwasher had talked to her, it had seemed like he had thought of Scott as some sort of force for good. Scott, who had cheated and lied and broken the law.

And it was that—the hope that maybe Scott had not been as reprehensible as she feared—as much as anything that had drawn Mia back here.

The back door opened with a squeal. She peeked around the Dumpster. A man she didn't recognize came out caring a sloshing metal pot. It slopped onto his already stained white uniform, and he let out what must be a curse in Chinese. While Mia pressed herself even tighter into her hiding spot, he propped open the lid of the trash receptacle—unleashing a new set of smells—and poured in the fetid slop. It was hard to believe that the delicious food they had eaten would ultimately become the source of this horrible stench.

When Mia was beginning to despair of ever seeing him, the dishwasher finally came out. He leaned against the wall and lit a cigarette. In the flare of the lighter, his face was drawn and thin.

Mia made a hissing noise. He straightened up and she hissed again, then stuck out one hand and beckoned.

He looked both ways before coming back around the Dumpster. When he saw her, he seemed both fearful and eager.

Mia held out her phone with the app already open. "What is your name?" she said. "If you talk into the phone, it will speak to me." She pressed the button and then handed him the phone.

His expression changed as her phone began to speak in Chinese. After a pause, he rattled off a series of words, all the while shaking his head and looking back over his shoulder. Then he stopped and looked at the phone expectantly.

Since he hadn't pressed the button, she did.

After a pause, the tinny voice said, "My name is Lihong. What are you doing here? This is not you and me security." The evenly accented words stripped the message of any urgency.

"Do you mean it's not safe?" Mia asked. "Why is it not safe?" She waited impatiently while the machine translated her words into Chinese and his into English.

"Zhong is a bad person. He hurt us." Lihong nodded as the computer spoke for him. "He would hurt me to talk to you. If he knows we said, he will be very angry. But you must complete your husband start."

"I don't understand," she said. "What did Scott do for you? How did he help you?"

"We still need someone to help us this terrible man." Lihong's eyes never left her face as the voice spoke for him. "You need that person."

Mia was getting a headache—and she was also beginning to understand why people used human translators instead of apps.

"You need me to help you?"

Lihong nodded emphatically. "His pay, so they will look the other way. Your husband is trying to help us."

"Look the other way? What are they looking the other way about?"

A man started shouting from the back door. Lihong's head whipped around. His eyes were wide with fear.

Mia froze. Her heart was beating so loudly it was a wonder they didn't hear it in the kitchen.

The man called out again. He sounded like Kenny Zhong. He also sounded closer.

Lihong pointed at his chest and then inside, put his finger to his lips, and backed away.

Mia risked peeping around the corner of the Dumpster. When Zhong saw Lihong, he shouted at him again, then slapped him full force across his left ear. The dishwasher cowered, holding the side of his head.

From her hand, the phone began to speak the words Kenny had yelled. "Who were you talking to?" Mia frantically pressed the volume. "Do you want to live . . ." Finally the mechanized voice died away to nothing.

Zhong had stopped speaking. He stood with his arm raised over Lihong, but he was staring right at Mia.

Or had been. Because she was running back to Charlie as fast as she could.

CHAPTER 53

SUNDAY

When his phone rang at one in the morning, Vin groaned. Nothing good happened at this time of night. He resisted the urge just to let it ring.

"Hello?"

"I have a problem," his boss said. A long sigh. "And I need you to clean it up."

"What is it?" He was already stepping into his pants, reaching for his gun.

"It is not my fault." The man was really too old to whine, but he was whining now.

"What's not your fault?" Since no one could see him, Vin rolled his eyes.

"She is always after me. Always. And whatever I give her, it is never enough. Tonight we had a fight. She kept saying she wanted to go back to where she was before. That she was tired of living a secret life."

The boss's girlfriend. A blonde, but not really. Big breasts that the boss had bought and paid for even before she left Scott Quinn to become his full-time girlfriend. Pretty, but not stupid. Or not stupid enough. She had snagged herself a rich businessman, but not one who could afford to flaunt his riches in a way that would attract the tax man. But she was the kind of poor and pretty girl that dreamed of being photographed, of being gossiped about, of her own reality show. The kind of attention that someone living on the wrong side of the law most certainly didn't want.

His boss had more money than he knew what to do with. From the outside, his home looked modest. Inside, it was filled with expensive rugs, antiques, artwork, and furniture. The girl had designer clothes on her skinny back, expensive rings on her fingers, diamonds around her neck and in her ears. Occasionally she even demanded that Vin be her driver, like he was a chauffeur. And then she filled his ears with nothing but complaints.

She hadn't been happy with any of it, not even the loads of cash his boss dropped on meals and trips to exotic places.

She wanted a nicer house. A much nicer house. Say an Arts and Crafts style, something in the three-million-dollar range. Or one of those electric roadsters. A Tesla, was that what they called it? George Clooney had one. She didn't seem to be able to get it through the thick skull underneath all that dyed hair that cash transactions over $10,000 had to be reported to the IRS. That George Clooney made his money legally and everyone expected him to flash it around. So of course he had an Italian villa.

His boss had managed to buy her a boat. An actual yacht. Found a private buyer who was willing to accept cash and look the other way. But she still wasn't happy.

The girl wasn't that old, but she must have figured out that her sell-by date was fast approaching. And that maybe she didn't want to spend what was left with a man who was at least twice her age.

"She saw what was coming and she actually jumped out of the

car," his boss continued. "But she didn't get far in those stupid heels of hers. I always told her those things would kill her." A laugh like a seal's bark. "It seems I was correct. Now I need you to make her go away. I took her purse, took the rings from her fingers, took anything that might identify her."

That wasn't enough, which he was sure his boss knew as well as he did. She still had a face. She still had teeth. She still had fingerprints.

He was going to have to change all that. And fast. And then dump the body someplace where, with luck, it might not be found, at least not for a long while.

These things should be done with finesse. Planning. If you wanted to kill someone, you thought about it beforehand. You did not get into an argument with a piece of fluff. And when she made you angry and ran from you, you did not impulsively shoot her down and then call someone else to clean it up.

Seven months ago his boss had been so hot for this girl, with her blond hair and her snub nose like a child's. Her arms and legs, perfectly shaped and flawless as a doll's. Now he had broken her.

"I wish you had let me handle this from the beginning," he said. His boss liked to keep those soft hands of his clean. He was tired of his boss making messes and expecting someone else to pick up after him.

There was a long silence from the other end of the phone. Long enough that Vin had time to regret what he had just said.

CHAPTER 54

When dispatch called at a little after three a.m., Charlie resisted the urge to pull the covers over his head and ignore the shrill trill of the phone. Nothing good happened at this hour of the morning.

In this case, a homeless man searching an industrial area for a place to bed down had instead found the body of a young woman. The report was a little garbled, but it sounded like he might even have surprised the killer in the act.

In Charlie's experience, people were more afraid of crime than ever, even though the reality was that by year's end fewer than thirty people would be murdered in Seattle. This girl would be number twenty-three, maybe number twenty-four, something like that.

Of course, if you were one of the dead, that statistic was of no comfort.

When Charlie got to the scene, he found a half dozen patrol cars parked near a long ribbon of yellow crime-scene tape. He talked to Kirk Snell, who had been the first uniform to arrive. He had frozen the scene and interviewed the witness, a middle-aged guy with a matted, grizzled beard that hid most of his face. Now the homeless man stood shivering in a dirty sweater, pants held up with what looked like a purple bathrobe tie, and worn boots without laces.

"The medical examiner and the CSIs are on their way," Kirk said.

"Did you find anything other than her body?"

"She was shot, but I didn't find the gun. There's pruning shears and a hammer next to the body, though. And two of her fingertips are missing."

Charlie winced. "What's her head look like?" Someone had obviously gone to some work to make her anonymous.

Kirk shrugged. "No idea. The RP"—he meant reporting party— "put his coat over it. Even though her fingers weren't bleeding, I still checked her wrist for a pulse, just in case. But she's for sure dead, and I didn't want to disturb the evidence. Then I called it in, put up the tape, and called you." He turned and looked at the yellow tape. "You okay with where it is?"

Charlie eyeballed the distances. His back-pocket rule was to rope off at least one hundred feet from the farthest item of visible evidence. Here the crime-scene tape was at least two hundred and fifty feet from the body, so that was good. It was easier to decrease the size of an area than to increase it, and he didn't need any press onlookers destroying any evidence. If this had been a high-traffic area, he would have had Kirk set up a second perimeter, one where bigwigs and the press could feel like they were getting better access. But few people came to this industrial area.

Right now, Charlie's money was on her being a prostitute. It was even possible the mutilation hadn't been done to hide her identity. A few years earlier a serial killer in Oregon had killed prostitutes and cut off their feet for twisted reasons of his own.

"What's the RP like?" he asked Kirk. They both looked over at the guy, who was blowing on his hands trying to warm them.

"For someone who probably drinks all day, he seems pretty with-it," Kirk said. "He had to go about half a mile before he managed to find someone with a cell phone. Then he came back here and waited for me. There're a couple of cars patrolling the neighborhood, looking for the guy he spooked. But I'm betting whoever did this is long gone."

"Do you think he could ID him?"

Kirk twisted his lips. "You could try asking him, but I don't think he was ever close enough."

Pulling on vinyl gloves he took from his belt, Charlie ducked under the crime-scene tape. He turned on his flashlight and swept it back and forth over the tarmac. All he saw were a few pieces of windblown trash, which would still have to be collected in case they turned out to be evidence. Finally he reached the dead woman and let the flashlight play over her. She lay on her back next to a loading dock, her head only a few inches from the concrete ramp. She wore black high-heeled boots, skintight dark-wash jeans, and a tight red sweater that showed off both her outsize breasts and the two-inch hole over her heart. Judging by the pool of blood she was lying in, she hadn't died right away. There was enough blood that the smell hung in the air and the coppery taste furred Charlie's tongue.

No coat, even though it was too cold not to wear one. The coat that covered her head had to have come from the guy who found her. It was stained and matted with layers of food and dirt.

Her left hand drew Charlie's eye. Three fingers bore a French manicure. The other two, the pinky and the ring, had been cut off at the first knuckle. He leaned down until he was a few inches away. White skin at the base where rings had been. Had the fingers been chopped off to make it easier to rob her? But even the intact fingers still showed the ghosts of rings. Whatever the reason, Kirk was right—there was very little blood. That meant the injuries had been inflicted after she was dead, or postmortem, as the medical examiner would phrase it.

Charlie scanned the ground but didn't see the fingertips. A bloodstained pair of pruning shears lay on the asphalt next to a hammer. It was all too easy to imagine what was under the coat—a face smashed into pulp, teeth turned into chips of ivory.

But he wasn't going to look. While the scene was Charlie's to investigate, the body belonged to the medical examiner. Charlie wasn't allowed to move it, take property from it, search its pockets for ID, or fingerprint it. Those tasks were the medical examiner's.

Whoever she was, someone had hoped to make her anonymous. A few minutes more and he might have succeeded.

He dipped back under the tape and went up to the homeless guy. "I'm Charlie Carlson with the Seattle PD. Homicide." He offered his hand.

"Hey, man. I'm Tom Lyle." He was shivering in the brisk breeze, which smelled of diesel fumes.

"Can you tell me what you saw tonight?"

"I was walking around that corner"—Lyle pointed—"when I saw this dude bending over someone lying on the ground. He had something white clamped between his knees. His hands were bright yellow, like maybe he was wearing dishwashing gloves. And in one of them he had some kind of big pair of scissors. About then is when I realized he was cutting off someone's finger." He raised his eyebrows.

"What did you do then?"

"I didn't know what to do. I didn't know if the person was alive or dead. But I also figured that somebody who would cut off someone's fingers probably wouldn't care too much about hurting me. So I stepped back around the corner so he couldn't see me, and I made my voice real deep and I said"—his voice dropped an octave—"'Police! Stop right there!' And when I looked again, he was booking the other way. After I was sure he was gone, I went over to see if I could help, but she was dead. At least she didn't feel what he did to her."

"Would you recognize the guy if you saw him again?"

Lyle blew air out of pursed lips. "He was white. That's about all I know."

"Big? Small?"

"Average."

"What color was his hair?"

"He was wearing a black knit hat. All his clothes were black."

Charlie was getting nowhere fast. "So you saw him run away? Was there anything distinctive about his run? A limp or anything?"

"Nah."

"Did you see a vehicle?" Charlie asked. "Hear it?"

"Sorry."

"Did you hear or see anyone else?"

Lyle shook his head.

"And why did you put your coat over her head?"

"I felt bad that somebody done her like that," Lyle said. "It just seemed right to cover her face."

"So her face is pretty messed up?"

"What?" Lyle looked surprised. "Nah. She's a pretty thing. All he done to her was cut her two fingers off."

So Lyle must have surprised the man just as he was beginning his work.

Charlie imagined Lyle shrugging out of his coat, laying it over the woman's face as tenderly as a mother might cover a sleeping child. The charity of it surprised him. "We're gonna need to keep your coat, I'm afraid. When we're done here, I'll see if one of the officers can run you over to a shelter, maybe get you another."

"I'd appreciate that." Lyle rubbed his hands up and down his arms. "Not the shelter—I don't like them—but a coat would be nice. It's cold."

Which was an understatement. Charlie made a note to ask if any of the officers might have an old blanket in the trunk that Lyle could use in the meantime. His old coat would go into a clean evidence bag. The girl would go in another. Locard's Exchange Principle said that whenever there was contact between two items, there would always be an exchange, even if it might not be visible to the naked eye. So the coat would have left some fibers on the dead girl, and the dead girl must have left something on the coat, even if it was just a hair or two. They needed the coat to rule it out as the source of anything else they found on the body so they would know it hadn't come from the killer. It was even possible that the killer had left some trace evidence on the girl, which had then been transferred to the coat. To help sort it out, the medical examiner would want Lyle's fingerprints as well as a sample of his hair.

And speak of the devil. Here was the medical examiner, Doug Pietsch, his bald head gleaming in the lights that one of the CSIs was setting up. He and Charlie nodded at each other, then walked back together to look again at the corpse.

"Judging by the blood loss, I would say she was killed here." Doug leaned down and wiggled her knee with his gloved hand. "Within the last two hours, maybe a little longer." He started to straighten up, then stopped and pointed. "Hey, what's that?"

Charlie lifted the beam of his flashlight and a chill went down his spine. There was blood on the wall. Not the fine mist from the gunshot. Not cast off from the amputations. No. This was deliberate. Someone had left a scrawled message behind. With gloved fingers, Charlie lifted the girl's wrist and looked at her intact right hand. Like the left hand, tan lines at the base of every finger showed where rings had once rested. But it was her index finger that he focused on. It was a solid red to the second knuckle.

Before she died, the dead girl had written in her own blood, dipped her finger to the wound in her chest or to the puddle she lay in. Left behind a message so important that she had spent the last few seconds of her life writing it. In wavering letters three inches high, it read:

9310

The only problem was that Charlie had no idea what it meant.

CHAPTER 55

inety-three seventy," Doug read aloud. "What do you think that means?"

Charlie stared at it, suddenly wishing he had a big cup of coffee. Ideally, with four shots of espresso. "I have no clue," he told the medical examiner. "I guess it could be a house number. Or maybe a locker number."

"Or the number of a safe-deposit box," Doug contributed. "Or maybe the combination to a lock?" He leaned forward, his big head tilted to one side. He looked more interested than Charlie ever remembered him being. Dead bodies, even those missing two digits, were his workaday reality. But four numbers scrawled in blood? That was new. Or at least newish.

Each number was shakier than the last. Maybe the actual number was even longer but the victim hadn't had the strength to finish. "Maybe it's part of her Social Security number?" Charlie guessed.

"Or two of the winning Powerball numbers." Doug grinned. "Maybe she's trying to tell us we need to play them."

"It's got to have been pretty important for her to write it in her own blood."

"Maybe it's some kind of code, in case the guy noticed what she had done," Doug said. "She might have figured that if he didn't understand it, maybe he wouldn't try to destroy it."

"If every letter is a number, then ninety-three seventy would be"—Charlie counted on his fingers—"I, C, G, and I don't know what zero would be. I guess that wouldn't work anyway. Not with twenty-six letters and only ten numbers." An idea teased him, then faded when he tried to pin it down. "If it is a code, it won't do us much good if we can't figure it out."

While they were speaking, two Seattle PD criminalists—a man and a woman—drove up and parked outside the perimeter of the crime-scene tape. They got out of their car and began to put on shoe coverings, hairnets, and white Tyvek suits they took from the trunk. The white suits would keep them from leaving trace evidence, as well as protect them from any biohazards, which was what they called all the liquids that leaked out of dead people. Although as scenes went, this one wasn't bad.

It was going to be a long day. In his head, Charlie ran through everything he would need to do. He needed to walk around the scene again, picking out what he wanted the criminalists to photograph or process. He would note places where they should look for fingerprints, maybe even shoe impressions if there were any patches of dirt.

When it came to photos, his rule was to document everything, even things that didn't seem important. You only had one chance to work a scene. A photograph might offer the only clues they would ever have. It wasn't like a lab sample that could be tested again as long as you hadn't used it up. Once the photographs were done, Doug would bag the woman's hands—or what remained of them—to preserve any trace evidence. He would then place the coat and the corpse in clean body bags.

Meanwhile, Charlie would be assigning officers to search nearby Dumpsters and the warehouse itself, even though it looked like it had been shuttered for years. Closed didn't necessarily mean empty. Empty spaces attracted human pests just as much as animal and insect ones. He also needed to re-interview Tom Lyle in more detail.

It might be hard to figure out what was trash and what might be evidence. When in doubt, take it all, was Charlie's motto. But his gut told him they would be lucky to find anything. In many ways, this felt like the work of a professional. Whoever it was had come prepared with gloves and tools. Most people would have had to work their way up to snipping off fingers, but Charlie had seen no hesitation marks on the girl's hand. And there was no sign of his shell casings or the girl's fingers, so he must have taken them away. What kind of man could slip two fingers in his pocket as if they were as commonplace as coins?

Then again, if this had been planned, why hadn't the killer taken the victim to some isolated place where she might never have been found and killed her there? Even if he had planned on dumping the body once he was finished obliterating any easy way to identify her, he would still be leaving behind a big pool of blood that would surely draw questions if anyone noticed it before the rain washed it away.

Charlie needed to walk the neighborhood, looking for evidence and witnesses. Stop to talk to laborers and forklift drivers. The victim's lack of a coat pointed to her coming here in some kind of vehicle. His mental to-do list got longer. Check with taxi companies. Check the registration of any parked cars in the area to see if they belonged to her. Seek out nearby security cams to see if they had any relevant footage. Send out a notice to law enforcement agencies. Check with missing persons.

With luck, once Doug got her back to the morgue, the fingerprints on her remaining fingers would match someone in the system.

If she was a prostitute—and the inflated breasts, high heels, and missing rings made him think she was—she had probably been picked up before.

Whoever she was, once the victim had been identified, Charlie would learn everything he could about her. It was like a spiral, the beginning of the yellow brick road. You started at the center, with the victim, then worked your way out in a logical order, making wider and wider circles. And somewhere along the path you figured out the why, even if it really only made sense to the killer. Then you figured out the who.

He and Doug backed off while one of the criminalists took establishing photographs of the body, Lyle's coat still across the head. Then she took midrange photos, close-ups, and finally more close-ups of the bullet wound and the mutilated hand with a paper ruler laid down for scale. When she was finished, she called Doug over to lift up the coat so she could take photos of the woman's face. After Doug moved her, they would take photos of the ground where she had lain.

But when Doug slowly peeled back the coat with his gloved hands, Charlie sucked in his breath. "Wait a minute." He leaned closer.

He'd seen her only in pictures, but he was sure of it, even though her hair was now a brighter blond that looked nearly brassy in the bright lights the criminalists had set up. Even though the painted lips were no longer curved up in a smile.

"I know this girl."

Doug and the criminalist were watching him curiously. "Who is it?"

"Her name's Betty Eastman." The girl Scott had been having an affair with. The girl Jared said had disappeared the same night Scott was killed. "Her boyfriend told me that he hadn't seen her since April fourteenth."

But this body was fresh. Clearly she hadn't died that night seven months ago.

Charlie tilted his head as he regarded Betty's slack mouth and half-open eyes. Where had she been for the last seven months?

Even if Betty had once been Scott's killer, now she was someone else's victim.

CHAPTER 56

Eli got to the Tilikum Place Café before Mia. Even though they only liked to seat complete parties, he talked the waitress into letting him snag the last table. While the restaurant wasn't very big and every seat was now taken, the high ceilings and front wall of windows made the space feel larger than it really was.

Five minutes later Mia walked in, cheeks pink from the cold. Under a long black North Face raincoat, she wore black pants and a turquoise sweater that set off her blue eyes.

Eli stood up and stepped around the table to pull out her chair for her. As she sat down, she turned to smile over her shoulder at him. He was close enough to smell her hair.

"What are you going to get?" he asked as she perused the menu. He poured her coffee from the carafe he had ordered.

"A Dutch Baby." It was the specialty of the house, cooked in its own individual frying pan. Eli had been considering ordering it, but then the waitress arrived and described the special: a house-made biscuit split open and filled with Beecher's flagship cheddar, arugula, an over-easy egg, and bacon. And it came with home fries.

"I'll have that," he said. "And she'll have the Dutch Baby." He looked at Mia. "Do you want orange juice?" When she nodded, he added, "And two large orange juices."

"So has there been a lot of fallout from your decision not to charge them as adults?" Eli asked once the waitress had left. His hope was to get Jackson the help that he so clearly needed. The boy still had a spark of promise inside him.

Mia looked around and then leaned close. "Oh, you mean besides Dominic Raines saying this was the proof the voters needed to kick Frank out of office?" Her voice was so low that Eli leaned in too. "I think people at the office are worried I've just pushed more votes Dominic's way."

"Is Frank D'Amato one of those people?" Just the thought made Eli angry.

"He said it was my decision and he would stand by it. But he didn't look very happy." Mia sighed. "The thing is, the public doesn't understand how our office functions. Raines is saying we're letting criminals off lightly. A lot of people have the misconception that offenders have been pled away. They think a plea is a reduction, but in King County a lot of people plead as charged. So that saves everyone time and money. But Raines talks about plea bargains like they're bad things."

"What will you do if he wins?"

"I don't know. Even if Raines is elected, I'd still have a few months before he was actually sworn in. And I doubt he'd push me out the first week." She gave him a crooked smile. "But maybe by the second."

He thanked his lucky stars that in Washington public defenders were appointed, not elected.

Their food came, and for a minute they were too busy eating to say much. Eli's sandwich was amazing: salty, savory, crunchy, chewy, cheesy, and delicious. Judging by the way she was closing her eyes and smiling while she chewed, Mia's food was equally good.

He spoke around a second mouthful. "Would you ever think of

going into private practice?" Many a former prosecutor had, touting their insider knowledge of what it was like on the other side. "Maybe corporate law?"

"One thing I know I couldn't do is civil law." She made a face and Eli mirrored it.

Civil cases could last years, with hours devoted to the finer points of civil procedure. The rest of the time went to the process known as "discovery," where lawyers got into huge fights over inherently uninteresting documents like tax returns. Once they finally obtained these documents, they then spent days, weeks, or months reading them—but most would never find their way into a trial.

"Criminal law is way more interesting, that's for sure," Eli said.

"I can honestly say I enjoy every day at work." Mia pointed her fork at him. "How many people can say that? Every case is different. And the facts can be exciting or bizarre or tragic. But they are always interesting. And they are never the same."

"I totally get where you're coming from." Eli nodded as he spoke. "I could never work for a white-shoe law firm. For them, everything is the bigger, the better: the bigger house, the bigger car, the bigger salary." That's the way Lydia had looked at the world. She had thought it was a waste for Eli to pour himself into his cases, working harder and harder even though the money would never get any better.

Mia snagged a home fry off his plate, and he mock swatted at her. After popping it into her mouth she said, "This might sound sappy, but I kind of like causes."

Eli thought of Rachel, who would be going to college in a year. He still wasn't sure how he would be able to afford that. "Still, there's something to be said for money."

"I should have told you"—Mia gave him a smile—"I'm paying for my half. Wouldn't want anyone to accuse me of a conflict of interest."

"So you're saying you could be bought for a Dutch Baby?"

"When you put it that way, it really sounds wrong. And besides, you're forgetting the home fries." She snatched another one from his plate. "And the coffee."

A single blond curl framed her blue eye. Eli suddenly wanted to lean forward and kiss her in the worst way. Right here in the restaurant.

Maybe she sensed it, because she sat back and said, "How long have you been divorced?"

"Lydia left a little over a year ago," he said, which was mostly the truth. "She thought we got married too young."

"Did you?"

"I was nineteen, she was eighteen. So, yes, we were both too young."

Eli had volunteered for the army after high school graduation. The army, in its infinite wisdom, had trained him to be a paralegal, which actually turned out to be a pretty good fit for him. On one of his leaves, Lydia got pregnant. She was still in school. She graduated, but she was four months along when she walked down the aisle of her high school auditorium in a cheap green satin graduation gown. And five months pregnant when she married him, this time wearing a cheap white satin gown.

Lydia had always complained that she had just moved from one house to another. She had never gotten to live on her own, never gotten to be independent. She had gone from being a child to being a mother.

"You must look at Rachel and think about how young you guys really were. I mean, she's, what, only a year younger than your wife was when you got married?"

Eli did think about it, but he still felt defensive. "At the time, it seemed like the right solution." He didn't spell out the pregnancy, figuring Mia could read between the lines. "But Lydia always felt she missed out on being a teenager. So she started acting like she could still be one. The summer she left I would come home from work and find her hanging around the pool with our daughter and her friends." In a bikini, no less. "Rachel was embarrassed, but I think the boys thought it was cool. One day I caught Lydia smoking pot with two of them." His face flushed as he remembered.

Mia winced.

"I had already realized that Rachel was getting off track. But it wasn't until that day that I realized it was my wife who was the one leading her down the garden path. She'd practically whisper in Rachel's ear: 'You're young, you need to go out and have fun while you still can.'" He blew air through pursed lips, remembering. "I asked Lydia to go to counseling at our church. She refused, and then she stopped going to church." He had pleaded, begged, promised— but it hadn't done any good. And then she was gone. "And that was pretty much it."

Mia was silent for a long time, cradling her coffee cup in her hands. "Did you love her?"

He was surprised. "Of course I did. You can't live with someone for seventeen years and not love them. Of course, you can't live that long with someone and not hate them too. And find them annoying and boring and wonderful and surprising and funny. I finally gave her a choice. Me or her new lifestyle." He bit his lip. "She chose the lifestyle."

"So how's Rachel dealing with it?"

"She doesn't say much, but it's been hard. When her mom left, she didn't just leave me, she left Rachel too. And the poor kid can't help thinking it has something to do with her. When it's really all about her mom. When we were still living in Portland, Rachel started getting into trouble, hanging out with a bad group of kids. So I decided to move up here, get a fresh start."

"Has it worked?"

A heaviness settled in his chest. "Maybe. I don't know." He spoke before he had a chance to consider whether it was a good idea to tell the truth. "The other day I'm pretty sure she was high. Her eyes looked swollen and she couldn't stop giggling. Then she tried to put her plate in the upper rack of the dishwasher even though it obviously wouldn't fit." He had watched her keep trying, though, while his dinner turned into a leaden lump in his stomach.

Mia leaned forward. "Gabe's had his problems too. A few months ago he was with a group of kids that robbed a convenience store. He didn't take anything, and he came forward afterward, so he wasn't charged. I just worry which way his life is going to go. What other choices he's going to make."

Eli felt relieved. There were times when he talked to other parents, even other single parents, and he felt like a loser. Their kids, at least according to them, always got good grades, never got into trouble, and volunteered to clean up without being asked. They even did real volunteer work.

"It's hard to be a single parent. And it's hard to be a kid and not have two parents." He hesitated. "You told me earlier that you thought your husband might have been murdered."

"Charlie has a theory," Mia began.

Eli nodded. He hadn't been too impressed with Charlie, with his slouch and long hair.

Mia explained it to him while Eli tried to look like he was keeping an open mind. Maybe homicide detectives started seeing murder everyplace they looked. The whole thing seemed complicated. Newton's first law of motion? Plus, Eli had a feeling there might be parts Mia was glossing over. Still, she was an open book compared to Lydia.

"If Charlie's right and Scott was murdered," he pointed out, "then whoever did it is not going to be happy that you're trying to figure it out."

"I'm thinking it's related to something Scott did. Not me." She bit her lip. "I'm wondering if this restaurant owner who was one of Scott's clients was involved. I was kind of sneaking around yesterday, talking to one of his employees, and then I actually saw the owner hit the poor man. He didn't know I was there. I'm thinking of calling the state department of labor, only I'm worried I'll just make this guy lose his job."

Sneaking around trying to solve Scott's murder? This was exactly the kind of thing Eli was afraid of. "But, Mia, don't you see that this can be—"

Her phone rang, interrupting him. She looked at it, her finger hovering over the button to dismiss it, then she took a closer look and picked it up instead.

"This is Mia." As she listened, the smile fell from her face like a plate from a shelf. Eli felt himself tense as she asked a series of questions.

"How did she die? . . . In her own blood?" Her voice was filled with disbelief. "What was the number?" Then she repeated, "Nine three seven oh. That doesn't mean anything to me either . . . Okay, I'll talk to you soon." She ended the call and then looked up at Eli. "Sorry about that."

"I couldn't help overhearing. Did someone you know die?"

The look she gave him wasn't easy to decipher. Embarrassment, anger, fear? A little of everything? "My late husband's girlfriend."

CHAPTER 57

TUESDAY

Mia had spent the last few days in a blur. Everyone was still adjust-ing to having two more people in the house. Charlie was keeping her up-to-date on his hunt to find Betty's killer, but so far it was coming up empty. Today was the election, and tempers were run-ning high at the office as everyone wondered whether they would wake up to the news of a new boss.

On her way home from work, Mia started sneezing. Great. She was getting a cold. Leaning forward, she rummaged through the glove box for a packet of tissues, careful not to take her eyes off the road. Instead, her fingers touched the black jewelry box that held the engagement ring Scott had planned to give Betty. She had put it there after meeting with Oleg, not able to bring herself to bring it back into her house.

But what if one day Gabe rummaged for a tissue or a pair of sunglasses? Even though it was so small, it felt like the box gave out a toxic glow, like something radioactive that would slowly poison bones and blood.

When Oleg had told her the truth about the ring's value, Mia had originally thought she should keep it to remind her of Scott's bone-deep perfidy. Not only to her, but even to his mistress.

But really, what was the point of that? Every day she was reminded of how he had lied to her, how he had already begun to abandon her and their children. She was reminded when she worried about whether she could afford new tires for the car. When she wished that her kids would stop growing out of their clothes. When she had to pay a bill that Scott had run up. For all she knew, this ring had been put on one of the many credit cards he had left behind.

Mia hadn't yet gotten on the freeway, so she pulled over and Googled "jewelry stores" on her phone. There was one only a half mile away.

Located in a small shopping area with stores on three sides of a parking lot, Streeter's Jewelry wasn't nearly as nice as Oleg's Jewels and Gems. But it had a sign in the window that said, "We pay cash for your jewelry," and that was all she cared about. Oleg had told her Scott had paid seven or eight hundred for the ring, that the setting was 18-karat gold. She thought of the heft of it. Once you pried out the cubic zirconia, the rest could be melted down.

A bell jingled overhead when she walked in. It was a small store, with glass cases on three sides of the room. A man stepped out from the back. He was older, Hispanic looking, with a dark suit like a banker's and long silver sideburns to show that he also had an artistic side.

"May I help you?"

"I'd like to sell this ring." She held out the black box. It was a relief to put it in his palm.

"Oh?" He raised an eyebrow.

She said evenly, "It reminds me of a past relationship." Just not hers. "Could you tell me how much it's worth?"

Screwing a jeweler's loupe to his left eye, he snapped open the box, then plucked the ring from inside and leaned down to look at it under a light.

Even though it would be a relief to be rid of it, realistically, how much could she expect to get? Oleg had probably exaggerated the value, trying to help a widow in need without embarrassing either of them.

Then again, even a couple hundred dollars would be welcome. And it would be out of her life, which was even more important.

He lifted his head and took the loupe from his eye. "It's a beautiful piece," he said slowly. "The cut, the clarity, the color. Of course, we can only offer you the wholesale value, not the retail." His eyes were a very light brown with gold flecks. "To be honest, you might try selling it as a private party. You might be able to get more for it."

"I'd feel kind of strange about that," Mia said. "I mean, I would tell them right up front that it's a fake, but I'd still feel like one of those men with the watches hung up inside their raincoats."

His eyes narrowed. "What are you talking about? This is no fake."

"What?" The room seemed to be rotating around her, and she put her hand on the counter to steady herself. "Are you saying it's real?"

"Very much so. I could give you maybe twenty thousand for it, but if you sold it as a private party, you could probably get thirty."

"But I was told by another jeweler that it was a fake. He said it was a very good fake, but still a fake."

He snorted. "He was right about it being very good. Just not about it being fake. Let me ask you something. Did he offer to take it off your hands?"

Mia remembered how alarmed Oleg had looked when she had started laughing at the news. "He told me he could buy it back if I was having a problem with money."

"Buy it back?"

"He has two shops. One sells gems, the other costume jewelry. He said my husband had bought the ring from the costume jewelry one."

"He lied to you," he said flatly. "He was trying to cheat you. You should report him to the Better Business Bureau."

Mia felt off balance. What else might Oleg have lied about?

CHAPTER 58

Charlie sat at his desk staring at a photograph of the number: *9370*. Betty had used her last few heartbeats to leave a message, a message so vital that she had chosen to write it in her own blood.

But he had no idea what it was.

He typed **9370** into Google.

It was a BlackBerry model number. So had Betty been trying to hint they needed to look at a phone?

But it turned out to also be the model number of a radar detector, an International truck, and an IBM mainframe computer released in 1986. In addition, it was the name of a gene that was involved with metabolic and hormonal processes. None of these seemed like anything Betty would care about.

Remembering Doug's theory that it might have only been a partial number, Charlie Googled 937 to see if it was an area code. It was—in Ohio. 937-0. So had she wanted them to call the operator in Ohio?

The number was the only real clue he had. As for Betty herself, there was no yellow brick road to follow. She had no family and had grown up in a series of foster placements. The clothes she had been wearing when she died were expensive, but not exclusive enough to be traced back to a single buyer. The last friend she'd had seemed to have been Jared. And according to him, Betty had dropped out of sight the day Scott was murdered. April was also the last month she seemed to have had a cell phone contract, a job, any activity on her credit cards, or gone to school.

So something must have happened to Betty around the same time, or even the very night Scott died. Both airbags had been deployed, so if she had been in the car and wearing her seat belt, she could have survived in much better shape than Scott had. Especially assuming no one had taken a club to her head afterward. Had someone caused the accident, taken her, and then gotten tired of her?

With a groan Charlie pushed himself back from his desk and walked over to the break room. He came back with a cup of sludgy coffee that smelled like it had sat on the burner since Monday. His grandma would have said it was the kind of coffee that would put hair on your chest.

He walked around his desk to get back to his chair, his eyes still on the photo.

And suddenly Charlie saw what Betty's last message had been.

He pictured Betty, her heart pumping erratically, lying on her back, not strong enough to get to her feet. Not even strong enough to sit up or roll over. Dipping her finger in her own blood, reaching back, writing her note with the last of her strength. Her brain already affected by a lack of oxygen before it finally shut down altogether.

She had written it so that it was right side up for her.

It wasn't 9370.

It was OLEG.

CHAPTER 59

Vin waited for the three men to emerge from the workroom. As required, they had stripped before they walked into the room as naked as the day they were born. Inside the room, his boss supplied everything they needed: the bunny suits, the gloves, the breathing masks. As well as the hammers, the gaudy necklaces, the scales, the packaging.

Even with the masks, when they were done they would still stagger out of the room with pupils so wide they looked like those Japanese cartoon characters that he thought were called anime. Then he would search them, put his own gloved hands on their sweating, trembling bodies to make sure they hadn't hidden any of the precious commodity in an orifice.

From inside the room the rhythmic *tap, tap, tap* still echoed. Each of the men gently striking one of the huge necklaces shaped like hearts and covered with rhinestones. The necklaces that had been chosen not for any sense of beauty, but solely for how much they could hold.

There was a cracking sound as one of the necklaces finally yielded. Revealing its own white, powdery heart.

Pure cocaine.

Then his phone rang.

In the old days everyone knew if you wanted something done right, you went to Vin. A bank robbery that happened minutes after the casino made a deposit? He was your man. Did you want someone dead but no one to be suspicious? Let Vin take care of it, and no one would even guess it was a hit. He had been responsible for five "accidents," two missing persons, and one businessman who was believed to have run off with his mistress.

The key to being successful, to keeping out of prison, was to plan everything in advance. Before you did any kind of job, whether it was a hit or a robbery, you began by familiarizing yourself with the routine you planned to disrupt.

You figured out one quick escape route, but you also had another, longer one, in case some Joe Citizen looking for a merit badge decided to follow you and you had to shake him loose. You mapped and timed both primary and secondary routes. You stole license plates from parked cars. You stole parked cars. You rented garages to park the stolen cars with the new stolen plates.

When you did a job, you never carried anything that if dropped could later be traced back to you. No cell phones. No scraps of paper with your girlfriend's phone number. No nothing, up to and including your wallet. And you never touched anything with your bare hands.

The last time he had done a job in haste, it had gone wrong. Terribly wrong. Nineteen years of prison wrong. He had gone in a strong man, a man in the prime of life, a man who could scare people just by looking at them, and had come out an old man.

But it wasn't like he had a pension plan. He was going to have to work until he was dead.

Now all Vin's rules, produced by years of careful study and thought, kept being broken. Not because of anything he did, but because of his new boss. Oleg was unpredictable. Oleg made messes. Oleg was jovial, until very suddenly he wasn't.

Vin was just Oleg's errand boy. Sixty-two years old and this was what he had been reduced to. Shakedowns, threats, bribes. Low-level muscle. Sometimes even playing the part of a driver, dressed in a black suit that was too tight across the shoulders. He was also the guy who pulled on vinyl gloves and did cavity searches. And, very rarely, there was the termination that called for his special skills. Planning Scott Quinn's murder, making sure it looked like an accident, had been the most interesting thing he had done all year.

Now what Oleg was demanding of him was hasty, pulled together far too fast for Vin's taste. It was too haphazard to even be called a plan. He didn't like the sound of it at all. It was one thing to be sicced on someone who should have known what they were getting into, but civilians were a different matter. They had their world, and he had his. He didn't like overlap.

Of course there were people who tried to straddle both sides. Like that Scott Quinn. Letting himself be eased from one thing to the next until one day he woke up and had second thoughts a little too late. Tax evasion was one thing, he had actually told Oleg, but cocaine was another.

In the last few seconds of his life, as Vin took a baseball bat to his head, maybe he had realized they weren't that far apart.

CHAPTER 60

Mia parked her car in the U-Dub parking lot, then got out and went over to the passenger side. As she leaned in to gather her papers and books, she was overcome with exhaustion. The last thing she wanted was to teach tonight.

She realized a man was standing behind her. Too close. With a gasp, she straightened up and whirled around. Then she recognized him. It was Alvin Turner. The older man who had stopped and tried to help Scott. Tried to help him even after Scott had bullied him.

Only why was he here? At the University of Washington?

And something about his face had changed. It was harder somehow. Except for his blue eyes. For some reason, they just looked . . . dead.

"Alvin?" she said uncertainly.

"Call me Vin," he said, and then pressed the gun into her side.

CHAPTER 61

Eli pulled into the law school's parking lot. A few rows ahead of him, he saw Mia. She was standing next to the passenger side of her car. An old man with white hair and a ruddy face was talking to her. As Eli watched, Mia's hand flew to her mouth and her eyes went wide.

Was something wrong? Had the man brought her bad news? Eli squinted. Was that guy maybe Mia's dad?

Still talking, the old man took her left arm just above the elbow and pulled her closer to him. Then the two of them began to hurry through the parking lot and away from Eli. Mia moved oddly. Her body was stiff and her feet scuffed the ground.

Eli slowly got out of his car, his eyes never leaving them, still trying to figure out what was happening. The two got into an old blue Ford. The weird thing was they both got in on the passenger's side, Mia first and then the older man. Then she scooted over—it must have a bench seat—until she was behind the wheel.

Eli felt the hair rise on the back of his neck. Something was wrong. He didn't know what, but he had learned to trust that sixth sense. Instead of going into the law school or even calling Mia on her cell, he got back in his car and followed the Taurus back out of the lot and onto the street.

Mia was driving a little too fast. Soon they were heading west. Eli tried to keep two cars between them, even though he didn't think either of them knew he was there. The old man wasn't turning around to look behind him, and Mia seemed to be staring straight ahead. It looked like she was talking.

At a stoplight Eli yanked out his phone and dialed Mia's number. No answer. He was staring at the back of her head and she didn't even move. But the times he had been with her, she had kept her phone on vibrate mode. Maybe she hadn't noticed his call. Maybe she was busy talking to the man about whatever urgent business had caused her to leave campus when her class would be starting in only a few minutes. He hung up without leaving a message.

If Eli called 911, what would he say? That this woman he knew slightly was now driving off with a man he didn't know at all? Instead, he called 411 and asked for the number for the Seattle Police Department. When he got through, Eli said, "I need to speak to a detective in the homicide department. His name is Charlie . . ." What was Charlie's last name? He ground his teeth in frustration.

"Carlson," the woman supplied.

"Yes, yes. Carlson. And it's urgent."

"Carlson," the guy growled into the phone a few seconds later. Eli felt a nibble of irritation. It sounded like Charlie had watched one too many movies about tough-guy cops.

"Charlie, this is Eli Hall, from the public defender's office." Charlie started to say something, maybe to mention something about the shopping cart case, but Eli overrode him. "Mia and I were supposed to be teaching together tonight at U-Dub. But as I was driving in, I saw her getting into a car with this older guy. It wasn't her car and I've never seen the man before. And there was something about his face and her body language. Like he had hold of her arm and they both got into the car on the passenger's side, and then she scooted over to drive. Maybe I'm crazy, but I don't think she's going willingly. I tried calling her, but she didn't answer."

Charlie's voice sharpened. "What does this guy look like?"

Eli felt both relieved that he believed him and worried that he wasn't dismissing him out of hand. "Older. He had white hair."

"Did you notice anything else about him?"

"He had a reddish face. Like maybe he had bad skin a long time ago."

Charlie swore. And then swore again. "Did you get the license number of the car?"

"Hold on a sec." Eli pressed down on the accelerator. "I'll see if I can get close enough to make it." He cut around a white Jetta in front of him, then winced when it honked.

"Wait a minute," Charlie said. "You're following him?"

"Yes." Eli got into the left lane, hoping the change looked natural. He didn't want the guy guessing Eli was on his tail.

"Not a good idea. Not a good idea at all." Charlie was now talking between gasps. It sounded like he was running.

"I'm not leaving her." Eli felt ridiculous, like he was saying, *You're not the boss of me.*

"Think about it. What if you're right and something is wrong? What if you spook him?"

"Look," Eli said as he squinted at the back of the car, "do you want his license number or not?"

"Yes. What is it?"

Eli rattled it off.

"Okay," Charlie said. "Great. Now you need to back off and let the professionals take over."

"What, are you telling me you can get a squad car here right this second? I don't think so. And if I let them drive off, then we'll have no idea where she is."

"If he realizes you're tailing him, he might panic. And people who panic tend to do stupid things. So back off!"

Eli started to ease up on the accelerator. But as he did, something inside the other car caught his attention. Did the old man have something in his hand? He squinted, and then his insides turned to ice.

It was definitely a gun. But it wasn't pointed at Eli.

It was pointed at Mia.

CHAPTER 62

Where is he?" Mia spit the words at the old man pressing a gun into her side. "Where is my son?" Her hands were slick and hot on the steering wheel. She barely saw the cars around them.

They had Gabe, Vin had told her a few minutes ago. They had Gabe, and the only way they would keep him alive would be if Mia went with him. Right then.

"Have you hurt him?" Her voice cracked. "If you've hurt him . . ."

"Don't worry about that," he said tonelessly. "Shut up and keep driving." There was no passion in his voice, as if he wasn't even invested in their conversation. As if what she had to say didn't matter. The kindly old man who had apologetically told her about Scott's last few minutes had disappeared as if he had never been. Which Mia supposed he hadn't.

Should she even ask about Brooke? Would asking only serve to draw attention to her? Or was Vin keeping silent because something irrevocable had already happened to her daughter? Four-year-olds were not known for obeying orders. A gunshot might be the quickest way to silence a crying child.

No, Mia told herself, her gorge rising. *No. The reason he's not saying anything about Brooke is because they don't have her.* Maybe had even forgotten or not known about her. It was better to keep quiet.

But she couldn't keep absolutely silent. The wheels were turning in her brain. "You killed Scott, didn't you?"

Beside her, Vin shrugged. Still, it felt like an admission. All he said was, "Turn left at the light."

But before they got there it turned red, giving her a moment to think. Was there anything she could do?

"Don't make eye contact, don't call out, don't do anything to draw attention," Vin said, pressing the gun more firmly into Mia's side, just below her ribs. She had seen enough crime-scene photos to know what would happen if he pulled the trigger. If the bullet didn't kill her outright, the infection from having her intestines ripped apart probably would.

As ordered, Mia kept her face pointing straight ahead, but still she concentrated on what she could see in her peripheral vision. The person closest to her, a girl in the passenger seat of an SUV, was texting on her phone. Even if Mia rolled down the window or ran out of the car, what could that girl do? What could anyone do? If Mia tried anything, she would be dead within seconds.

The light turned green and she took the turn. "So I guess you were a little more than just a passerby who happened upon my husband's accident," she said.

"Look, Mia." The sound of her name in his mouth made her shiver. "When you lie down with dogs, you get up with fleas. Your husband decided he was too good for certain things. Like he could pick and choose. Fraud and tax evasion were okay, but selling coke wasn't? We didn't need him getting a conscience. Don't worry, I made sure it was fast. Fast and smart. And I covered my tracks. No one had to know. But then you had to come along and start asking questions."

So the Jade Kitchen was selling more than Chinese cuisine. Mia wondered how Kenny Zhong did it. Four restaurants meant a lot of people coming and going. Maybe he hid drugs in takeout boxes?

But Kenny hadn't done his own dirty work. The man sitting beside her, sitting close enough that she could hear his slow exhalations, had swung a bat at Scott's head so hard that it had shattered his skull. And Alvin Turner—or Vin—still seemed to think of himself as the good guy. The chances of appealing to his sense of human decency were slim.

"I have a diamond ring worth thirty thousand dollars," she said. "You can have it if you let me and my son go." It was in her purse, the purse still strapped across her shoulder, but Vin didn't need to know that.

"Good to know." His voice was laconic.

"Please, if not me, then my son. Let Gabe go, and I'll tell you where the ring is."

He sighed. "There's no point in talking. This whole thing has gotten way past the point of talk."

He was never going to let her go, that was clear. She had seen his face. Knew his name, at least if the name he had told them was true. People who were dead couldn't talk.

The same was probably true for Gabe. Was she really helping her son by following Vin's orders?

Could she crash the car into something and get out and run? Mia looked up the road. There. Where the road turned. It wasn't a line of trees like Scott had crashed into, but there was a telephone pole. She wasn't wearing a seat belt, just as Scott hadn't. How badly would she be hurt? She remembered Scott's torn aorta. At least the pole was closer to Turner's side. Maybe the two of them would die together.

The pressure of the gun was gone from her side, but before she could react, the barrel was pressed just under the hinge of her jaw.

"Stop thinking about how you're going to get out of this," Vin said. "Don't make this harder than it has to be."

"Don't make this harder!" she repeated, anger singing through her veins. "For who? For me or for you? Because I'm getting a feeling this is going to be pretty dadgum hard for me."

To her surprise, Vin made a muffled snort.

Had that been a laugh? But then the nose of the gun pressed into the spot under her jaw even harder than ever.

Following the directions he barked at her, she turned into the parking lot for Puget Marina. As she parked she looked around for someone who might help her. But there were only a handful of cars and no people to be seen at all. On an August afternoon there wouldn't be a free parking space. But it was a different story on a blustery late afternoon in November.

There was no point in relying on someone else to save her. If Mia was going to live, she had to figure it out by herself.

CHAPTER 63

Driving this fast was probably not a good idea. Especially when he was trying to track a moving dot on an app on the tiny screen of his phone. The phone was propped behind his steering wheel against the control panel, just below the dial that showed his speed. Charlie was trying to pay attention to the first and ignore the second.

He radioed dispatch, raising his voice to be heard above his siren. "I need you to run a name for crim hist."

"Go ahead."

"A guy named Alvin Turner. I'd say he's over sixty and local." His chest felt tight.

Maybe he was wrong. Maybe Mia wasn't really in trouble. Eli's description of a man with white hair and a ruddy face—that could be anybody. It didn't have to be the guy who had witnessed Scott's accident. Or who had claimed that he had. And just because Eli thought he had seen him pointing a gun at Mia, that didn't mean that was what was really happening. Maybe it had been . . . something else. Charlie cast around for what that something else could be. A cell phone. Even a pack of cigarettes. There could be an innocent explanation. Couldn't there?

If Turner was in the system, his criminal history would show his arrests—by penal code number as well as the name of the crime—and whether each had resulted in conviction or dismissal. It would also list if he was currently incarcerated or had been, or if he was on parole or probation.

Hardware. Wasn't that what Turner had said? That he was retired from the hardware business?

It only took a minute, and then the dispatcher was back.

"Got it. It's pretty long."

Charlie's stomach dropped. He felt like he was on a roller coaster and just starting to fall. "Hit the highlights for me, would you?"

He remembered how Turner had told them about Scott's speeding past him, described coming upon the accident and trying to find his pulse. Probably none of that was true. And the old guy had forgotten to mention the part where he bashed Scott in the head, snapping his jaw.

Charlie was going flat out now, car after car pulling over as traffic parted before him like water. He never stopped scanning for that one driver who would refuse to pay attention to the lights or the siren, for someone too befuddled or too stubborn to pull over.

For all his speed, the dot of Mia's phone was still a couple of miles ahead of him, heading due west. Pretty soon it would reach Puget Sound and have to head north or south. He had goosed the car up to eighty-five and it didn't seem nearly fast enough to close the distance.

The dispatcher was silent for a second as she searched the records for the most recent and most violent offenses to give Charlie a hint of what he was about to deal with. "He was released from Lompoc fifteen months ago. Served nineteen years for bank robbery. Past crimes—and there's a lot of them—include hmm . . . extortion, kidnapping, and, um, murder."

Charlie was an idiot. The patrol officer could be excused for not running Alvin Taylor's name for what seemed to have been an uncomplicated accident. But once Charlie figured out it was a murder, he should have looked at everyone. But no, he had trusted that white hair and those sagging blue eyes. But even criminals got old. And now Mia was going to die because of his mistake.

But why had Turner killed Scott? And what did he want with Mia? The only thing in Charlie's favor was that Turner was alone with her. Once Charlie threw himself into the mix, he could shift the balance of power.

The dot seemed to have stopped. Charlie nearly clipped a pulled-over black Blazer as he risked squinting at the cell phone's miniature map. Instead of turning north or south, it was at—he looked closer—Puget Marina. Puget Marina was just one of the dozen marinas bordering Seattle, a city that liked its water at least as much as it did its land.

A half mile away he cut his siren but left the lights on. Less than a minute later, Charlie barreled into the marina's parking lot, tires squealing. It held only a few cars. This certainly wasn't boating weather. As he hit the speed bumps fast enough that his teeth clacked together, he grabbed his phone. The dot was close. Maybe a couple of hundred yards away. He scanned the parking lot for the old blue Ford Eli had described.

There!

But when he ran over, gun drawn, it was empty. Charlie radioed dispatch to send in all available units but to have them come in without lights and sirens. After a second's thought, he also asked dispatch to alert Harbor Patrol to send the closest unit.

Holding the phone in front of him, he began to run toward the dot of Mia's phone. He loped down a flight of metal stairs so fast it was more of a controlled fall than a run. He scanned back and forth, looking for Mia on one of the boats, the pier juddering under his long strides.

According to the app he was very close, but still there was no one around. The only sounds were the soft lap of the waves and the crows and seagulls calling overhead.

His dot and Mia's now overlapped. He was right where the phone showed her as being.

Or as having been. Because as he watched, the display changed to: "Old location. Currently unavailable." He pushed the refresh button, but the words didn't change. And his dot was right on top of her last location.

He was at the end of the pier, right next to an empty space. He squinted and looked out over the water.

A boat. Heading out into the sound.

Not just a boat. A yacht. White. Gleaming. Sleek. And fast.

Very fast.

CHAPTER 64

Vin scooted closer to Mia, close enough that she could smell him, sweaty and sour.

"Get out. Slowly. Stay right by the car. Don't try anything. I'll have a gun on you the whole time. A bullet can outrun you."

Mia did as she was told, but as she put her feet to the ground, she tried to position herself to slide around to the far side of the door. Maybe she could slam it closed on him. But Vin was as close as her shadow, his breath hot on the back of her neck. "I told you not to try anything."

Mia didn't bother denying her half-formed plan. She was already trying to figure out what she could do next.

"Okay, we're going to take a little walk. And if we meet anyone, you're not going to say anything. Or both you and them will die." Vin grabbed her arm with iron fingers and pressed the gun into her side. If she managed to live through this day, her body would be pockmarked with bruises.

"You're taking me to Gabe?"

"Not if you keep asking questions. Not if you don't do exactly what I say."

Vin might be marching her forward, but he couldn't stop her head from turning. Couldn't stop her eyes from searching. Surely there had to be someone here who could help her. Or maybe not help her, but at least call the police. But there was no one. The only sign of life was the birds crying overhead.

They walked down a ramp, past boat after boat. All of them, on this blustery afternoon, empty. She kept wondering when he would tell her to stop. Was he planning on marching her into the ocean? Then they reached the last yacht.

And there was Oleg Popov. Not Kenny Zhong. Oleg. Mia tried to recalculate.

"Come aboard, my dear," he said.

"Where's Gabe?" she demanded as she climbed aboard. "I need to see my son. Now." Was he tied up below? There was nothing on the deck but a stack of concrete blocks.

He gestured. "Come down below."

They went down into the yacht's living quarters. Vin shadowed Mia's footsteps, his gun still inches away from her. Everything was compact and immovable. The highly polished table was bolted to the floor. For seating there were leather banquettes and two fixed swiveling chairs. Even the art on the walls was screwed down, reminding Mia of the mental hospital where they had talked to Manny.

"I'm afraid your son is not here," Oleg said.

"What?" Mia put her hand on her chest. What was he saying? Had something even worse happened to Gabe?

"I knew you wouldn't go with me unless you thought it would help one of your kids," Vin said.

Mia's knees sagged. "They're safe, then?"

Vin shrugged. "I don't believe in visiting the sins of the fathers on the children. Or the wives. But you—you gave us no choice."

Oleg put out his hand. "Please give me your purse."

Mia tried to think of something to do with it—could she swing it at him?—but in the end, she simply lifted the strap over her head and shoulder and handed it to him. After rummaging through it, he found her phone and turned it off, then set it down on a banquette. He also found the ring box, looked at her for a long moment, then slipped it into his pocket. He walked over to the helm and, after flipping a few switches, started the engine.

"What are you going to do to me?" She had to raise her voice. Vin watched her. He held the gun easily, as if it were a tool he used daily.

"It is a sad story really, Mia," Oleg said. "You killed yourself. Drowned yourself in the Sound." The yacht began to move forward.

He was speaking as if it had already happened. As if she were already dead. Mia held herself very still. She would not let them see how afraid she was. "Anyone who knows me will know I would never leave my children."

"Ah, but you've only recently discovered that your husband had a mistress. In fact, you tracked her down over the weekend and killed her."

They were outside of the harbor wall now. Bile flooded her mouth. How deep was Puget Sound? Surely hundreds of feet.

"Vin is going to go back and move your car next to the water. On the seat, they'll find your purse and your keys. On top will be the gun you used to kill the poor girl. Her name was Elizabeth Eastman."

She didn't have time to think about the girl being dead. "Everyone knows I hate the water."

He smiled, and her blood turned to slush. "What better way to punish yourself for what you have done? However, I am afraid we are going to have to tie you to those cement blocks outside. I am sorry, but it must be done."

"How are you going to explain away the cement blocks? That certainly won't look like a suicide."

"We will not need to. The blocks will ensure that they will never find your body."

Her heartbeat was slamming in her ears. "Don't do this. If you have a soul, don't do this."

"You forced my hand. You would not stop asking questions. You would not let the dead bury the dead." He made some adjustments to the instruments, and the sound of the engine changed. Mia could feel the yacht slow and then stop. The engines idled.

At a nod from Oleg, Vin prodded her with the gun. "We're going back up now."

Oleg nodded. "My advice would be not to fight this. Vin will shoot you if he has to. I do not want him to—it will make a hell of a mess."

Mia's tongue was a piece of leather in her mouth. "It would be faster for me, though."

Vin laughed without mirth. "There're plenty of places to shoot you that will only leave you disabled and in a lot of pain. But all you have to do when you go into the water is take a nice deep breath and it will all be over."

Mia looked around for something she could use to fight back, but there was nothing extraneous, nothing loose, nothing that could tip over or come loose during a storm. When Vin poked her again with the gun, she climbed the stairs and went out onto the aft deck. The ocean was all she could see, stretching all the way to the horizon on every side. So many of her nightmares had been just like this.

Oleg took a piece of wire and began to thread it through a block. Wire. Not rope. Nothing that she could hope would stretch once it was wet. If anything, it would cut into her skin.

Mia did the only thing she could think to do.

She leaped over the side and into the water.

CHAPTER 65

As Mia leaped off the yacht, time slowed down. While still in mid-air, she uttered the oldest prayer of all. "Help."

The shock of the icy water stole all the breath from her body. She sank through the gloom. Her lungs demanded air, but she denied them until they turned hollow, until they felt as if they were turning inside out. She heard the muffled sounds of bullets stitching the water.

Her eyes were open, but it made no difference. She was no longer sure what was up or what was down. She couldn't breathe, couldn't move, couldn't focus. She was going to die here in the dark, and then drift slowly down, down, down until the pressure crushed her bones.

No! Mia began to thrash blindly, her arms and legs flailing at the water. Finally her head breached the surface. She drew in a ragged breath that was a painful mix of air and water. Salt water burned her nose and throat. The light was bleeding from the sky.

Where was the yacht? She dog-paddled in a frantic circle. There it was, about forty yards away. As fast as she could, she swam away from it. A spot between her shoulder blades itched. Any moment she expected a bullet to punch through her. Did she need to dive down again, to avoid being shot? Or was it more important to gain distance? She chose distance.

When she snatched a glance over her shoulder, the yacht was about a hundred yards away, and Vin and Oleg were turned away from her, looking into the distance. Were they worried that the sound of their guns had carried? Or maybe they had decided that there was no point in trying to kill her if the water would take care of things soon enough.

No matter what the answer was, they had stopped shooting at her. She thought it likely she was now out of range. And Mia was already tired. So tired. She arched her back and tried to float. But water sheeted across her face, filling her mouth with the ocean's briny, bitter taste. Coughing, spitting, and snorting, she instinctively jerked up as if she could somehow sit up, sit up on top of the ocean. Instead, she began to sink again.

The panic surged back. She fought the water that burned her nose and throat. And suddenly she was vomiting into the ocean, vomiting ocean water and her lunch and, it felt like, even her breakfast and last night's dinner. Her arms and legs were churning, keeping her afloat, but she was moving too fast. There was nothing to hold on to. The only way she had managed to learn to swim as an adult was by reminding herself that the water was contained with a pool, that the pool was finite, that she could always make her way to a point where she could stand up, or to a ladder she could climb up, or to a lip she could cling to. Even then, she had always picked an outside lane for practice. Now there was nothing for miles. Nothing but water.

She knew the sea couldn't be sucking her down, but it felt like it was. And soon it would win.

No! Mia told herself. She could not afford to panic. She could not afford to lose her strength. She continued to move her arms and legs like eggbeaters, but she deliberately slowed down, trying not to waste energy.

Last year Mia had seen part of a special on drowning. She caught it as she was flipping through channels and then watched the rest, horrified. In one home movie, shot by someone unaware that he was also filming a death, children played in the waves, splashing and frolicking while a man just a few feet behind them drowned.

It wasn't like it was in cartoons, when the victim called out or waved for help before going down for a third time. The man's head had been low in the water, unmoving. Even so, his mouth was open, a small dark dot. His hair hung over his eyes. One hand appeared for a second, then the other.

"The victim," the announcer intoned in a sonorous voice, "is using all his energy and oxygen just to keep his mouth above water. As is common in these types of cases, he appears to be climbing an invisible ladder. He doesn't have enough air to call out. He doesn't have enough energy to swim toward shore or to wave for help. All he has is less than a minute before he goes under—for good. The last thing that will happen is he will lose consciousness and make a final effort to breathe. This is known as the terminal gasp. Water will then move passively into the airways. Death will follow."

That documentary had featured prominently in Mia's nightmares for months.

Now she was living it.

If only something would float by that she could cling to. Wasn't the ocean supposed to be filled with garbage? Where was some when she needed it?

If only she had a life vest.

Although that's stupid, she berated herself. *Why not wish for a helicopter with a guy from the Coast Guard in the basket?*

Her arms and legs were even slower now, and not by her choice. Slower and heavier. Heavy as lead yet limp as noodles. She told herself she was conserving energy.

What good had jumping off the yacht done her? No good at all. She was alone in the middle of Puget Sound. Pretty soon she would stop being able to tread water and she would die here. Would it be a calm death? she wondered. The way Vin had half promised? Or would she be panicking to the last, even if she was too weak to show it?

Maybe when the end came, it would be easy to let go. To take that last breath.

Then she pictured Gabe's face. The face he wore when he forgot that he was supposed to be a surly teenager. Forgot that he was supposed to be the man of the house. When he showed that he was what he was—still a boy, a boy mourning his father. A boy who needed a steady adult to guide him.

And Brooke? She was only four. Scott had almost faded from her memory. Mia certainly hadn't had enough time to shape her, to teach her, to love her.

She had to figure out a way to live. If she could make it to sunrise, maybe someone would venture out, a fishing boat or even a pleasure craft, and spot her. She thought longingly again of life jackets. Remembered the last time she had flown, the flight attendants going through their spiel about slipping the vest on over the head and blowing into the tubes on either side.

And that gave Mia an idea. Her raincoat! She shrugged out of it, her head dipping below the water each time she pulled an arm free. She knotted the two sleeves at the end, then managed, after a long period of fumbling with stiff fingers, to refasten the zipper and pull it all the way up. As if it were a life jacket, she stuck her head between the tied together sleeves, with the knot resting against the back of her neck. Then she took the bottom edge of the coat and spread it open with her hands. She lifted it high overhead, legs still kicking, and slammed it down toward the water, bagging air.

It worked! The body of the coat was swollen with air. She laughed in triumph. She had done it. She had created a makeshift life vest. Holding the bottom of the coat tightly closed, she let herself rest on top of the air trapped inside.

Only then did she realize that her toes were going numb from the cold.

Mia wasn't going to die from drowning. She was going to die from hypothermia.

CHAPTER 66

Staring after the yacht, Charlie berated himself. He had come too late. He had come too late and now Mia was in the hands of killers and he had no way to follow her. His voice tight with urgency, he radioed dispatch. "Tell Harbor Patrol I need that unit to meet me on the northernmost pier. We have an active kidnapping situation."

He was still releasing his thumb from the button when he heard footsteps pounding toward him. Sucking in a breath, he pivoted while grabbing for his gun. A man was running toward him, swinging a long metal boat hook.

Charlie was aiming for center of mass when he realized who it was. Eli Hall. He let his arm fall by his side. Panting, Eli dropped the hook. Then he leaned down and braced his hands on his knees.

"You're too late," Charlie said. "They're gone." He gestured at the sleek white yacht, which was speeding out of the harbor. "And they've got Mia."

"You're the one who told me to keep back," Eli said between gasps. "By the time I got here that guy was marching her down the ramp and into the yacht that used to be here. I went to find something to use as a weapon." He lifted his head to glare at Charlie. "If I hadn't listened to you, I might have made a difference."

"You also might have got Mia killed," Charlie said. Then he realized how stupid it was to stand here arguing. "Did you get a name or a number off the yacht?"

Eli shook his head. "I didn't get close enough."

They both turned at the sound of the Harbor Patrol. It was a sleek aluminum craft, the high bow cutting through the waves, the word POLICE written on the side in four-foot-tall black letters. It entered the far side of the harbor and raced toward them, sirens sounding and lights blazing. As it got closer, Charlie could see two cops on board.

Instead of stepping back, Eli was sticking right next to Charlie. Acting as if he had become part of things. Charlie shook his head. "Oh no. You're staying here."

"No, I'm not." Eli was just as adamant. "And you don't have any time to argue with me. We don't have time to do anything but go after her."

Charlie's only answer was a growl, but Eli was right. There wasn't any time to waste.

The cop at the helm, a tall black guy, cut the motor and expertly glided in next to the end of the pier. The other cop, a redhead with masses of freckles, leaned forward to offer Charlie a hand.

"Charlie Carlson, Homicide," Charlie said as he clambered aboard with Eli right on his heels. Eli even introduced himself as if he were central to the process. The first cop was named Johnny Crashaw and the second Gordon Ploughman. The four of them moved into the bow of the boat. Charlie pointed out across the water. "A yacht just left here. There's a hostage on board. She's a King County prosecutor. And there are two suspects with her. Maybe more."

"And at least one of them is armed," Eli added.

"Who is this guy exactly?" Gordon asked Charlie with a frown, staring at Eli.

"Eli Hall. He's a witness," Charlie said. What Eli really was, was a nuisance.

Eli said, "I'm also the hostage's boyfriend."

"What?" Charlie jerked his head around. Was Eli serious? There hadn't been any hint of a relationship between them when they interviewed Jackson. He shook his head, clearing his thoughts. There was no time to think about what Eli had just said, or about why his own first reaction had been jealousy. For right now, he had to keep his feelings about Mia compartmentalized or he wouldn't be any good to anyone.

They were now out of the harbor and in the open water of the sound. The boat skipped over the waves, the powerful engines thrumming.

Charlie squinted. "There it is." The police boat was so fast it made the yacht look like it was standing still. Then he realized it really was. Two men were standing on the back deck, but Charlie didn't see Mia, and the portholes were too small to reveal anything.

He was so focused on finding Mia that at first he didn't notice that the two men on the yacht both had guns in their hands. At the sound of the Harbor Patrol's approach, they turned and began firing.

"Get down!" Gordon yelled at Eli. While Charlie and Gordon drew their guns, Eli dropped to his knees and scuttled into the cabin, where Johnny was grabbing a handheld microphone.

"This is the Seattle Police," Johnny said. His words were broadcast a split second later. "Come out with your hands up."

Instead, the two men on the yacht—Charlie could see now that one of them was Turner—opened the door and both of them ran down into the yacht's main living quarters.

They were alongside the other craft now. Johnny cut the engines and ran out on deck. All three of them had their guns drawn.

Where was Mia? Charlie was frantic with worry. Was she tied up inside the boat? Had they hurt her? He moved into the bow and leaned closer to the yacht, squinting as the Harbor Patrol boat bobbed up and down. Through a porthole he saw movement, but it was too hard to tell what he was seeing. He just prayed that she was still alive.

He looked down. Their bow was right next to the yacht's back deck, which was about the same size as his bathroom at home and had cement blocks stacked in one corner. The waves were two or three feet high, maybe more. That meant the two decks were moving as much as six feet up and down from each other.

Even if Charlie had been a twenty-two-year-old Olympic athlete, the idea of trying to land on the yacht was ridiculous.

He took a deep breath.

And then he stepped over the rail, bent his knees, and jumped.

CHAPTER 67

It was clear to Vin that things were going south in a hurry. He and Oleg stood in the yacht's tiny living area, staring at each other. Blindingly bright beams of light from the police boat cut through the portholes. Outside, orders blared, telling them to cut their engines. Telling them to come out with their hands up.

Where there was one unit of Harbor Patrol you could bet there would soon be more. Eventually with the addition of the Coast Guard and Homeland Security. It wouldn't be long until they were surrounded. Any opportunity to escape was quickly slipping away. But Oleg seemed rooted to the spot.

"We've got to get out of here!" Vin yelled at him.

Oleg shook his head and muttered to himself in Russian. Vin wanted to shake him. If Vin just knew how to drive this stupid boat, they would have been long gone by now.

They both jumped as something heavy landed on the aft deck, shaking the whole yacht. What had the cops tossed on board? Some kind of anchor? A flash-bang grenade to temporarily disable them?

But then the door at the top of the stairs opened and Vin realized it had been a person. All he could see was a black shadow silhouetted against the bright lights. Moving to put Oleg's bulk between himself and the intruder, Vin raised his gun and fired. Oleg did as well.

The small space of the cabin rang with the sound of multiple gunshots.

Oleg screamed like a girl and crumpled to the floor. The cop tumbled down the stairs and then landed half on and half off a suede banquette. Blood was gushing from his face, and his right arm was twisted at an odd angle.

Neither the cop nor Oleg was moving.

Vin ran for the controls. There were dozens of dials, sliders, switches, and what looked like gearshift handles. The only thing he was sure how to operate was the metal steering wheel. He set down his gun. The engines were still thrumming, but he needed to make the boat go forward. Desperately he began to shove and push at the levers. If he could just get back on land, he might still stand a chance. He didn't care if he ran this stupid thing up onto the rocks and tore off the bottom. He just had to turn tail and get out of there while there was still time.

But instead of revving, the engines abruptly cut off with a clunk that he felt as much as heard.

No! He was not going to be trapped in here. He was not going to die in a space hardly bigger than a prison cell.

Vin ran out onto the deck, his eyes nearly closed against the blinding light, not paying any attention to the amplified commands being shouted at him.

Someone punched him in the shoulder. Vin spun around to see who it was. But no one was there. His arms pinwheeled as he lost his balance. As he fell back off the deck, he only had eyes for the neat round hole in his chest.

The water closed over his face before Vin even had a chance to be surprised.

CHAPTER 68

"Get inside," Gordon had shouted at Eli when the two men on the yacht started firing. "And get down!"

On his own, Eli had already decided that this was a great idea. This realization had coincided with everyone else's guns coming out. The last time Eli had spent any real time with a weapon was basic training. Now he realized that fieldstripping a gun and firing at a paper target was no preparation for having someone earnestly trying to kill you. He just prayed that Mia was out of range of the guns. Out of range and safe.

He dropped to his hands and knees and crawled through the door to the boat's cabin, flinching each time he heard a bullet whine by. The cockpit seemed like it would offer the most protection, so he huddled as close to it as he could.

A screen next to him drew his eye. The display was made up of different shades of gray. It reminded him of looking at ultrasound pictures when Lydia was pregnant with Rachel. At first you had no idea what you were seeing. And then the lines and curves and shadows resolved and you realized you were looking at a baby on its back, curled up like a shrimp.

Only in this case, what Eli was seeing was . . . was what? Something out on the water. A bright white oval floating above a dark gray background. Two lighter gray lines on either side of it moved slowly back and forth. They were longer and paler, appearing insubstantial when compared to the nearly white oval.

It was like watching a video of a ghost. But what it was, Eli realized, was a real live person. A person as seen through some kind of thermal imager. Judging by levels of brightness, the person's head was still warm, the arms less so. No wonder, given that their owner was floating in the Puget Sound in November.

And that person must be Mia. If Eli's guess was right, she wasn't on the yacht at all. She was in the water on the other side of the Harbor Patrol boat. He squinted. Was she clinging to something? As he watched, the glowing oval drooped forward. And was it his imagination, or was the brightness slowly draining away from it? Eli's heart contracted. Could he be watching Mia die?

He risked getting to his knees. Peering out over the cockpit, his eyes scanned the water. *There! On the left! That must be Mia, floating.* But now she seemed motionless. Was she even still alive?

He scuttled back to the door and called out, "Charlie! Charlie!" He risked poking his head out.

But Eli couldn't see Charlie. He could only see Johnny, standing with his arms out in front of him, his hands steadying his gun. When he heard Eli, he flicked an annoyed glance over his shoulder.

"Get back inside!"

"But I see Mia. I see her in the water. On that imager thing on the dash."

Just as Eli finished speaking, more gunfire broke out. It sounded muffled, though, not like it was directed at them. Even so, both he and Johnny flinched.

"What!" It wasn't a question but a verbal swat. "Listen to me. Get back inside and stay down. We can't worry about that now!"

But Eli was most definitely worried.

He scooted back inside, but once there, he again rose to his knees. He scanned the water until he spotted her again, a black spot on the steel gray of the sea. Mia was about a hundred yards away. She still didn't appear to be moving. The cold water must be sucking all the heat from her. Even if she was alive, how long could she survive?

Hadn't he seen a life ring on the other side of the cabin? He crawled back out the door, but this time he scuttled to the far side of the boat. The white life ring was fastened to the railing. He undid it and the coil of rope it was attached to. In one quick motion Eli got to his feet, pulled the ring behind his back, and then hurled it with all his strength toward Mia. As it flew straight through the air, the line played out to its full length. The life ring landed with a splash.

It was still at least fifty yards short.

Had Mia's head lifted at the sound, just a little bit? Hope made Eli dizzy. Still, even if she was still conscious, she appeared far too weak to swim to it.

Without giving himself time to think, he toed off his shoes and dived in.

The water was shockingly cold. But Eli was a strong swimmer, and he put all the adrenaline already pumping through his veins to good use.

When he reached her she was lying with her eyes closed, her cheek resting on something black. He realized it was her coat, which was somehow keeping her afloat like an air-inflated pillow.

"Mia!" Eli shouted.

Her eyelids fluttered. "Charlie?"

It was a ridiculous time and place to feel jealous, treading water in the ocean while behind him people were doing their best to kill each other, but Eli did.

"Lie on your back and I'll tow you." He left her coat in place—she seemed to be using it as a makeshift flotation device—and grabbed the collar of her shirt. With one arm, he began to stroke through the water, dragging her to the life ring. By the time he finally reached it, his shoulder was burning and his legs were as heavy as if he were wearing lead boots.

"Okay, Mia, here we go. I'm going to get this ring on you." But when Eli released her, she began to sink. He grabbed for her again, hauling her up out of the water. She didn't move, didn't respond in any way. The phrase *dead weight* popped into his mind. Eli slapped one pale cheek. "Come on, Mia!" She didn't stir. He slapped again, harder. "Stay awake! Keep fighting! Don't you quit on me!"

Her head was back, exposing the long ivory column of her throat. Her eyes were open a fraction of an inch, showing the white rim. She was as still as a corpse.

"Mia!" He shook her. Her head wobbled loosely in the water. "Wake up! Gabe and Brooke need you."

That got a response. Her eyes opened and she feebly began to struggle. He lifted the tied-together arms of the coat over her head and let it slip away. Then he managed to wrestle the ring over her shoulders and arms.

He heard a shout and turned. It was Gordon, leaning over the railing. Johnny was next to him. They began to tow Mia in, hauling the rope in hand over hand. Swimming, Eli followed at a slower pace. If the two cops were helping them, he figured everything else must be under control. He had never been more physically exhausted in his life. When he got to the boat, Charlie was there too, although something about him didn't look right. Eli was too spent to figure it out or even to care.

Working together, Johnny and Gordon hauled Mia on board while Charlie watched. Eli managed to get his forearms on the back of the boat, but then he just hung there, half in and half out of the water. He was shaking with cold and adrenaline, but he didn't have enough energy to get himself fully out. Then Gordon offered him a hand, and Eli finally managed to get a knee up, then the other. He crawled forward to where Mia lay on her back.

Johnny was on the radio, requesting assistance, including an ambulance to meet them at the dock. Gordon lifted his fingers from the
side of Mia's neck. "She still has a pulse, but it's too slow. She's hypo-
thermic. We've got to rewarm her."

"Get those wet clothes off her," Charlie said. "They're sucking
all the warmth out of her." He made no move to help, and then Eli
saw why—his right arm hung loose and at an odd angle. At least one
of the bones in his forearm looked broken. Charlie's face was very
white and his teeth were gritted against the pain. An ugly red gash
marred his chin where something had dug a chunk out of it.

Gordon was already tugging off Mia's pants. Eli tried to unbut-
ton her blouse, but the buttons were too small and his fingers too
clumsy. He gave up and pulled hard, popping the buttons. Against
the ivory color of her bra, her skin was tinged with violet. Her lips
looked blue. Eli rolled her from side to side to get the sleeves off,
then started running his hands up and down her arms, trying to
warm her. Her skin was as cold as if she were a corpse in a refriger-
ated locker.

"Stop that!" Gordon snapped as he stood up. "Leave her arms and
legs alone. That's where the cold blood pools. If you massage them,
you could send it right back to her heart and give her a heart attack."

"But we need to get her warmed up," Eli said. "Don't you have
some blankets or a sleeping bag?"

"That won't work," the cop said as he rummaged in an overhead
compartment. "She's not shivering, so she's not even generating her
own heat anymore." He came up with three gray wool blankets.
"We can't just wrap her in a cold blanket. We need something to
warm her." He looked from Eli to Charlie. "Two somethings. Both of
you get down to your skivvies and cozy up. I'll wrap these blankets
around you."

Eli ended up having to help Charlie out of his pants. He left the
broken arm alone, although he managed—with Charlie swearing a
good deal—to bare his other arm and torso.

It was so cold. Eli's teeth were chattering as he shivered so hard he practically vibrated. Gordon spread one blanket on the deck, rolled Mia into the center, then directed Charlie to lie down on one side and Eli on the other, pressed close together so they were a tangle of arms and legs. The second and third blankets went over the first, and then Gordon tucked them in, wrapping them up like a twelve-limbed papoose. Well, eleven, because he left Charlie's broken arm free. Even though Eli still felt like he was freezing to death, when he pressed his legs and torso against Mia, he was far warmer than she was. She felt like she still belonged to the sea.

"What happened to the guys who took her?" Eli asked Charlie.

"They're both dead." His voice was flat, as if it was a simple fact with no emotion behind it. Eli might be one kind of cold, but Charlie was another.

Eli tried to press himself even closer against Mia and ended up with his mouth resting against her bare shoulder. *Come on*, he urged her in his thoughts as he pressed his lips against her. *Warm up! Live! Live, Mia, Live!*

She stirred. Eli went up on one elbow. When Mia's eyelids flickered and then opened, he felt like he could breathe again. She was alive. She was alive and they were all going to be okay.

But then her eyes focused, not on Eli or Charlie, but on something at the end of the boat. Eli watched as they went wide.

"Watch out," she slurred. "It's Vin. He's here."

Eli turned to follow her gaze.

"I shot him, Mia," Charlie said. "He's dead. You're hallucinating."

"No she's not!" Eli said. The old man with the red face stood on the deck, water sheeting off him, his white hair plastered to his head and his shirt slicked to his torso. There was a small hole in his chest. And a gun in his hand.

Then he raised it and fired.

CHAPTER 69

The King County courtroom was packed. Some of the people crowded into the benches were the media, but most were Mia's colleagues. She could feel them behind her, feel them silently giving her the strength to do this.

Frank was in the thick of it, shaking hands and accepting praise until the last possible moment to take a seat. He had eked out a victory over Dominic Raines, and even people she was sure had voted against him were now finding it politic to pay their respects. Mia still didn't know whom she had overheard him talking to that evening at the office, the person who most certainly hadn't been his wife. She told herself that she didn't really want to know.

At the back of the courtroom, Charlie sat with his arms folded and his face expressionless, scanning the room. He had gotten his cast off a few days earlier, and the bullet graze on his chin was now marked by shiny pink skin.

From the other side of the room, Eli smiled and gave Mia a little wave.

As she looked from one man to the other, heat climbed her cheeks. She had only vague memories of being sandwiched between the two of them, all of them stripped to their underwear. It was still embarrassing to think about.

Even when down to just his boxers, Charlie had kept his gun nearby. Which had turned out to be a good thing. After having fallen off the yacht, Alvin Turner—or Vin, as he apparently had gone by in the rest of his life—had grabbed a line hanging off the police boat and then managed to clamber on board with his gun tucked in his waistband. But the bullet Vin had fired at them had missed, and the second time Charlie shot him had proved truly fatal.

Coho County had reopened Scott's case. The blood drawn from his chest tap had been stored at the medical examiner's office. Once it was tested, the lab report said it contained massive amounts of opiates. Oleg's home had yielded ground-up methadone as well as a nearly empty bottle of Everclear—a potent and tasteless alcohol. They had also found evidence linking Oleg to the murder of Elizabeth Eastman, who had also gone by Betty and Bets. She had turned Scott from an employer to a lover, and then when the two of them had met Oleg, she had set her sights on the wealthier man.

On Vin's computer they had discovered evidence that he had bribed the IRS agent who had been investigating Oleg. Vin had used both the carrot—a cash payout—and the stick—Scott's death—to help the agent decide which path to take.

Now the crowd started to murmur as Bernard Young entered the courtroom. Mia's scalp prickled, the hair rising on her head and neck. She fought the urge to run. Young shuffled forward one slow step at a time, his ankles shackled together, his handcuffed wrists connected to his waist with a belly chain. Still, there was a deputy in front of him and a deputy behind, with a half dozen more scattered throughout the room.

Young raised his head and glared at her. Chin held high, Mia matched him stare for stare. He took his place next to his new defense attorney. True to his word, Rolf had refused to continue to represent him.

Judge Rivas took the bench. He nodded at her, the silver hairs in his buzz cut catching the light. "You're looking well, Counselor. It's good to have you back in my courtroom under happier circumstances." He looked over at Trevor. "And special thanks to Mr. Gosden, our courtroom deputy clerk, for making it possible for you to be here today."

Applause broke out from those assembled, and Judge Rivas let it go on for a few seconds before banging his gavel and putting on a stern face. "I would ask for silence. This isn't a sporting event." Then he was back to business.

He offered the opportunity to make statements to the families of the two girls Young had killed. One girl's family just shook their heads, all of them weeping. But the other girl's mother took the witness stand.

"I will never forgive the act," she said, her voice so low and trembling that even with the microphone Mia had to strain to hear her. "But I am slowly finding it possible to forgive you, Mr. Young. If I don't, then I might as well have died with my daughter."

As she spoke, Mia was watching not her face, but Young's. Was there the tiniest flicker of emotion in his eyes? Was it possible to still reach someone whose soul was as dark as midnight?

Looking at Young made Mia think of the three boys who had sentenced Tamsin Merritt to a different kind of prison, the prison of her own body. Still, Tamsin was slowly breaking free. She could now walk and talk and dress herself, even if all of these things were done slowly. Mia had gone to visit her a week ago in the rehabilitation facility. The other woman had trouble enunciating, and she cried easily, but then again she had twice faced death, once at the hands of her husband. The doctors said she had some short-term memory loss and that it was impossible to say if she would ever be back to normal. Still, Tamsin had been sure that Mia had done the right thing in not charging the boys as adults. She had spoken passionately, one painful syllable at a time, about the economic conditions that she felt had contributed to the three boys going off track.

Now Judge Rivas looked at Young. "Mr. Young, this afternoon you have the right to address the court prior to the imposition of sentence. You are not required to say anything, should that be your choice, but the law does afford you that opportunity. Is there anything which you wish to state to the court this afternoon?"

Rivas looked at the two families, and then at Mia. But when he opened his mouth, all he said was, "No."

A few minutes later Young was sentenced to life, and then it was all over.

Both Charlie and Eli got up and headed in Mia's direction. The two men had little in common, other than Mia. Both had saved her life. Both had become her friends. And both, she sometimes thought, might want to be something more. She looked from one to the other.

But then the courtroom doors opened and Brooke and Gabe came in—and it was for them that Mia opened her arms.

READING GROUP GUIDE

1. Mia's work as a public prosecutor is extremely important and demanding, as is her work as a single mother of two. Have you ever struggled with work-life balance? Discuss the difficulty of doing well at work while also maintaining personal relationships.

2. When Charlie approaches Mia about the inconsistencies of her husband Scott's death, Mia says, "Let the dead bury the dead." Have you ever wanted to move on so badly that you didn't care to know the truth? Is knowing the truth about an event essential to coming to grips with it?

3. The justice system is the arena for Mia's work, yet she is often asking what justice is supposed to look like. How do you define justice? Is the point of justice punishment for wrongdoing? Rehabilitation for criminals? Preventing future crimes? All of these things?

4. Mia's discoveries in the basement make her believe that her whole life with Scott had been a lie. Have you ever experienced or discovered something that made you question the most foundational aspects of your life?

5. When handling the shopping cart case, Mia can't help but compare her own son to the teenagers involved. How does her

role as a mother affect her viewpoint and her actions? How would you have handled the case?

6. At many points during Mia's investigations, she feels that she is finding more questions than answers—and that truth itself is "as slippery as a silver bead of mercury." Have you ever searched for the truth, only to come up empty-handed?

7. While Mia works to prosecute criminals, her friend Eli works to defend them. In your opinion, which position would be more difficult, and why?

8. Even though Mia is overwhelmed by responsibilities, she manages to make room for Kali and Eldon in her home. What makes her so sympathetic toward Kali and her circumstances?

9. Scott's unethical accounting practices led him down a slippery—and eventually deadly—slope. Have you ever found yourself trying to justify smaller offenses, only to find yourself knee-deep in bigger ones?

10. Hindsight is 20/20 for Mia once she learns the whole truth about Scott, his work, and their marriage. Like Mia, have you ever been in long-term denial about a situation in your life? How differently would things have turned out if Mia had confronted Scott about her concerns?

ACKNOWLEDGMENTS

Thank you to the readers of the Mia Quinn mysteries! I so appreciate your jumping on board and following her adventures. It is both humbling and gratifying to be able to share her story.

This is a novel, and yet accuracy and research are key. So thank you to Jaydra Perfetti of the IRS, for clarifying how IRS audits work; Robert Payton Morris, for explaining so much about yachts, drowning, and harbor patrol; Robin Burcell, author and former police officer, for answering procedural questions; CJ Lyons, author and physician, for answering questions about ventilators; and to the many federal and state law enforcement officers and prosecutors who consulted without attribution.

Thank you O'Reilly, from Wiehl. And special thanks to John Blasi, the smarts and vision behind billoreilly.com. And thank you Deirdre and Don Imus. Your friendship (off camera) means the world to me. And Roger Ailes and Dianne Brandi.

Thank you to the ceaselessly stunning publishing team! Daisy Hutton, vice president and publisher, is wise well beyond her years; Ami McConnell, senior acquisitions editor, so honored to call her my friend; Amanda Bostic, editorial director, brilliant; LB Norton, line editor, with the keenest of pens and the sharpest of wits; Becky Monds, editor, keeps the whole team on track with a smile on her face;

ACKNOWLEDGMENTS

Jodi Hughes, the ever on-target associate editor; Kristen Vasgaard, a brilliant manager of packaging; Laura Dickerson, marketing manager, is inspired; Kerri Potts, marketing and publicity coordinator, and the inspiration behind my Facebook; and, of course, special thanks to my dear friend Katie Bond, director of marketing and publicity. We're so proud to be part of this team!

Special thanks to our book agents, Todd Shuster and Lane Zachary of Zachary, Shuster, Harmsworth Literary and Entertainment Agency and Wendy Schmalz of the Wendy Schmalz Agency, who have worked tirelessly. We couldn't have done this without your amazing vision.

And always, Mom and Dad, thank you does not even begin to express how I feel.

All the mistakes are ours. All the credit is theirs. Thank you!

AN EXCERPT FROM *SNAPSHOT*

PROLOGUE

APRIL 10, 1965

Fort Worth, Texas

Special Agent James Waldren reached around his jacket and felt the Smith & Wesson .38 Special concealed at the small of his back. He scanned the pedestrians up and down the street before responding to the tugs at his sleeve.

"Daddy, look. Daddy, I'm skipping." Lisa took off in an awkward hop and skip up the sidewalk.

"Wait for me," James said, picking up his pace. The camera hanging around his neck slapped his chest as he reached out for her arm. "Hold my hand now."

"And look both ways," Lisa said as they reached an intersection. The light turned green, and they crossed the street with a growing crowd hurrying forward.

James was keenly aware of the glances, and of how people moved ever so slightly away—some even crossed to the other sidewalk—when they saw him. This wasn't a neighborhood where a white man and his blond-haired daughter would normally be seen. Lisa skipped along, oblivious.

The sounds of cheering and shouts echoing through a bullhorn increased as they closed in on the throng of people. As a tall man raced by, the placard he carried clattered to the sidewalk. Lisa released James's hand to run a few steps ahead, reaching the sign as the man bent to pick it up.

"Here you go, sir," Lisa chirped. She picked up the edge of the sign that had FREEDOM NOW painted in bold red against the white.

The man glanced from Lisa to James, then back to the child. She pushed the end of the wooden pole as high as she could with two hands.

"Thank you, li'l miss," the man said.

"You're welcome, sir," Lisa said, smiling back as he picked up the placard.

He gave James a tentative nod before racing up the street, sign in hand.

As the sidewalk congestion grew, James scooped Lisa into his arms, eliciting a joyful squeal. She rested in the crook of his elbow, and her soft hand reached around his neck, curling her fingers into his hair.

At the corner, the streets lined with tall brick buildings opened to a small park and public square. The air was electric with the energy of the growing crowd.

James surveyed the plaza where at least a hundred people lined the adjacent street, waiting for the approaching marchers: women in Sunday dresses, many with hats and white gloves, pantyhose, and dress shoes; men in crisp button-down shirts and slacks, some with ties and jackets even on this warm spring morning.

"Where is the important man, Daddy?" Lisa craned her neck.

"We'll see him very soon," James said, moving closer toward the parade route. His eight years with the Bureau had altered training into instinct, but in the eighteen months since President Kennedy's assassination in Dallas, every important event held the threat of danger, no matter how peaceful it was planned to be.

James had spent countless hours and overtime investigating the JFK assassination. He was assigned to the killer, the deceased Lee Harvey Oswald—his activities, friends, coworkers, family, and especially his Russian wife, Marina Oswald. Good ole cowboy country hid numerous underground connections and secret groups throughout Dallas, Fort Worth, and outward from the South and across the nation. There were Russian expats with connections in the USSR, hidden KKK members in political positions, and a growing group of black freedom fighters.

But today James tried to blend in. Just another bystander, a normal guy who'd brought his daughter to witness a historical event. Just any white dad who happened to have a revolver and FBI credentials in his wallet. The truth was, James couldn't be just a bystander. A special agent with the Federal Bureau of Investigation was never off duty, and an event like this had layers of possible intrigue. His wife would be furious if she knew he'd brought Lisa with him. She thought they were going to the park.

"Here he comes." James lifted Lisa onto his shoulders. She patted the top of his head, bouncing up and down with the cheers erupting around them. "See that man, the one in the middle?"

"The man with the big hat?" Lisa leaned down toward his ear. The girl was hat obsessed. She'd wanted to break out her Easter bonnet today, but his wife wanted it saved for Easter Sunday.

"Not that one. The shorter man with the red necktie." He lifted his camera with one hand and snapped a picture, then advanced the film and snapped another.

"I see him," she said, bouncing again.

"He's an important man, a very good writer and speaker."

James took pictures as they watched the progression down the street. Benjamin Gray was surrounded by marchers holding signs, the cry for freedom and equality on their lips. The crowd took up singing "We Shall Overcome." Benjamin Gray carried a Bible under his arm and slapped his hands together as he joined in the singing.

Lisa wiggled on James's shoulders, trying to slide down just as he spotted his partner, Agent Peter Hughes, up a block and across the street.

"Want down, Daddy," Lisa said.

The marchers made a sharp turn and moved into the square where Gray and other leaders would speak to the crowd.

James set Lisa on the ground, holding on to her arm, but she tugged away from him.

"Wait!" he called, weaving through the crowd after the blond head.

James watched as Lisa stopped a few feet from a little black girl close to her age who sat on a cylindrical concrete seat. The girl stared back at Lisa, then smiled when his daughter waved. Lisa clambered up the seat, pushing higher with her toes. It seemed that thoughts of parades and important men were pushed aside by the more interesting distraction of a potential playmate.

"I'm four," Lisa said as she held up three fingers, then the fourth.

James didn't hear the other girl but saw her show Lisa four fingers back. A nearby woman in a large white hat kept a watchful eye from an adjacent, slightly taller bench.

"Can I take a picture?" he asked her.

She leaned back, studying him and then the two girls before winking and breaking into a smile.

"Go right ahead," she said, and returned to watching the progression of marchers as they looped from behind them to curve around James toward the central square at his back.

He clicked several photos, struck by the poignancy of the images. These two little girls, one white and one black, sitting side by side, were the symbol of today's event.

James snapped another picture as the two girls leaned close, smiling and talking as if already friends.

A gunshot pierced the air. Then another.

James jumped to shield Lisa as he grabbed his gun. He moved the two girls directly behind him. His eyes jumped around the crowded plaza behind him, where the shots had come from.

The rally turned into instant chaos, with people running in all directions.

The black girl's mother screamed at James, hitting him with her purse as she reached for her child.

"It's okay, I'm FBI." He flipped out his wallet with the large letters clearly visible, but the woman continued to cry out, gloved hands at her mouth. James passed the child to her, and they were immediately enveloped into the crowd and out of sight.

"They shot him! Help, please help!" someone screamed.

Through the commotion James glimpsed a man on the ground. Beside the body, a Bible lay covered in blood.

James pushed forward with Lisa held against his chest. "Close your eyes," he demanded.

The faces around him reflected terror and confusion.

As he turned toward the man on the ground, James was certain that Benjamin Gray was already dead.

The story continues in *Snapshot* . . .